Victorious!

A Story of Faith, Family
and Football
in the Heartland

Victorious!

Cover photo: Rochester coach Derek Leonard (left) shakes hands with his father, Sacred Heart-Griffin coach Ken Leonard before the "Leonard Bowl" game in 2017 at Rocket Booster Stadium in Rochester. *(Photo by Justin L. Fowler, USA Today Network)*

Dedications

This book is dedicated to my family. To my late parents, John and Iona Leonard that taught me how to be a great husband, father, and man. My father's great example instilled confidence in me to be the best at whatever I did. To my siblings, Curt, Mary Kay (deceased), Sheila, Barbie, and Phillip for their support throughout my life. To my late wife Liz, who raised our three sons, Phil (deceased), Derek, and Bradley with love and teaching them to treat everyone with love and respect. She allowed me to coach and be gone from home to do my job as a football coach and athletic director. To Derek and Bradley and their wives, Lindsey and Becky, thank you for being such wonderful parents to our grandchildren, JP, Blake, Julia, and Austin. To our granddaughter, Savannah (Phil's daughter), we can't wait to meet our new great grandson, Phoenix. The Lord put Angie and me together after we both lost spouses, and I am grateful for the role Angie plays in our family and as a coach's wife. She loves being "Grandma Angie" to our grandchildren. The Lord picked the perfect wife for me to end my career with and for our retirement together.

To my former coaches, Ed Thomas and John Eliasik, thank you for setting such great examples of being a head coach. To all my former assistant coaches, players and parents, thank you for your dedication, time, support and hard work. To all the administrators and staff that I worked with at Sacred Heart-Griffin, thank you for your support and encouragement for 39 years.

Most importantly, I want to thank Jesus Christ, my Lord and Savior, for calling me to this life I live.

In Christ Alone,
Ken

I am dedicating this book to the many people who have been so important in my life and my career. First, I am dedicating it to my mother and father, who are the reasons I am the person I am today. To my two brothers, Bradley and Philip, and the rest of my family, my wife Lindsey and to my sons Blake and Austin – without their love and support, I would not be able to do what I love to do. Also, to those who coached me and coached with me over the years – and to all the young men I have had the privilege to coach. Most importantly, to the Lord Jesus Christ for making this story and all things possible.

Derek

Victorious!

Acknowledgements, Apologies & Preface

I never intended to write a book after careers in newspapers and state government that often required me to type things. I never could find "home row" in typing class and to this day type with only two fingers. I probably peaked at about 70 words per minute in my younger days, but my brain only operates at about 35 wpm. A wise editor once pointed out that I should never type faster than I think.

Three years ago, I started having a nagging thought to write about the incredible coaching careers of Ken and Derek Leonard. The idea kept resurfacing, each time with more of an emphasis on their faith and family stories than their football accomplishments. Ken and Derek graciously gave me hundreds of hours of their time. I only knew Ken professionally from my days as sports editor of the *State Journal-Register*, but getting to know him and Derek better the past couple of years has been one of the most rewarding parts of this journey. They shared behind-the-scenes glimpses into key moments in the football histories of Sacred Heart-Griffin and Rochester. They also shared stories about their faith journeys and navigating through family sorrow. I never met Ken's wife Liz Leonard. I wish I'd had the opportunity to benefit from her grace because it became obvious to me that she had a profound effect on those whose lives she touched. The other thing that became clear to me in writing this book is that what you see is what you get with Ken and Derek. Their faith is genuine and has withstood the test of family tragedies. About the only thing Ken approaches with more zeal than he did coaching football is proclaiming Jesus Christ as his Savior.

When Ken and Derek talk about their players, it sounds more like they are talking about their own sons. If you want to know their secret as coaches, I have concluded that it is more about how deeply they care about the young men they coach than any football strategy they have devised. Their competitiveness runs about as deep as their faith. They both have a burning desire to come out on top in everything from cards to playing a game of H-O-R-S-E to seeing who can pick the most winners in the horse races at the State Fair and, of course, those memorable "Leonard Bowl" games.

I hope this book accurately depicts the story of the Leonards. It began as an attempt to tell of their historic coaching accomplishments. Indeed, you will find lots of football stories and lore on these pages. But at some point, I felt the urge to pray that God would give me the words to properly glorify Him in the telling of this story. It's not God's fault if I failed; I still sometimes type faster than I think. I want to thank the Rev. Roger Grimmett of Springfield First United Methodist Church and the Rev. Clint Cook of Real Life Church in Springfield. They don't know it, but they helped shape the spiritual parts of this book from their sermons to having Dr. Grimmett read some excerpts to make sure I wasn't misrepresenting the Bible.

My heartfelt apologies to anyone whose name should have been included in these pages but was not. Ken and Derek combined have probably coached more than 5,000 players. A large number were All-Staters, and many others did remarkable things on the field. Some people who gave of their time, memories and thoughts only appear briefly, if at all. I owe them my thanks because every interview helped provide context for what appears in these pages. It would have been easier to write 5,000 pages, but then only the strongest could have picked the book up and even fewer would bother to read it.

Trying to write a book about faith probably surprises some who know me. It did me. On the other hand, love of sports is likely in my DNA. My paternal grandfather owned a truck line in Cairo, Illinois, and he also owned a Brooklyn Dodgers Class D baseball team based there in the 1949 and early 1950. The St. Louis Cardinals even conducted spring training there in 1943 because of World War II travel restrictions to preserve resources like fuel for the war effort. My maternal grandfather was the groundskeeper for that minor league team, and he started taking me to Cardinal baseball games when I was about 4 years old. I saw Stan Musial's National League record 3,630th and last hit – a ground ball single past a Cincinnati Reds rookie second baseman named Pete Rose, who 18 years later would break that record. By the time I realized I would never make a living playing any games, writing about them seemed to be the best Plan B. I got paid (not much) to cover the games I loved.

Merle Jones, the legendary and colorful sports editor of *The Southern Illinoisan* in Carbondale, gave me my first chance to write sports when I was in journalism school at Southern Illinois University. My interview consisted of only one question: "Can you type?" Those were the Ice Age days of typewriters, and it seems he once hired a guy who turned in handwritten stories. I fibbed. For the first three weeks of covering high school sports in my part-time job, I would dictate the stories to my wife Peggy. She remained supportive in all other ways but suggested that if sports writing was going to be my career, it might be unprofessional to bring her to the office to type my stories for me. That's when I adopted the hunt-and-peck method that earned me strange looks in every job I've had.

I got the opportunity to come to Springfield when a *State Journal-Regis-*

ter editor named Paul Povse called to see if I would be interested in applying to become assistant sports editor. Paul and I had become telephone friends because he was an avid SIU fan and had read my coverage of Saluki college basketball, football and baseball. Paul became one of my best friends until his death in 2018, and I owe him for the many good things that have happened to me since I moved to Springfield in 1986. Sports editor Larry Harnly gave me that chance to become part of his staff, and I was privileged to work with some of the best of the best, including guys like Dave Kane, Hal Pilger, Jim Wildrick, Robert Burns, Gene Seymour and Hall of Fame sports editor Jim Ruppert, to name just a few.

Special thanks to Ruppert, who was my right hand when I was sports editor of the Springfield paper and then succeeded and surpassed me in that role. He is a walking encyclopedia when it comes to the last four decades of sports in the Springfield area. He declined my invitation to co-write this book, saying he didn't want to work that hard in his retirement. He then proceeded to put in time to provide information and tips, read the manuscript, and give me the unvarnished truth when the writing wasn't good enough. I also want to thank former SJ-R photographer Justin Fowler, who continued in the tradition of great photojournalists who have worked at the Springfield newspaper. Most of the photos in this book were taken by Justin. Thanks also to Scott Hanson, host of the wildly popular NFL RedZone show. Scott took time out from his chaotic schedule to write a deeply personal foreword for this book. Thanks also to attorneys James Fahey and Michael Horstman Jr. of the Sorling Northrup law firm in Springfield for their guidance related to the business aspects of this project. Horstman played for Ken Leonard, both had sons play for the coach, and both were on his coaching staff at SHG.

One of my colleagues for more than two decades in state government was Julie Beamer-Pfeifer, an English major from Millikin University. She is the absolute best when it comes to proofing and editing. I depended on her to correct my misspellings and turn my "grammer" into grammar whenever I had to write important government reports or correspondence. I turned to her again on this project. If there are spelling, style or grammatical errors, they are only because I failed to properly hit the Save All Changes button in the Word documents Julie edited. My sister-in-law Dawn Summers, who had no prior connection to either the Rochester or the Sacred Heart-Griffin football programs, also read the manuscript. Her perspective improved the final product.

Taylor Pensoneau is a Springfield-area author who has written 11 books, including "Brothers Notorious: The Sheltons: Southern Illinois' Legendary

Victorious!

Gangsters," which sold more than 21,000 copies. Mr. Pensoneau shared valuable advice on how to go about writing and self-publishing a book. That meeting took place in 2021, and he asked me what my time frame was to complete the project. I told him I thought I could wrap it all up in about three months. He told me I'd better allow more like two years, and that was without him knowing about my typing deficiencies. I thought he was underestimating me. Well, it's 2023 as I type this sentence.

Thanks to Karen Reilly for laying out the book and for her meticulous editing. Thanks also to Brad Books and his staff at Capitol Blueprint, especially to Jeremy Garcia for his design of the cover.

As the title suggests, this is a book about faith, family and football. I learned by spending so much time with Ken, Derek and other football experts that I really didn't know as much about the inner workings of the game as I thought I did. I'm still a work in progress when it comes to my faith. But I do have some experience with families, having been blessed with a great one that I dearly love.

My wife Peggy and I celebrated our 50th wedding anniversary in June of 2023. She remains my best friend in life. We have two grown daughters, Angela and Cindy. The highest compliment I can give them is that they are like their mother in all the important ways. Angela is married to Craig Foxall, a good enough athlete at Galesburg High to go on to play football and baseball at Monmouth College, where he held the career home run record for more than 20 years. They have a son, Jacob. Cindy is married to Devon Warren, and they have a blended family of six children, including Avery Warren, Aubrey Warren, Brynlee Warren, Jori Fleck and identical twins Kale and Liam Fleck.

I now understand that I often went overboard trying to climb higher in my various jobs, and maybe even diving down so many rabbit holes in researching and writing this book. As I get older, I realize on a more conscious level that all those extra hours I invested in my pursuits meant I had less time and attention to give to my wife and kids. On the positive side, my wife having more direct influence in the raising of our daughters and, by extension, our grandchildren, turned out to be a very good thing. Ken Leonard might even call it a God thing.

Thanks to all who helped in any way with this project. Thank you for reading it.

Mike Chamness

Foreword

Football. The No. 1 sport and premier form of entertainment in our sports-mad American society.

Family. The grouping of lives through biology and relationships that builds and binds human civilization.

Faith. It can mean a million things to a million different people. To me, it's a personal relationship with Jesus Christ...trusting fully, without seeing perfectly, that my salvation begins and ends with His perfect work.

It wouldn't have happened for me the way it did without Ken Leonard.

Before I became the host of NFL RedZone (a role described by some as being "Touchdown Santa Claus") I had the privilege of working at WICS-TV, then the NBC affiliate in Springfield, Illinois. I arrived there in 1995. High school football was king in the area, regularly leading my nightly sportscasts from August through November. It quickly became clear to me that when the calendar turned to football season, all eyes turned to Sacred Heart-Griffin and the Cyclones' stone-jawed leader, Ken Leonard.

Ken was direct, firm and demanded his players strive for excellence. The

Scott Hanson was born and raised in Rochester, Michigan. He knew he wanted to become a sportscaster at a young age, and he pursued that dream at Syracuse University's famous Newhouse School of Public Communications. His love of football compelled him to walk on the football team at Syracuse University, playing for four years (1989-1992) while achieving dean's list academic honors. Scott was captain of the Bishop Foley High School team in Madison Heights, Michigan in 1988.

Two years after graduation, Scott began working as the weekend sports anchor at WICS-TV in Springfield, Illinois. Other stops on his broadcast path included work in the Tampa, Philadelphia, and Washington/Baltimore markets. In 2007, Hanson began working for NFL Network, and in 2009 was named host of NFL RedZone, the extremely popular pro football "whip-around" show.

In the offseason, Hanson enjoys world travel. He has taken humanitarian aid/mission trips to Africa, India, Haiti, Russia, Serbia, the Philippines, Mexico, Peru, the Amazon jungle, and Southeast Asia. His world adventures include running with the bulls in Pamplona, and climbing Mt. Kilimanjaro.

results showed. Mind you, this was more than two decades before he'd become the winningest football coach in Illinois high school history. I would routinely interview him after games with an initial question along the lines of "Wow, Coach, a 49-0 win! Which was better today, your offense or your defense?"

Almost always, the first words out of his mouth weren't about the X's

Victorious!

and O's. They were about the Cross. "Well, I'd just like to thank my Lord and Savior Jesus Christ for the opportunity to coach these young men," he would say, not out of habit or to impress his employers in the Catholic hierarchy. Over time, I came to realize it came from a deeper place. You've heard it before on live TV. And many of you probably reacted the same way I did back in 1995…with an internal "eye roll" and a hope that we'd quickly move off of the awkward "religious stuff" and get back to football.

But something about those bold proclamations of faith stayed with me, even after I raced back to the TV studio to make sure they were edited out so they would not appear on the 11 o'clock news.

Talk with Ken Leonard for 10 minutes and you'll quickly perceive authenticity. He's a man with the rare gift of not being troubled when the paths of popularity and sincerity diverge. Little did I know that God was laying groundwork for me in and through a football coach.

In the spring of 1996, I went through an existential crisis. Through circumstances internal and external, I spiraled to the lowest point in my life. Society and my upbringing suggested I should just "man up" and suffer in silence until it passed. But I had begun reading the Bible in a pseudo-quest for peace or some nugget of wisdom that would help me feel good about myself again. Funny thing about the Bible, read it with any seriousness for a period of time and you'll note it almost seems to go out of its way to expose everyone in it – including the reader – as flawed, broken, lost… and, dare I say in this modern age of relative morality, sinful. Well, everyone except The One whom Coach Leonard would always credit in his postgame interviews.

With my head swirling in the midst of my troubles, this newfound religious curiosity, and the sense that maybe *God* was involved in this, I knew I needed to reach out and talk to someone. My childhood upbringing suggested that if you need to talk about "God things" then you go to a nun or a priest. In Springfield, I knew neither.

But I did know a person who seemed to like to mention God. Someone who was kind to me and always available. And, most importantly to me then, someone I respected professionally. Football coaches who kick butt and do it with integrity were always held in high esteem in the Hanson household. *"Call Ken Leonard"* was the thought that kept surfacing in the middle of my turmoil.

I summoned up the courage, which, believe me, took some doing. "What guy calls another guy out of the blue to ask questions about God?" was my archaic thinking. On a Tuesday afternoon, I called Ken's office at SHG. The conversation went something like this:

Ken: "Hello"

Me: "It's Scott Hanson from Newschannel 20"

Ken: "Hey Scott – what can I do for you?"

Me: "Well, Coach, I'm actually not calling for a professional reason. I'm calling about something personal."

Ken: "What's up?"

Me: "Well… Coach… (my voice weakened and my volume lowered) … I'm going through a really hard time right now. Nothing seems to make sense in my life. I've been reading the Bible… and I think I need to talk to someone. I think I need to talk to someone about… (long pause, and then, almost in a whisper) … God. Do you know what I mean?"

At this point, I was fearful I'd done the wrong thing, that Coach might laugh me off the phone and I'd have to live with the embarrassment of admitting weakness and need. Instead, I heard these words: "Yes, Scott. I know exactly what you mean. And almost four years ago, I went through the same exact thing."

WHAT?!?! I couldn't believe it. This rugged man's man, this football champion who everyone seemed to admire, had issues like me?!? This coach who used virtually every TV or radio sound bite opportunity to proclaim Jesus Christ as his Lord and Savior was once confused about who God is and what His purposes are?!?

I'm not sure to this day what I expected to come from that timid phone call. But Ken Leonard's kind tone and genuine concern were exactly what I needed. Had he brushed me off or told me to just toughen up, I don't know what the trajectory of my life would've been. Over the course of the next few days, Coach Leonard took time away from his coaching duties and his family to meet with a young man he knew only casually. He helped me sort through questions far more difficult than the ones I normally would ask him in those postgame football interviews: Is God real? Is the Bible actually true? Could this Jesus actually love me despite how badly I've messed up?!? The answers – a resounding Yes!!! – proved to be bigger and more important than winning a state championship or having a resume tape that would skyrocket a career to national TV.

Ken listened, sympathized, empathized, and he helped me to sift through what I thought was a damaged if not ruined life. He was strong but patient and humble every time he walked me through some principle in scripture. He never talked down to me.

Victorious!

"Scott," he told me during one of our meetings that also were convenient excuses to crush some cheeseburgers at a fast-food joint, "I'll do the best I can to help you. But know this: I don't have all the answers. And I'm capable of being wrong. But God is never wrong. His word is never wrong. Don't listen to a word I or anyone else says about spiritual matters unless you can find it in the Bible."

There was the coach, with the confidence of a play-caller who knows a touchdown will result, pointing me to life's Ultimate Playbook. Those talks with Coach Leonard and a friend of his who joined us along the way helped me to understand a message that has become the foundation of my life. It is a message specifically for me, but available to anyone. It cannot be earned; it's already been paid for. It just needs to be accepted. The message went like this:

"Scott, the Bible says there is a God – and He loves you – but through your own thoughts, words and actions, you've rejected Him. The Bible calls that sin… and says that every human is guilty before God. Even the ones you think are 'pretty good people.' Sin has a penalty, which is separation from God. In a word, that is Hell. But there is Good News. God's love is so great for us that He made a way. Christ paid the penalty. Through His perfect life and death on the cross, He paid the penalty that would be yours. Because of His resurrection, you can know that He is real, true and alive today. You can trust that His work, the free gift to you of salvation, is what you need to be right with God and to put you on the path of making you the man He intended you to be. Jesus is the way. The only way."

As heavy as that reads, imagine being told that while your whole world was shaking! I made the decision to put my trust in Jesus Christ on April 23, 1996. My life has never been the same! Not everything has gone smoothly or perfectly. That was never the promise, and I still am an imperfect human being. But, thanks to God's grace, I know I am eternally secured. I know that in large part because of a football coach who took the time to guide me to the right path – something he has also done for generations of football players by living out his faith as best he could in front of them.

I am excited for you to read about Ken and the remarkable Leonard family. My life was forever impacted by my interaction with them. You picked up this book for any number of reasons. Maybe you're a Cyclones or Rockets fan, and there are plenty of behind-the-scenes glimpses into their successes in this book. Maybe you're just a football fan who wants to learn more about one of the most successful high school football families in America and what makes them tick.

But perhaps there's something more waiting for you on these pages. You might be surprised – as a TV sports reporter seeking a sound bite was back in the 1990s – to find that something (and Someone) greater than us moves and works through wins, losses, joy, tragedy, family, friends, strangers and even enemies. Or that He might use a 100-yard football field to lead people to salvation.

Scott Hanson
Host of NFL RedZone

CHAPTERS

CHAPTERS

Victorious!

When One Door Closes...

A shutdown of the Gridley High School football program was inevitable. Even a 32-9 record that represented the school's best four-year run since the 1920s couldn't save football at the central Illinois school of fewer than 100 students. You simply couldn't run a football program safely with only 18 players, and smaller schools forming cooperative teams would not be an option in Illinois for another five years.

So, the decision by the Gridley school board to pause the varsity program after the 1983 season wasn't totally unexpected. Still, it hit hard when Superintendent Gene Cwick, himself a former football coach at the school, delivered the final verdict. Ken Leonard's first head coaching job in football, the only job he ever really wanted, was gone in that instant. It would turn out to be no more than a speed bump compared to some of life's detours he had already experienced in his 30 years of life:

- As a teenager, helping hold a fire hose on the embers the morning after his father's grain elevator family business in Chenoa burned to the ground;
- Living with two different families his senior year of high school after his parents moved to Indiana for work following another devastating business setback; and
- Exploring a path away from football after losing his position as the starting quarterback at Dakota State University.

His conversion as a born-again Christian wouldn't come until

1

years later, but those faith seeds had already been planted by his parents, John and Iona Leonard. They took Ken and his five siblings to Catholic Mass each week. Never giving up was also a life lesson. His father's words were permanently etched in his mind.

"My dad was from the Greatest Generation. He fought with the infantry in the Third Army under General George Patton in France and Germany during World War II. He was a man's man," Ken would recall years later. "He told us to have dreams, but don't just dream. Work to make them happen. I can still hear him saying, 'Don't let anybody tell you what you can and can't do. Just go prove it!'"

Ken Leonard also still remembers the October night in 1968 when he and his family were awakened shortly after midnight by a ringing telephone. Phone calls that time of night usually carry bad news, and the look on his father's face confirmed that something was terribly wrong. The volunteer fire department was only about a block away from the Leonard house, and the alarms and sirens there were going off, too.

Sheila was 12 at the time, three years younger than her brother Ken. Her bedroom window faced the Leonard Grain Elevator, a 100-foot-tall wooden structure a couple of blocks away near the center of town. Looking out her window, she saw that the whole town of Chenoa was lit by an eerie orange glow. Her father's grain elevator was engulfed in flames.

More than 50 years later, Sheila still gets emotional when she describes that night. "It was after midnight when the phone rang. When I woke up, I could see the fire through my window. Dad answered the phone and he left. The rest of us huddled around my window and just watched it burn all night," she says. "My parents were just devastated. How do you move forward from that? It's not like we ever had a lot of money to begin with. When I look back, knowing now what it takes to take care of a family, and there were six of us kids, I don't know how they did it. Our big treat was mom and dad taking us to the market on Sunday evening to pick out a flavored soda to take home and make an ice cream float. We never had anything extra, but we always had food and a lot of love in that house."

The Chenoa Historical Society files include clippings from the local weekly newspaper detailing the fire that was reported at 12:25 a.m., the wee hours of Friday, October 4, 1968. Volunteer fire departments from the surrounding communities of Pontiac, Lexington, Fairbury and Gridley assisted the volunteer firemen from Chenoa in battling the blaze for more than six hours, using more than a half million gallons of water to finally bring it under control and preserve the rest of downtown Chenoa.

The newspaper said citizens reported seeing the flames shooting from the top of the grain elevator from as far away as 30 miles. John Leonard told the newspaper that around 40,000 bushels of grain were stored in the elevator bin at the time of the fire, and he estimated the loss at more than $130,000, equivalent in purchasing power to about $1.1 million in 2023. Sheila's memory is that her father had developed and hooked up a new corn dryer at the grain elevator and that a short in the dryer was determined to be the cause of the fire. That meant that the insurance company would not pay for the loss.

Ken, then a sophomore in high school, was at the scene the next morning, holding a fire hose and helping firefighters water down the hot spots, a process that lasted more than 24 hours according to news reports. Ken played in a Chenoa football game later that Friday evening.

"I just remember how big that fire was," Ken says. "It was a really tall, wooden structure…and it burned completely to the ground. You can imagine what that looked like in the middle of the night. My dad took off to go to the elevator. My mom was crying. She didn't say it to me, but I found out later she talked to her friends about how worried she was for my father. We had been living comfortably, but we were living harvest season to harvest season, and this happened at one of the worst times for us. My mom worked some odd jobs, but she was mainly a stay-at-home mom. We had no money coming in. It was really a tough time for my parents."

John Leonard bounced back from that devastating fire only to see his business fail again when a company he had partnered with at the Chicago Board of Trade went bankrupt. The company had a contract to sell waxy maize corn to Japan, but that fell through. The company declared bankruptcy, leaving John Leonard not only metaphorically holding the bag, but also literally holding bins full of corn for which he now had to find buyers – buyers that would be paying far less than what the Japanese deal had specified, and also far less than what Leonard had contracted to pay the farmers.

"My dad could have also filed for bankruptcy, but he was determined to pay all the farmers he had made deals with to buy their crops. He wrote them checks and he had nothing left," Ken says. "He had fought his way across France and Germany and all the horrors of that. He finally had his own business and then, poof! It was gone just like that. Twice in a period of a couple of years he had lost everything. My parents had to move to Plymouth, Indiana, for him to take a job with a seed company."

Get knocked down. Get up. More than once. That's how it was for people who had lived through the Great Depression and two world wars.

Having his first coaching job evaporate would not end Ken Leonard's career. Resilience was part of his DNA. He would "just go prove it" by becoming the winningest high school football coach in Illinois history with 419 victories and six state championships by the time he retired after 43 seasons at the end of 2022. Putting those numbers in perspective, to reach 400 wins a high school football coach would have to *average* 10 wins a year for 40 years. A regular season has only nine games.

Being in any job for four decades is rare, but it's almost unheard of for a high school football coach. Coaching high school football has evolved into a year-round job with off-season weightlifting programs and the proliferation of 7-on-7 summer camps. The number of hours spent in scouting, film study, game preparation, practice and taking care of public relations add up to a coaching stipend that falls below the minimum hourly wage. That doesn't even factor in the whims of school boards and/or administrators and dealing with helicopter parents who believe their kid is the next Tom Brady. Hall of Fame Benton High and Southern Illinois University basketball coach Rich Herrin was asked later in his career if kids had changed during his 40-plus years in coaching. His answer was simple: "Kids haven't changed, parents have."

Victorious!

The Making of a Coach

Ken Leonard's path to becoming a football coach took some extreme twists and turns. He played all sports as a kid but became especially interested in football after watching his brother Curt, who was eight years older. Curt was a two-way starter as a running back/ defensive back at Chenoa High School before going on to play at Eastern Illinois University.

"I remember going to his high school games and seeing him score touchdowns and being kind of the star. Then dad would take me to Charleston to see Curt when he played at EIU. Back then, we played whatever sport was in season, playing pickup games all over town. But watching Curt really piqued my interest in football," Ken says. He also remembers watching the Green Bay Packers on TV, the Ice Bowl, and seeing Vince Lombardi prowling the sidelines ex- horting his players to dig deeper to achieve greatness. Ken Leonard has always been driven to excel. It is an internal force he says comes from watching his father persevere.

Ken was a catcher in baseball, a point guard in basketball and a quarterback in football – all leadership positions where you touch the ball on almost every play, control the action, anticipate what the opponent might do, and make split-second decisions. Even as a young boy, he was the organizer of those pickup games around town. Taking charge when it came to sports just seemed to come naturally. Clearly, he was destined to be a coach, but he was tugged a few different ways. He remembers completing catechism and think-

7

ing, however briefly, that he might even become a priest.

"God was working on my heart early on, but I was not by any stretch of the imagination living the Christian faith," he says.

His first thought about coaching was about basketball. While he was good at all sports, he says his first love in grade school was basketball. He may not have looked the part as a sophomore in high school – standing just 5-foot-6 and sporting black horn-rimmed glasses – but he was a skilled point guard and smart floor general in basketball. He was able to see the patterns of the game unfold almost as in slow motion. Playing in Illinois State University's Horton Fieldhouse in 1969 as a high school sophomore alongside four seniors, Leonard sank a series of pressure free throws late in the championship game to help win the McLean County Tournament. It was the first time in 20 years that Chenoa had won the prestigious county tournament, the last such victory dating back to when Stan Albeck of Bradley University and NBA coaching fame was a star player for the school.

Ken Leonard's first paid coaching job was as assistant coach in football and basketball at his high school alma mater in 1978. Innovation, especially in designing high-powered football offenses, is a big part of his coaching legacy. He says back then he was intense and a self-described "bit of a wild man." Take, for example, the out-of-bounds play called "Circus Circus" that he designed for his Chenoa freshman-sophomore basketball players to execute. They would line up across the free throw line and start doing flips or cartwheels in different directions to distract the opponents.

They ran the play during a game against El Paso, where Jim Cozzolino was the opposing coach. Six minutes into the game, neither team had scored. His team had the ball under the basket, so Leonard called for the "Circus Circus" play. One player cartwheeled to the left, another to the right, a third flipped backwards toward the top of the key, and the fourth somersaulted forward, caught the inbounds pass and laid it in the basket. Cheers and laughter erupted from fans of both teams. The referee was not amused. He wiped out the basket and called a technical foul on Chenoa.

"The ref said we were making a travesty out of the game. 'Coz' was even arguing with the ref. He said his El Paso team didn't want to shoot the technical free throws, that neither team scoring for six minutes was the real travesty!" Leonard says, chuckling at the memory. Cozzolino would later become Leonard's first defensive coordinator at Griffin High School before going on to coach and become athletic director at Lanphier High School in Springfield.

Despite his fondness for basketball (and "Circus Circus"), Leonard kept being drawn back to the football field. He admits he probably wouldn't have survived as a basketball coach because of his intensity and unorthodox ideas. He wanted his teams to go 100 mph, and he wanted to keep pushing the limits. The 84-by-50 foot basketball court was too limiting. The football field was a larger, better canvas for his coaching mind that was always exploring new ways to gain a competitive edge.

"I love everything about football," he says. "I love the toughness, the strategy and putting a game plan together. I love being in charge. As a kid playing pickup games around town, there were no parents involved, no one coaching us, and no referees. We figured it out on our own."

He played some varsity football as a sophomore and then was named the starting quarterback his junior and senior years. He credits head coach Ed Thomas with teaching him fundamentals and discipline and assistant coach Gary Steinbach with teaching creativity on offense. Those Chenoa teams were pretty good his sophomore and senior seasons, but he thought about quitting football before his junior season.

"We were gonna be really good in basketball but not in football that year because we only had three or four seniors. One of my best friends quit football, and he talked to me about quitting football and concentrating on basketball," Ken says. That notion was quickly squashed when he got home. "Dad sat me down and told me I was going to finish what I started, that no son of his was going to be a quitter. That was that."

When Leonard's parents had to move to Plymouth, Indiana, for his dad's new job before Ken's senior year, Ken talked his parents into letting him finish high school in Chenoa with his friends. He started that year living with the family of his best friend Ed Easley. That friend's younger brother Sam Easley later would become Ken's brother-in-law when he married Sheila Leonard. The Easley family moved to nearby Lexington, Illinois, midway through the school year, so Ken finished his final year of high school living with another friend's family in Chenoa. From there, he enrolled at Harper Junior College in the Chicago suburb of Palatine. That school was starting a football program, and Ken became the school's first quarterback. He lived with his brother Curt, who was working for Quaker Oats in Chicago at the time.

After two years at Harper Junior College, Ken was offered a full scholarship to play football at Indiana State University. However, about three weeks after signing day, Indiana State changed coaches. The new coaching staff wanted to install more of a wide-open passing game. Ironically, given his coaching legacy of bringing the spread offense and a fast-paced passing attack to high school football, Leonard had been a wishbone option quarterback in an offense that mostly ran the ball at Harper College. That meant Indiana State was no longer a great fit. Dakota State University needed a quarterback and offered him a full scholarship, so Ken, five of his buddies from the Harper College team and his future wife, Elizabeth "Liz" Brown, headed to Madison, South Dakota.

Ken was the starting QB. The team was doing okay, but the offense wasn't really clicking on all cylinders. Six games into the season, he lost his starting spot. "For the first time in my life, I wasn't 'The Guy' on a sports team," he says. "A freshman beat me out. He was good, not super good, but he deserved to be the quarterback. I hadn't totally bought into the training thing; I hadn't worked hard enough. In a strange way, I think that experience of failing in sports for the first time solidified me as a coach. I was a good teammate; I didn't go around complaining or bad-mouthing the coach. But I now knew what it was like not getting to play and the type of dedication it took to be good."

With his starting job gone, so was the allure of Madison, South Dakota. "I mean, I was from a small town, but this was real cowboy territory. When the weekends came, everyone went to rodeos or who knows where. It was like a ghost town back then. The only people left in town were the football players. That year was a great experience, but I knew then that wasn't going to be the place for me."

Turns out that South Dakota wasn't really the middle of nowhere for Ken Leonard. That would be Alaska, where the next chapter of his life would take him far away from college and football to work for his uncle's company.

Victorious!

North to Alaska

Ken still harbored dreams of becoming a football coach, but those were packed away with his belongings as he left Dakota State and headed to his parents' home in Indiana at the semester break. He moved to Bloomington-Normal and enrolled at Illinois State University, sharing an apartment with friends and working as a hot roofer carrying buckets of tar.

He thought about returning to the football field and had gone so far as to talk with the ISU coaches about going out for the team. But, as Ken says, "When you come up with a plan, I imagine God must be up there chuckling. He had other plans for me."

Oil had been discovered in 1968 on Prudhoe Bay, located at the northern tip of Alaska on the Arctic Ocean. The oil field contained more than 25 billion barrels of oil, making it the largest oil field in North America. Years of environmental, legal and political debates followed, but demand had surpassed supply, creating the oil crisis of 1973. The shortages sent gas prices skyrocketing. The resulting public pressure cleared the way for exploration.

How best to get the oil to the continental United States was a logistical puzzle. The answer was to construct an 800-mile-long, 48-inch-wide pipeline south to the Port of Valdez, the nearest port that would be ice free year-round. At full production, it would carry more than 2 million barrels of crude oil per day, easing the country's energy crisis. The Alaskan Pipeline was an engineering challenge because the steel pipe had to be able to withstand earthquakes, forest fires and other natural or even man-made disasters. It was also a daunting physical task for the construction workers as the pipeline had to travel across rough, often frozen terrain.

Without a football scholarship, Ken didn't have money for college, and he knew the financial struggles his parents were facing. He was intrigued when his uncle, who owned a pipeline construction company, offered him a job for more money than he had ever seen. He left Illinois State University in the summer of 1975 and headed to Alaska, where he would drag the pipeline up for the welders. He experienced a lot of things while in Alaska, working in locations such as Prudhoe Bay, Fairbanks and Valdez, not to mention desolate areas of what was known as The Last Frontier. Workers were far from home, laboring long hours in cold and isolated places.

"We would work seven days a week, 12 hours or more a day for 10 straight weeks, and then we'd have a week off. It was grueling work, dragging the line up to weld it. Even when we did have time off, there wasn't much to do," he says. "It was all men in the camp, no women and no bars. Most of the guys spent their time drinking in camp and playing cards or dice. Some guys would get Dear John letters from their wives or girlfriends. They would be depressed, missing family and friends back home. A lot of them turned to drugs or alcohol. I might have had a drink once in a great while, but I was working for Leonard Pipelines, and I remembered my dad and my uncle emphasizing that I better not shame our name. So, I spent a lot of time lifting weights during my free time. But they fed us well, and I made more in one year than I've ever made in any year since."

It was during one of the down times that Ken had a concerning phone conversation with his fiancée. "On one of my phone calls with Liz, she was telling me about feeling kind of panicky. She didn't feel very comfortable going anywhere outside of her apartment," Ken recalls. "I just thought it was one of those things where we were apart and she was struggling. I had no idea what it was and neither did she. She said she was heading into one of the larger rooms for class and just felt really nervous and shaky. She went back home."

It would be years before Liz would be diagnosed as suffering from agoraphobia, which for some can be an intense fear of becoming overwhelmed by new places, unfamiliar situations, crowds and other places they might not feel safe outside their home.

Ken worked almost two years in Alaska, earning a six-figure paycheck, before work on the pipeline started winding down in 1977. His uncle offered him an opportunity to go to Saudi Arabia for another job, but the Alaskan Pipeline experience and two years away from football had sealed Ken Leonard's career path stronger than any weld. He wanted more than ever to be a coach.

While in Alaska, Leonard met a guy named Joe Black, who worked on the pipeline one summer. Black had been a linebacker on the Arkansas Razorbacks' 1964 national championship team, playing alongside future Dallas Cowboys owner Jerry Jones and NFL Hall of Fame coach Jimmy Johnson. Black was a high school football coach in Piggott, Arkansas, and invited Leonard to visit and observe a few summer practices.

"I learned what toughness really was watching those practices," Ken says. "It's late July in Arkansas. It is hot, like 95 degrees, and the players are in full pads for two hours. One big ol' kid has a mouthful of Copenhagen dip. Everybody dipped tobacco in Alaska; I think I puked the first time I tried it. I said, 'Joe, how can he do that?' Joe said, 'KC – that was my nickname in Alaska because my middle name is Claude – KC, that's just how these boys are raised.'"

He may never have taken to Copenhagen dip, but Leonard's practices early in his coaching career were influenced by and, according to the accounts of his former players, rivaled what he observed in Arkansas that summer. Watching Joe Black work reaffirmed Ken Leonard's choice of coaching as his profession. He returned to Illinois State University with a new commitment. "It wasn't until I was taken away from football that I knew for sure I wanted to be a coach. I was okay in math, but in high school and my first few years of college, I did just enough to get by and be able to play," he says. "But now I was really focused on being a teacher and coach. I went

15

back to Illinois State and buckled down…and I made the dean's list for the first time in my life!"

His student teaching assignment in the fall of 1977 was at Streator High School, where his former college roommate Norm Eash was the offensive coordinator and line coach. Eash would go on to become head football coach at his alma mater, Illinois Wesleyan University, where he built a 225-121 record with nine conference championships in 36 years through the 2022 season. While he was a student teacher, Leonard also helped Eash as a volunteer assistant, helping coach the quarterbacks at Streator. That 1977 Streator Bulldogs team went 9-1 and made the playoffs.

After Streator, Leonard helped as a student assistant at Illinois State for a while. His first paid coaching opportunity came in 1978, when he was hired as an assistant coach at Chenoa by his old high school football coach Ed Thomas. Thomas ended up coaching 29 years at Chenoa, winning 179 games and taking nine teams to the playoffs. His 1979 team finished second in the state, losing the championship game to an undefeated Hampshire team. That was Leonard's second year as a "real" football coach. It was almost his last.

That 1979 Chenoa team was expected to be good and had won its first game. One of the starters had missed a practice the week leading up to the second game. Thomas, the head coach, questioned the boy about his absence the next day. "Whatever it was, I bet it didn't keep you from hanging around your girlfriend," the coach said. The boy dropped the F-bomb on the coach. Things escalated. "What did you say?" Another F-bomb. Thomas hit the boy with a forearm to the chest. The boy's parents took him to the doctor. Those were different times, but even in 1979 there were repercussions.

"My wife Liz and I lived in a little bitty house across the street from the grade school," Leonard recalls. "That's where they held school board meetings. We were asleep, and there was a knock on the door about midnight. It was the school board president. He said, 'We know you want to be a head coach. Here's your opportunity. We are letting Coach Thomas go.' I said, 'Yeah, I do want to be a head coach, but not this way.' I told them if they fired Coach Thomas I was quitting, too."

Ken and Liz lost a child, a baby girl, during Liz's first pregnancy. They had just learned she was pregnant again, this time with a boy they would name Derek. Quitting his first coaching job probably wouldn't have been his most strategic career move, but it was the only option in Ken's mind when it came to his old high school coach. "Loyalty was one of the big things my dad taught me. Just like when the corn deal went south on him because the company he had partnered with declared bankruptcy. My dad was loyal to the farmers he owed money to, and he refused to file for bankruptcy even when it left him with nothing," he says. "Coach Thomas had been my high school coach. He gave me my first coaching job. I wasn't going to abandon him."

Eventually, it was decided that Thomas would be suspended for one game. Leonard and another assistant coach were put in charge for that game. "Of course," Leonard says, "that was the only game we lost that year until the championship game." The episode left an imprint on Leonard. He didn't endorse Thomas' physical response when the player cussed at him, but he didn't think it warranted firing the longtime coach, at least not by the standards back then. "I'll never forget what Coach Thomas told me way back then. He said as a coach, the longer you stick around, the more enemies you make. A lot of people may support you when you're winning, but when you make a mistake, you'll find out who your friends really are."

Leonard's first head coaching opportunity came in 1980 in Gridley, a small town about eight miles due west of Chenoa. At the time, Gridley High School was known more for its basketball. Leonard interviewed with Cwick and the high school principal, Pete Meiss, who was also the basketball coach. Leonard got the job at age 27. "Probably," he says, "because no one else wanted it." Gridley had gone 9-27 during the previous four years.

"I think they had some football tradition back in the day, but it was one of the smallest schools in the conference, maybe one of the smallest schools playing football in the whole state. The fact they hadn't had a winning season in a while didn't matter to me," Leonard says, "It was the best thing ever to happen to me as far as being a football coach."

Marty Lomelino was a sophomore when Ken Leonard was hired at Gridley, and he was a two-way starter for three years as a fullback on offense and a linebacker on defense. He went on to become a three-year starter at Western Illinois University, being named the Most Valuable Player his senior season in 1986, when he was also an all-conference selection and honored as an Italian All-American. He served a couple of seasons on Leonard's staff at Griffin High School before becoming an assistant coach at Peoria Richwoods from 1994 until he retired from coaching in 2014. His day job was as a business services manager for the Illinois Department of Transportation.

To this day, Lomelino becomes emotional when talking about the role Ken Leonard has played in his life. "He has been a huge factor in any success I have had in my life. I had a great family growing up. Other than my father, he's probably had the most impact on my life," Lomelino says. "I mean, we spent so much time together with non-stop football. When I graduated from Gridley, I really didn't know what I wanted to do. He took me under his wing and helped me get a scholarship to Western Illinois. What he did for me, he did for a lot of other kids. He was like a second father to a lot of boys."

Lomelino confirms Leonard's self-assessment that he was intense at the start of his coaching career. "Have you seen the movie Junction Boys?" he says, comparing Leonard's football practices to the 2002 TV movie starring Tom Berenger as legendary Alabama coach Paul "Bear" Bryant – so nicknamed because he once accepted the challenge to wrestle a bear for $1 at a carnival. The movie depicts scenes in which Bryant, then a first-year coach at Texas A&M, took his team out into the scorching plains of Texas to see who was tough enough to survive. Gridley didn't have desert-like terrain, but

Lomelino remembers summer workouts in the high school gymnasium. In fact, he tried to quit football during one of those workouts before ever playing a game for Leonard.

"It was probably 120 degrees in that gym, and we kept running. I went up to Coach Leonard and said, 'Coach, football just isn't for me.' He looked at me and said, 'OK, get your butt back in line and get ready to run,'" Lomelino recalls. "I thank him every day of my life for not letting me quit."

Leonard's first game as a head coach in the fall of 1980 was a win against Chatsworth. By a 6-0 score. It was not exactly the fireworks show he was expecting. "When I interviewed for the job, I sold myself as kind of an offensive innovator, talking about my experience as an assistant working on the offensive side of the ball, and how I had all of these new ideas to bring a wide-open offense to Gridley. Then we won the first game six to nothing. Our defense might even have scored that touchdown as I think back on it," Leonard says. "I remember thinking *'Okay, maybe I'm not really the offensive guru I thought I was.'*"

In hindsight, Leonard says he probably had overworked his players in his zeal to prepare them for that first game. Nevertheless, there was jubilation afterward in the locker room. A win is a win. And the juniors and seniors had won a grand total of just three games the two previous seasons.

Gridley would win its next three games to go 4-0, prompting Leonard to think that coaching football might be easier than he thought. They lost the next four games. They won the final game to post a 5-4 record, the first winning record for Gridley football in five years. Leonard's Gridley team would go 10-1 the next season, making the playoffs for the first time. The 1982 team soared unbeaten through the regular season and won its first playoff game before losing in the second round. That was Lomelino's senior season. He remembers how special Friday nights had become during football season.

"We had maybe 1,200 people living in Gridley back then, and

I think almost everyone attended the football games. We had a pizza place in town, and it would be crammed full on those Friday nights after a game. Those were special times in that community," he says, adding that despite all of that, he could see that football might not be sustainable. "My graduating class had 21 or 22 kids in it, and we had 90-something in the high school. My sister was a freshman, and by the time she graduated, there were only about 80 kids in the school."

The 1983 team went 7-2. But, as Lomelino predicted, the participation numbers were not sustainable. That's when Gridley's varsity football program was shut down for what would turn out to be a two-year hiatus. The Gridley School District would merge with the El Paso School District in 2004.

...Another Door Opens

At the same time the Gridley program shut down, the head coaching job opened at Griffin High School, an all-boys Catholic school in Springfield, Illinois, 90 miles to the south. Griffin had a rich football tradition dating back to the 1940s and 50s, when it was known as Cathedral High School. It became Griffin High in 1959. The football program took off under coaches like George Fleischli, who posted a 45-12 record in five years, including a second-place finish in the state in 1975. Robin Cooper went 46-10 the next five years, qualifying for the playoffs each year and finishing second at state in 1982. Cooper left Griffin to start a football program at Mac-Murray College in nearby Jacksonville, Illinois.

Leonard decided to apply to become head coach at what had become one of the best high school football programs in downstate Illinois. He was undeterred by the fact he had only four years of head coaching experience, and that was in 1A, the smallest high school football division based on enrollment. "Football is football, whether it's 1A or 4A," Leonard said in an interview at the time. "The big difference is the number of assistant coaches you have. I had one assistant at Gridley."

He was one of 25 applicants, seven of whom were interviewed. At least one, Montini High School head coach Chris Andriano, was offered the Griffin job ahead of Leonard. At the time, Andriano had been head coach of the Catholic school in the Chicago suburb of Lombard for five years. He chose to stay at Montini. It was a deci-

21

sion that worked out well for both coaches. Andriano coached 38 years at Montini, winning 300 games and six state championships.

Andriano and Leonard remained closely connected as coaches, in charge of two of the most successful high school programs in the state. The two became good friends, laughing at times about the twist of fate that brought them together as opposing coaches. Twice, the two faced off in the state championship game. Leonard's 2013 Sacred Heart-Griffin team ended a four-year Montini championship streak 38-28, and the Cyclones repeated as state champs the following year, defeating Montini 29-14. Leonard's teams compiled an 8-2 record against Andriano and Montini.

With Andriano choosing to stay at Montini, Griffin turned to Leonard. Initially, Leonard considered declining the offer for reasons that weren't exactly clear even to him some 37 years later. Perhaps it was knowing he was second choice. Or maybe being a young coach taking over a successful program. Possibly even the low pay he was to receive.

In the end, he says he thought about the story Notre Dame coach Lou Holtz often told regarding Urban Meyer almost turning down his first head coaching job in college. It seems Meyer, who was one of Holtz's assistant coaches at Notre Dame, was having second thoughts about accepting the head coaching job at Bowling Green University because he didn't think it was a good enough job. Holtz had recommended Meyer for the job. As the story goes, Holtz explained the facts of coaching life to Meyer. "If it was a good job, the other guy would still be there. If it wasn't a bad job, why in the hell would they hire you?" Meyer ended up taking the Bowling Green job and from there went on to great success at Utah, Florida and Ohio State University and then to an ill-fated one-year stint as an NFL head coach of the Jacksonville Jaguars. It's not quite an apples-to-apples analogy because the Griffin job already was a good one, but Holtz's advice resonated with Leonard.

"No one was lining up to offer me other head coaching jobs," Leonard says. "I wanted to coach football, and it turned out to be a great opportunity in my life."

Leonard was introduced as the new head coach of the Griffin Cyclones at a press conference on May 18, 1984. Jim McMann was a freshman at the time. The room was filled with Griffin administrators, family members, some alumni and a few reporters. McMann still vividly remembers standing in the hallway at the back of the room with other players when Leonard was introduced.

"Like it was yesterday," says McMann, who became one of Leonard's assistant coaches in 1991 and served as the Cyclones defensive coordinator for the last two decades of Leonard's tenure at SHG. "He was wearing this plum-colored suit and he had big wig hair, like he had gotten a perm or something. And he's wearing cowboy boots. Now we're listening to him talk about toughness and what he was planning to do with the football program. We're all looking at each other and saying, 'Who is this guy? Is he John Wayne…or Liberace? We found out pretty quickly that summer that he definitely was more John Wayne."

The curly hair was natural, not a perm, Leonard insists. Indeed, any resemblance to the flamboyant pianist Liberace was purely cosmetic. That first summer, Leonard took his players to Camp CILCA, 225 acres of woodland and open fields a few miles north of Springfield. This was in the days before restrictions on the length or number of practices. There were practice sessions early morning, late morning, early afternoon and early evening. The sessions were rugged, with conditioning being one of the primary goals. Another goal was to weed out those who didn't have what it took to play for the Cyclones.

"I still have nightmares about that place," McMann says. "It was three days of pure hell. No mommas, no daddies, just football. But, looking back on it, Coach Leonard was kind of ahead of his time because of the way he broke those practices up and worked on different things. Whoever remained standing after those three days at Camp CILCA was going to be a champion."

McMann was almost not one of those left standing. A five-mile run was one of the things Leonard required of each player on the team. McMahan was a lineman, and even though they had slower time requirements than the backs and receivers, it was still grueling. At one point during his sophomore year, he decided to quit football. His story sounds much like Lomelino's from four years earlier.

"My freshman year, the year before Coach Leonard came, I remember football practices being tough, but this was a whole different deal. Now I would puke...and that was before practice, just thinking about what was coming," McMann says. "Sometimes my legs were so sore I felt like I could barely walk. This one day I went into Coach Leonard's office to tell him I was quitting. I still remember it as one of my worst days. I was shaking and I was like, 'Coach, I just can't do this.' For some reason – and I appreciate this to this day – he said, 'Take a day off and think about it.' My mom was upset with me, and my buddies were all telling me to get my butt back out there. I was just weak in the head and I made a bad choice. I will always be grateful that Coach Leonard gave me a second chance."

A few years later, Leonard would also give McMann another chance, this one an opportunity to join his staff at what had become Sacred Heart-Griffin High School. It came from out of the blue. Or maybe fate, depending on your viewpoint. McMann, a student at Eastern Illinois University (EIU) at the time, was on a spring break fishing trip to Arkansas with Steve Torricelli and Dan Callahan, a couple of friends from Springfield. Callahan was the head baseball coach at EIU, and Torricelli would go on to coach baseball at Springfield College (later called Benedictine University) and Lincoln Land Community College. Callahan would go on to coach at Southern Illinois University (SIU), where he became the second-winningest baseball coach in Saluki history before he died of a rare skin cancer in 2010. The university retired Callahan's jersey number 37 in 2023, and the Missouri Valley Conference renamed its annual coach of the year award for Callahan.

McMann called home one night during the trip to check in with his mother. "It was right around Easter, and my mom said 'I ran into Coach Leonard today. He said if you have time, he wants you to come out and coach some. He said to come in and talk with him when you get back,'" McMann says. He began as assistant defensive line coach in 1991, moving up the coaching ladder to be promoted to defensive coordinator in 2000. He doesn't teach at the school. In fact, his day job since 2003 has been as a Springfield firefighter, meshing his one-day-on, two-days-off schedule with his coaching duties, an arrangement that Leonard blessed.

The football coaching job has been more than a hobby or side job. Jim McMann has been part of most of Leonard's coaching tenure at SHG, first as a player and then, thanks to that chance meeting between his mom and Leonard, by his side as an assistant coach. That he has had a front-row seat and been a significant part of high school football history in Illinois is not lost on him. He says he bled purple and gold as a Griffin High Cyclone player and then black and gold as a Sacred Heart-Griffin coach. He has been part of the highest highs, including the six state championships, and some bitter losses.

He experienced two of the Cyclones' toughest losses in the playoffs, both against the same team and both in eerily similar fashion. The first was in 1985, his junior year against Washington, when Griffin was ranked No. 1 in the state in Class 4A. It was a second-round game, and the Cyclones led 18-14 with 17 seconds left to play. It was fourth-and-11 from the 12-yard line. McMann, playing on the defensive line, broke through Washington's line and had the quarterback in his sights for a game-winning sack. It had been raining, and the field had become a bit sloppy.

"I had the darn quarterback. I hit him, but I hit him too low and my arms slipped down to his ankles," McMann recalls with a grimace. "I can tell he has gotten the pass off. Now I'm face down in the mud. The Griffin crowd was on my right. But all I hear is crowd noise in my left ear. It was the Washington crowd going crazy." The ball was caught in the corner of the end zone for a touchdown and a 21-18 victory for Washington, which would go on to win the state championship.

Fast forward 33 years to 2018 and the second round of the Class 6A playoffs – again against Washington. One of McMann's sons, J.T., was a senior. The Cyclones led 21-16 with just seconds left. Washington had the ball, but this time about 45 yards away. Again, it appeared one of the Cyclones had a bead on the quarterback. "I thought no way in heck they could get a touchdown this time," McMann says, grimacing at the memory. "But just like what happened to me, the quarterback slips away from our tackler and chucks the ball toward the same darn end zone. One of their players comes from nowhere to catch it. It was just bizarre...same team, same end zone, and we lose 23-21. We were just shell-shocked."

In just a matter of seconds, a playoff win turned into a loss that ended the season and the Cyclones players' hopes of a championship. For the seniors, it ended their high school football careers. McMann still remembers how, amid the stunned silence and tears, Ken Leonard stepped into and addressed the postgame circle of players and coaches.

"He told those boys that everything was going to be okay and that it was only a football game, that God has a bigger plan and this is just part of that journey. He says, 'This part of the journey sucks, but it's only one small step in your journey of life. You might not see it right now, but you will all be better men because of this part of your journey,'" McMann says, reciting the same basic, consistent message he has heard Leonard preach to generations of his players after tough losses. He says Coach Leonard would use a slightly revised message about viewing the biggest wins through the same lens of faith. That message was used way more than the losing one. More than 400 times, in fact.

"It's crazy how time flies," McMann said shortly after Leonard announced that the 2022 season would be his last as a coach. "I could walk down and show you that cafeteria where I saw Coach Leonard at his introductory press conference. It seems like it was yesterday. I am so glad he stayed this long because he has had such a positive impact on so many kids in this school – I was one of those kids...and so were my sons, J.T. and Hudson

"More than 35 years of my 53 years of living have been with that man in there," McMann continued, nodding toward Leonard's office. "I probably spent more time growing up with him than I did my own dad. Other than my mom and dad, he's probably had the biggest influence on my life. And all those wins..."

More wins, with 419, than any high school football coach in Illinois history. Considering age and the number of wins accumulated, as of 2023 there were few coaches in Illinois with a legitimate shot at breaking Ken Leonard's state record. There was one coach who had already accumulated 184 wins and a public-school record eight state championships at age 42. That would be Ken's son, Derek Leonard, the football coach at conference rival Rochester High School.

Victorious!

The Rochester Beginnings

The Village of Rochester is a rural community located about seven miles southeast of Springfield, the state capital of Illinois. According to census records, Rochester had 3,670 residents in 2020. It also had one gas station, five sets of stoplights, five sit-down restaurants, six churches – and eight state football championships. Those state titles are even more amazing because they happened within a 10-year period that stands as the most dominant run of football success for any public school in state history. Rochester did not even have a football program until 1995.

Rochester celebrated its 150th birthday in 2019. The climax of the months-long observance was a Sesquicentennial Weekend Celebration in September that included a car cruise, a scavenger hunt, a walk/run, a carnival in the park, a pancake breakfast sponsored by the local Christian Church, the Miss Rochester pageant, a short historical play staged by middle school students, a performance by the high school drumline and fireworks. The festivities began in April with a tea, followed in May by the unveiling of a village poster, then a historical home tour in June, and a focus on agriculture in July to honor the village's beginnings as a farming community. The August highlight was the "Rochester Sesquicentennial Community Football Night."

A Kentuckian by the name of James McCoy is credited with being the first settler in Rochester, building a cabin there in 1819. Another of the early settlers was Lucetta (Putnam) Stevens. When her first husband Samuel Stevens died, a young lawyer from Spring-field named Abraham Lincoln helped her settle the estate. Lincoln was known to have visited the community on various occasions, even giving one of his earliest known political speeches there in 1832. For many years, until weather took its toll, a mural painted on a stone silo in the middle of town beside Illinois State Route 29 depicted a June 16, 1842, meeting between Martin Van Buren, the eighth president of the United States, and Lincoln, a state legislator who would become the nation's 16th president 18 years later.

Van Buren's term had ended a year earlier, and he was in the Springfield area to visit his first cousin, George Brunk, who lived near Rochester. According to the book "Life of Lincoln" written by Lincoln's law partner William Herndon, Van Buren's carriage wheels got stuck in the mud causing the former president to spend the night in Rochester. Although Lincoln was a member of the op-posing political party, he was known for his storytelling ability and was invited to entertain Van Buren during a reception in what is believed to have been a Rochester inn. The party lasted until after midnight as Van Buren shared political stories from his home state of New York and Lincoln spun tales about life on the western fron-tier.

Rochester was incorporated as a village on February 1, 1869, with some 250 residents and businesses such as sawmills, flour mills, a corn and carding mill and a post office. Rochester has evolved steadily but slowly over the past 150-plus years. For example, liquor could not be sold or served in the village until the 1990s. Anecdot-ally, it appears many of the families that have moved to Rochester over the years have done so because of the reputation of the school district. Continuity may be one of the reasons for the school dis-trict's success. In stark contrast to many school districts around the state, the average tenure was more than 15 years each for five su-perintendents who served Rochester schools from the early 1940s to 2018. At least for the past few decades, the town has seemed evenly divided between those who have lived there for decades and those moving into the subdivisions that have sprung up from farm fields around the village. The community also seemed divided when the subject of starting a high school football program came up in the mid-1990s.

With an enrollment approaching 500 students at the time, Rochester was one of the largest schools in the state to not offer football. According to a timeline written by Steve Taft, who graduated from Rochester High School in 1973, there had been several attempts to start a football program over the course of four decades. Perhaps the best-known effort was when a local businessman brought Green Bay Packers quarterback Bart Starr to town in the late 1960s to speak to an assembly and visit with school administrators. Everyone loved the future NFL Hall of Famer, but football remained a no-go.

"I really would like to have gotten to play in high school, but you don't really miss what you never had," says Taft, whose family name is synonymous with Rochester. The road into the first subdivision as you enter the village coming from Springfield on Route 29 is Taft Drive.

The impetus for Steve Taft to take up the challenge of bringing high school football to Rochester was a business trip in the fall of 1993. He was in the fundraising business at the time and was making a sales pitch to a booster club in Knoxville, Illinois, a rural community of similar size about 120 miles northwest of Rochester. He listened as members of the booster club talked about an upcoming parade and other festivities planned in conjunction with their homecoming football game. Football was the focal point around which all sorts of events orbited, involving virtually the entire community in one way or another.

"I had a lot of windshield time on the drive back home that night," Taft recalls. "Our school had a homecoming dance, but never a community-wide homecoming celebration like the people in Knoxville were talking about. I thought if Knoxville – a community much like ours in many ways – could do it, why not Rochester? That seed was just planted in my head, and the thought wouldn't go away.

I ended up calling (Rochester Athletics Director) Bill Derks when I got back. I went over to his house and said, 'What do you say we run it up the flagpole one more time?'"

It wasn't very long after the proposal went up that proverbial flagpole that it started catching flak. On the pro side were all the things Taft had heard being talked about in Knoxville as well as the obvious: an opportunity for students who wanted to play football, as Taft himself had wanted to do 20 years earlier. On the other side of the ledger was the reality that football is by far the most expensive high school sport when you consider the number of players and coaches, the cost of football helmets, pads and uniforms and liability insurance. The potential for injury to players was another concern that was voiced. One person even brought a gold Sacred Heart-Griffin football helmet to one of the public meetings, pointing out that the helmet had a manufacturer's sticker stating the helmet would not prevent injury. Taft responded by pointing out that baseball batting helmets include the same disclaimer.

"As I look back, I think it boiled down to the money and the safety issue," Taft says. "Bill Derks said if we were going to do this, we needed to form a group to study it." The "Rochester Seven," as the group would come to be called, was formed in November of 1993. Along with Derks and Taft, it included Mike Jeffers, Bob Thomas, Jack Messmore, Ron Wiggins and Mike Long, whose sons Drew and Kurt would be among the first in a long line of talented quarterbacks for the Rockets.

Jeffers was a 1973 graduate of Rochester High School. He ran track and played baseball and basketball, remaining among the top 10 career scorers in basketball some 50 years later with more than 2,000 points. "I would have played football, no doubt. I would have loved to get the chance to play," says Jeffers, who was an eighth grader when Bart Starr spoke at the school assembly in 1969. "But we didn't have football. Really, no one in our conference had football at that time." That would change soon after Jeffers graduated, with schools like Chatham Glenwood, Riverton and Williamsville adding football.

The group made its first of several appearances before the Rochester School Board in December of 1993. The board, in exercising its due diligence, asked for the group to come back after doing research on expenses, injuries, facilities, gender equity and potential effects on academics. The group offered a donation of $25,000 to help start the program. The board countered by asking the group to completely fund all expenses associated with the football program for a period of five years. Those expenses included paying for equipment, insurance, coaching stipends, game officials and travel plus the cost of off-duty police officers and an ambulance and crew of EMTs at the home games. Those costs averaged about $30,000 a year.

"The seven of us signed an agreement to put the money up to pay for the program those first five years," Jeffers says. "In the end, we didn't have to pay anything out of our pockets." The original agreement gave the group gate receipts for the home football games and track meets. The group found business owners in the Springfield area and others willing and eager to financially support the program. They also raffled off items, including an autographed Michael Jordan jersey. A golf outing to raise money for the football program began in 1995 was still going as one of the program's annual fundraisers almost three decades later.

It turned out that getting the money was the easy part. Public opinion was a different matter. There were letters to the editor, pro and con, as well as radio and TV interviews, mailers, and some face-to-face confrontations. One particular day, the local weekly paper included letters ripping Steve and his group for the football idea – and another letter criticizing his wife Robin, a Hall of Fame girls track coach at Rochester who died in 2023, for voicing her opinion that athletes should be allowed to participate in only one spring sport to open up as many participation opportunities as possible for students.

"Our son Aaron was in grade school, and he came home upset

because he said no one wanted to play with him on the playground," Steve recalls. "I told him not to worry, that no one wanted to play with mommy or daddy that day either. It started to feel personal. If I'm being completely honest, that just made me more determined."

Jeffers says that Taft was the main target of those opposed to bringing football to Rochester. "Steve was kind of the spokesperson for us, so he bore the brunt of the pushback," says Jeffers, who opened a Subway store in Rochester in 1992. "The controversy didn't hurt my store any. It was easy for the rest of us because everyone went after Steve. Some people even suggested he was making money off football because he had a food business. The truth is, he never made a penny off the sales at the concession stand. We got nothing from the concession sales."

The debate culminated with a town meeting in the school library in April of 1994. Taft remembers that the library was packed with between 200 and 300 people who showed up to present differing viewpoints about what had become the village's hottest topic. Two weeks later, the board voted 5-2 to implement a football program, with the caveat that the "Rochester Seven" would agree to pay the bill for five years and that the board would then reassess whether to continue the program. He can laugh about it now, but that doesn't mean Steve Taft has forgotten some of the things that were said in the heat of the moment.

"Some of the people talked about how taxpayers were going to have to pay a six-figure bill each year to have football, which simply wasn't true then or now," he says. "There was one farmer, who since has passed away. I knew him well. We were in the hallway right outside the boardroom after the board voted. I was doing an interview with Channel 20, and he just started reading me the riot act. His grandson went on to be one of the first really good football players at Rochester...and the man never missed a game."

Jeffers says the football program has been nothing but a positive from his viewpoint as a Rochester alumnus and a business owner in the village. "On a Friday night during football season, you will see virtually the entire community at a game. In addition to the players, you have the band playing, the cheerleaders, the pom squad and a student section that is full," he says. "It involves so many of the students, and that means many of their families are there, too."

Dan Cox, who became superintendent at Rochester in 2019, believes the success of the football program has a cathartic effect on the entire student body and on other programs. The district tag line – *"A Tradition of Excellence"* – is not meant to apply just to football.

"No question, football moves the needle in our high school and in our community," Cox says. "But what people on the outside think we are – what I thought Rochester was – is not really what we are. The football program always has very high expectations, but we have those same expectations for our fine arts program, for our academics, and for all our programs. Derek Leonard might be the most well-known coach we have, but we have so many other outstanding coaches and leaders in other sports and in other programs. When I first became superintendent here, I was invited to a Madrigals performance. My jaw dropped open at how good that performance was; it was of college-level quality. From the outside looking in, people may think we are just a football school. That's just not true."

Adding football offered a participation opportunity for players with different body types and a variety of skills that might not translate as well to other sports. Jeffers uses Taft, who was a classmate of his, as a prime example. "Steve played other sports, but he would have been so good at football. That would have been his best sport," says Jeffers, noting that Taft was on the junior high basketball team but never got the chance to start. "One time, the coach got ticked off at some of the starters for some reason and decided to bench them for the next game. Steve was supposed to start. The day of the game, it snowed so much the game was called off. By the time we played again, the coach forgot what he was mad about, so Steve never got to start a game." Taft's son Aaron would get the opportunity to play football for the Rockets, playing for the program's first coach, Dave Jacobs, from 2001-2004. During those four seasons, the Rockets posted a 30-15 cumulative record and made the playoffs each season.

Having had no feeder program for football, it was decided that Rochester would start with a junior varsity team in the fall of 1995 before playing a varsity schedule beginning the following year. A large caravan followed the team bus to Pana for that first junior varsity game in August of 1995. The Rockets lost 33-12, but no one cared much about that result. Rochester finally had football.

The board had hired Jacobs, who had coached at Illiopolis and New Berlin. With a 43-48 record in nine years at Rochester, his name could perhaps be the answer to a trivia question and just a footnote in the Rochester football history books. But those close to the program say that Rochester football might never have ascended to the heights it did without his original leadership. "I will always say that Dave was the right guy for that time," Taft says. "He started out teaching kids how to put shoulder pads and a football uniform on – and that's no joke if you've ever tried to do that. Five years later, we were in the playoffs. That was really an impressive effort."

Jacobs left after nine years coaching the Rockets, leading them to playoff berths each of his last five seasons, to coach at Champaign Central. Jacobs retired from teaching and coaching in 2021 after a 33-year career with various coaching stops in central and southern Illinois, including coaching playoff teams at Champaign Central and Jerseyville. He was inducted into the Illinois High School Football Coaches Association's Hall of Fame in 2019 and in 2021 received the Ray Eliot Award for service to the organization that he for years helped lead.

Steve Taft remembers feeling a mixture of anxiousness, happiness and sheer relief the afternoon of the Rockets' first-ever varsity football game on Friday, August 31, 1996. It truly would be "Friday Night Lights" Rochester style because over the summer a group led by longtime football statistician Chuck Scharf erected lights at the football field, making it the first lighted athletic field of any kind in Rochester. Taft wondered how many people would turn out for that first game. The bleachers were pretty full. He hoped the team would be competitive and that no one would get injured. Also, that there would be no lingering hard feelings in the community. Whatever anxiety he might have felt disappeared when he entered what now is known as Rocket Booster Stadium.

"It was just a sigh of relief," he says. "The fundraising, the community debate, the hiring of a coaching staff, getting the facility ready, the people who got the lights put up, and those kids who came out to play football, just everything it took to get to this point. Watching that first varsity football game ever was really a neat experience."

That first game was an overtime thriller, the Rockets beating Litchfield 21-14 when sophomore running back Tony Hord scored from 10 yards out. For the trivia-minded, the first ever snap of a football for Rochester was from senior center Brett Cox to sophomore quarterback Drew Long. Long scored the first-ever TD on a 1-yard run. The first pass completion was from Long to Hord – for a 7-yard loss. In fact, the Rockets did not complete a pass for a gain in the game. The first rushing attempt was a 3-yard gain by senior Jim Covert. There were 63 players on that first roster, including 17 seniors, two juniors, 18 sophomores and 26 freshmen.

The Rockets traveled the next week to Riverton, a 24-6 win that included the first pass for a gain, a 13-yarder from Long to senior Adam Mueller. As of 2023, that win stands as the only football game ever played between the two Sangamon County schools that have been rivals in most other sports. The football thing must have seemed pretty easy to the casual fan, with the Rockets winning their first two games.

They would not win another game for nearly two years. None of the 63 players on that squad would ever experience a winning high school football season. But they laid the foundation for what would become one of the most storied football programs in state annals.

Victorious!

Born to Coach

Those who know him best are not surprised that Derek Leonard became a football coach. Nor are they surprised that he has become arguably the most successful public school football coach in state history. His coach-in-training regimen began when he was 4 or 5 years old, hanging out at his father's football practices at Griffin High School and serving as a ball boy during Cyclones games. Despite his age, roaming the practice fields and sidelines, he felt a part of his dad's teams as they experienced that old tag line from ABC's "Wide World of Sports" – *The Thrill of Victory... and the Agony of Defeat.*

It was after a lopsided loss to Rock Island Alleman that the youngster approached his father on the sideline and plaintively asked, "We don't have to play that green team again, do we?" Indeed, it was against those same green-clad Alleman Pioneers some 20 years later in 2005 that Ken Leonard and the Cyclones would earn their first-ever state football championship. That also happened to be Derek Leonard's first year as head coach in Rochester. Five years later, Derek would lead Rochester to its first-ever state championship – over the same "green team" that as a little kid he never again wanted to play.

Derek says he cannot point to any "Aha!" moment when he knew he would become a football coach. But he also cannot remember a time when he didn't want to be a football coach. Even as an elementary school student, he would diagram football plays and present them to his father for consideration. "He always seemed glad to get them, but I don't know if he ever used any of them," says Derek, adding, "I've got a few of them in my playbook. My sons Blake and Austin have drawn up some plays just like I did for my dad."

Derek's wife Lindsey recalls sitting in a current events class beside her future husband at Sacred Heart-Griffin High School and wondering how he was going to pass the class. "Just the way the seating chart was designed, Derek was seated in the row next to me. I would glance over, and he would be drawing on a piece of paper," she says, now recognizing the drawings to be the same football plays he still diagrams at the kitchen table. "Other times, he would get recruiting mail from colleges, and the envelope with the school logo would be on his desk. He would make sure I was watching, and he would sign his name like he was signing a recruiting letter of intent, I guess to impress me."

Lindsey remembers that her first impression of Derek was not entirely favorable. She was a junior cheerleader, and Derek was a senior point guard on the SHG basketball team. "He wore number 23 – Michael Jordan's number – and he would make a three-pointer and backpedal down the court pumping his fist in the air. I thought he was kind of arrogant," she says. "When I got to know him, I found out that he is anything but arrogant. He has such a great personality, and he makes me laugh. He's also a wonderful father. Everyone else talks about those championships, but he really doesn't. There are newspaper clippings on his office wall, but he didn't put them there."

Visitors to Derek Leonard's office in the Rochester Athletic Complex across the parking lot from the main high school building would be shocked. And not by its grandeur. It is about the size of a broom closet. There are ragged newspaper clippings documenting the eight state championships that have been randomly taped to the walls by players. There is also a crayon drawing fashioned by his older son Blake when he was 5 or 6 years old. It is of a giant-sized basketball player wearing Michael Jordan's number 23 and a tiny-sized Lebron James, representing Blake's editorial view of the GOAT (Greatest of All Time). Above the door to the office, which is positioned just off one of the practice basketball courts, is a small blue cross formed by two pieces of blue painter's tape and the following, again in simple painter's tape: "Mr. Coach Derek Leonard, Lover of God."

Acknowledging that his football coaching success has provided him with a faith platform that most might not have in a public school, Derek says, "I didn't put the tape there...but I didn't take it down." Probably because he says his personality is much more like his mother's, Derek is pretty low-key and nonconfrontational, at least off the football field. But don't mistake that for a lack of competitiveness.

One of the family drawbacks to Derek getting the Rochester job, one that wasn't the case when he first took the job, was that a few years later the Rockets would join the Central State Eight Conference, meaning that he would face his father's team at least once a year in what came to be known as the "Leonard Bowl." The father and son normally talked by phone several times a week, but never in the week leading up to that game. It was not fun for anyone in the family, least of all Liz. "She didn't want either of us to lose, and that included the players, because she considered them part of her family, too," Derek says. "She would remind whoever won to be graceful in victory toward the one who lost. She would just love on the one that lost."

"Liz had a knack for making everyone she came into contact with feel like they were really important," says Ken Leonard, acknowledging that she provided a much-needed balance to the competitive fire that burned inside of him. "With her, there never was competition...everyone else came first."

When it comes to being competitive, Derek might finish second in his own household to his wife Lindsey. She was a talented enough softball player to be promoted to the SHG varsity as a freshman. She says competitiveness can be hard to tame for the wife of a coach, even one as successful as Derek has been at Rochester. It was advice from Derek's mother that she follows.

"Liz told me a story about that. She often would come to the games after they had started. She said during one game, a couple of men were sitting a couple rows below her and were pretty loud in their criticism of Ken's play-calling or something," Lindsey says. "The person she was with asked her what she was going to do about it. She said, 'Nothing. God will take care of it.' Well, shortly after the game was over, those guys were still there when Ken came walking up and sat down next to Liz. They were mortified to learn that they had been spouting off in front of the coach's wife. God took care of it!"

The Road to Rochester

Lindsey Leonard remembers having a premonition about ending up in Rochester. It was the fall of 2003 and Lindsey was the cheerleading coach at Sacred Heart-Griffin, riding on a school bus to a game in Taylorville. She had just gotten engaged to Derek, who had been hired for his first paid job as an assistant football coach at Prairie Central High School in Fairbury, about 90 miles northeast of Springfield.

"I remember thinking, 'Gosh, it would be cool if he could coach at Rochester because then it would be local, our families are here,'" she told *The State Journal-Register* sportswriter Ryan Mahan in a 2021 interview. "I knew nothing about Rochester at the time. And then a couple of years later it happened. It's been great!" Call it timing. Call it fate. Call it God's plan. Whatever you call it, Rocket fans are thankful that Lindsey's dream scenario fell into place. There were a few reasons it might not have happened.

Derek's first season at Prairie Central under head coach Brian Hassett was in 2003, and the team had its most successful season in school history, finishing second in the state in Class 4A. The Hawks won their first 13 games before losing the championship game 37-21 to an unbeaten Addison Driscoll squad. Derek worked mainly with the quarterbacks that first year, and the Hawks averaged more than 37 points a game, a two-touchdown improvement over the previous year.

The assistant coaching job at Prairie Central had kind of landed in his lap thanks to an ice storm that hit Springfield. The hazardous conditions caused Derek to cancel plans to travel to Chicago to see his uncle. Instead, he decided to accept his father's invitation to attend a coaches' clinic being sponsored by a local sporting goods store at a hotel near the Springfield airport. "Dad was speaking at the clinic, so he said, 'C'mon to the clinic. You need to look for a job anyway,'" recalls Derek, who had just graduated from Illinois College. "I was stuck in town, so I went to the clinic."

One of the speakers was Brian Hassett, the head coach at Prairie Central in Fairbury, about seven miles from Chenoa, where Ken Leonard grew up. Because of the storm, Derek was one of only a handful of people in the room when Hassett spoke about filling an opening on his staff. "He asked if anyone taught PE and might be interested in an assistant coaching job. Boom! When he got done speaking, I headed up to the podium and introduced myself. God kinda put me there." Three weeks later, Derek Leonard had his first coaching job.

"Brian Hassett has been a special person in my life. Obviously, he gave me my first chance to coach. He did a great job of putting me in my place but was also someone who would listen to a young coach. They were transitioning from a power-I running offense to more of a spread passing offense, and I guess I was kind of an avenue to that." Hassett, who quarterbacked Kankakee Bishop McNamara to two state championships in the mid-1980s, coached 16 years at Prairie Central, posting a 98-68 record that included 10 playoff berths. He was selected for induction into the Illinois Football Coaches Hall of Fame in 2021.

Knowing he would be getting married and wanting to be closer to his and Lindsey's families, Derek applied for the head coaching job in Riverton in 2003 after his first year at Prairie Central. With only one season as an assistant coach on his resume, he knew it was probably a longshot. Partly because of Mother Nature and the way in which Leonard ended up on Hassett's staff, he had never been through a formal job interview. "I was kind of nervous interviewing for that Riverton job," he says. "I probably did not do great." In what turned out to fall into the great "What If?" category, Riverton passed on the opportunity to hire Leonard. The coach who was hired lasted just two years, going 5-13.

"It's kind of like the lyrics to Garth Brooks' song Unanswered Prayers," Derek says.

Sometimes I thank God for unanswered prayers
Remember when you're talkin' to the man upstairs
That just because he may not answer doesn't mean he don't care
Some of God's greatest gifts are unanswered prayers

"With some decisions in life, you're almost glad your prayers aren't answered. It's not that I don't believe in myself, but I'm not sure the same thing could have happened in Riverton. Rochester was just a perfect storm."

Leonard returned to Prairie Central for a second season, this time being elevated to the role of offensive coordinator when the previous coordinator, Matt Fox, took a job at Bradley Bourbonnais. The Hawks went 10-2, again averaging more than 30 points per game. With his marriage to Lindsey now less than a year away and with her having been hired to put her business administration degree to use at a Springfield real estate company, Derek was even more intent upon getting a job in the Springfield area. Rochester's first football coach, Dave Jacobs, decided to leave after his ninth season to take a job at Champaign Central High School. Jacobs mentioned his job change to Ken Leonard. One of Jacobs' assistants at Rochester, Charlie Brown, phoned Derek.

"I had gotten to know Charlie through some coaching clinics. He called me and told me he was not going after the head coaching job, but he thought I should apply," Derek says. If the Prairie Central job found him, and the Riverton attempt was just one interview, the process at Rochester was anything but simple. It involved meeting with four or five different groups, including school administrators, school board members, parents and even some players.

The Rochester superintendent of schools at the time was Tom Bertrand, whose career had included stints as an assistant football coach at Quincy College and head coach at Pittsfield High School. There are at least two things about interviewing Derek Leonard that remain vivid in his mind. One was that Leonard was sporting what clearly was a new suit – obvious because the price tag was still attached. "Derek is not a suit-wearing kind of guy," Bertrand says. "The only other time I can remember seeing him wear a suit was at his mother's funeral. But, yeah, the price tag was still on the suit. The secretary motioned for him to come over, and she clipped off the tag before he came into the room for the interview."

The other thing that stood out to Bertrand was a little harder to spot than the dangling price tag. There were two other candidates with more impressive resumes than the 24-year-old Leonard, who had only two seasons as an assistant coach under his belt. The other two finalists had been successful head coaches for years. "Derek just had the 'it' factor," Bertrand says. "I don't even know how to describe it, but you know it when you see it."

Bertrand was especially intrigued by Leonard's plans to implement a wide-open, up-tempo offense with lots of passing and hard-to-defend schemes that would be an especially cutting-edge approach at the high school level. "His was a totally different mindset, and one that we very much needed with the type of athletes we had. We didn't have the power, three-yards-and-a-cloud-of-dust sort of players," Bertrand says. "I also was impressed with what I saw as Derek's ability to build relationships, which is really so important in today's culture."

Derek's ability to connect with people is something he gleaned from observing his mother. "My mom had this way of making everyone feel like they were the most important person in the world. People knew she cared about them," he says. "I learned football from my dad. I learned how to be who I am with people from my mother."

Derek's ability to relate to people is not limited to his football players. Rochester administrators long have directed students with special needs to his PE classes. Bertrand recalls Derek's special bond with a student named Faith, who was non-verbal around almost everyone except Derek. The night of her graduation, she was hesitant to walk across the stage to receive her diploma, crying until Derek escorted her.

Dan Cox, who became superintendent in Rochester in 2019, also quickly recognized Derek's connection with students from varied backgrounds. "It was my first year at Rochester, and I walked over to the gym on Friday morning to shake hands with Derek and wish him luck for that night's game," Cox recalls. "Some football coaches are so locked in on game day that you can't talk to them, but that's not Derek. A couple of high school special needs students were walking in the gym, and one came over and gave Derek a hug while we were talking. Their teacher started to apologize for the interruption, but Derek smiled and said, 'No worries, it's okay!' Pretty soon another and then another student came over for a hug from Derek."

Cox had been a school superintendent in the Jasper County school district for five years and then at Staunton for five years before coming to Rochester. He had a football background, having been a standout offensive and defensive lineman at Newton High School, then going on to play left tackle at Millikin University. He was an assistant football coach at Warrensburg-Latham High School and Argenta-Oreana High School before becoming a school administrator. So, he knows football and has been around several football coaches. He said Derek Leonard was not at all the sort of coach he expected to meet when he arrived in Rochester.

"Viewing it from the outside, seeing all of his success and knowing his coaching pedigree, I expected to find this larger-than-life figure, and maybe even someone with a pretty big ego," Cox says. "Derek is the exact opposite. Don't get me wrong, he is a straight-out competitor. His practices are intense, and he commands respect. He has confidence, but he also has humility. His relational skills are the things that impress me the most. He cares about kids, and not just the kids on his team."

During the hiring process, Tom Bertrand was blown away by Derek's creative offensive mind and enthusiasm. He laughs when he recalls the reaction of Steve Taft, the guy who led the effort to finally bring football to Rochester, when Bertrand introduced Derek at his first public event. "The first words out of Derek's mouth were, 'Oh boy, I've wanted to be a football coach ever since I was a little kid!' I looked over at Steve and he just said, 'Oh, my…what have we gotten ourselves into?'"

Indeed, the Rockets and their fans were in for a very wild ride. That first season under Derek the Rockets were 3-6 – his only losing season through 2022 – and the next two seasons were both break-even 5-5 campaigns. Bertrand saw promising signs, especially in that third year, when Rochester pushed a loaded Bloomington Central Catholic team to the limit before losing 42-37 in a conference game. Central Catholic would go on to finish second in Class 4A that year and then win the state title the next year. Two years later, in 2009, the Rockets would demolish Central Catholic 49-12 in Rochester's final year in the Corn Belt Conference. That also would be the season when the Rockets lost by one point in the semifinals to Metamora, the precursor to the incredible decade in which Rochester won eight state championships.

"You know, it's really kind of funny, but the two games that stand out to me the most, the games that convinced me great things were about to happen, were both losses," Bertrand says. "That game against Bloomington Central Catholic, we had no business hanging with them based on the talent they had, including a future NFL player and other Division I college players. Schematically, they could not stop our offense. Then, in 2009, I really thought we outplayed Metamora but just got some bad breaks. Metamora won the state championship game the next week by like 50 points. Of course, the highlights were all of the championships that followed. But it was those two losses when I just knew we all were going to be in for something really special."

There was one other twist that, had he known about it, would have caused Derek Leonard to have second thoughts about coming to Rochester. In 2010, the Rockets moved from the Corn Belt Conference, a league of 4A-sized schools, to the Central State Eight Conference, a 5A/6A-size league in which Rochester would be the smallest school. "I absolutely would not have taken the Rochester job if I had known we would be going to the Central State Eight," Derek says. "When that happened, I thought, 'Man, what are we doing?' I understood why we made the move because the travel in the Corn Belt was brutal with all the schools being around Bloomington or farther away. But I had my doubts we could compete in the Central State Eight. It's one of the best conferences in the state."

There was one fact that gave Derek optimism that Rochester might be able to compete in the Central State Eight. Taft and Terry David had started the Rochester Junior Football League (JFL), and the JFL was in good shape. Brent Tackett, who was on Derek's Rochester coaching staff, was one of the first JFL coaches. Kids were being taught football fundamentals and techniques at a young age, and the JFL was beginning to churn out class after class of developing football players. The success of the Rockets continued to fuel that JFL system into the 2020s under the leadership of Kevin Gade as scores of boys in Rochester aspired to become Rochester football players.

"That JFL program has been the lifeblood of Rochester football," Derek says. "I knew we had some good groups coming, and I knew as far back as 2007 that we were going to be pretty good for the next few years. But you never really know until it actually happens, and at a school our size in a league like the Central State Eight, you know you're probably going to have some down years."

In the first 13 years since joining the Central State Eight – from the 2010 season through the 2022 season – the furthest "down" the Rockets would fall were four years in which they lost two games each season. Their overall record for those 13 seasons was 152-16. No one in the Central State Eight would be shedding any tears for Rochester or Derek any time soon.

Philip's Story

Ken Leonard had finished his morning run and was sitting in his office talking with SHG basketball coach Jim Drew. It was about 8:30 the morning of February 3, 2000. He noticed a blonde woman enter through the doorway across the common area of the athletic department offices. At first glance, he thought it was one of the teachers from the main school building. But this woman was accompanied by a police officer. She wasn't a teacher. She was Sangamon County Coroner Susan Boone.

"She told me that our son Philip had been killed in a car accident down near St. Louis where he was working and living. It had happened the night before, but because his last name was Pearson, it took the authorities a while to figure out that he was our adopted son," recalled Ken some 22 years later. "My first reaction was pure anger. I threw something against the wall. Then the Holy Spirit took over and assured me of everything I believed. I knew I had to be strong. I needed to go over to Graham (Elementary) School and get Liz out of class and tell her. My God, that was horrible. She was completely distraught."

Philip Pearson was dead at age 23. According to reports, he had been one of three passengers in a car driven by an intoxicated young man who had filled the car up at a gas station and sped away without paying. The car flipped over at a very high rate of speed, killing everyone except the driver.

Philip had overcome great odds just to graduate from high

51

school. He bounced from foster home to foster home from the time he was about four years old until the Leonards took him into their family when he was 11. His birth mother was in prison. Ken says the story he was told is that she killed one of Philip's cousins in front of Philip and a half-brother, one of nine half-siblings who ended up spread out among foster homes in different cities. In addition to the emotional scars, there were the physical marks Ken noticed on Philip, which the boy said were from some of his mother's boyfriends.

Derek Leonard was three years younger than Philip, but the boys played basketball together at Dubois Elementary School. Philip was someone the other boys tended to gravitate toward, in part because of the survival skills Philip had acquired at a very early age. He had the ability to charm, smooth talk and manipulate people. Philip could, as Ken described it, "talk anyone into giving you the change out of their britches." Derek recalls that at first Philip would come over to their house after school along with other kids. The Leonard house was modest, but it had makeshift sports venues and was a landing spot for boys from the neighborhood and the school. It was a home Derek remembers as "a living playground." Ken was still living there upon his retirement.

"We didn't allow any of the computer stuff after school back then. They played ball outside. We had a basket up on the side of the house, and they beat the crap out of the siding," says Ken.

The loving environment at the Leonard home was indeed a gift for a kid with Philip's background. He had been living in what was termed an "attention home," a group home for kids who had been delinquent or had no family home in which to live. It is no wonder that Philip asked to grow the after-school visits into an occasional overnight visit and then weekend visits. Liz worked more than 25 years as an elementary school teacher's aide in the Springfield school district. That's how she had gotten to know Philip and learned about his situation. She and Ken started discussing adopting Philip, and they began attending foster parenting classes. "It was more Liz than me at first," Ken recalls. "One thing they stressed during the training we went through was that it was not going to be easy, that people needed to go in with their eyes wide open because many of the kids had come from very rough situations. One of the discussions Liz and I had was that if we got him, we would be all-in. There would be no going back on our commitment."

Bryan McKenzie, one of the leaders in the Fellowship of Christian Athletes (FCA) organization and a close friend of Ken Leonard, was not surprised that the Leonards decided to add Philip to their family. Years later, McKenzie would officiate at Philip Pearson's funeral. "For some, a kid from the type of background Philip came from might seem unlovable, but not to Ken and Liz. I saw a couple that loved a young man that needed a whole lot of love," McKenzie says. "They treated him just like they treated Derek and Bradley. He was one of their sons. They had a structure in their home and rules that everyone had to follow. Today a lot of parents don't have that structure because of a fear that their kids won't like them…and then they end up losing their kids to things like drugs and alcohol."

Even in the best of situations, marriage and raising children can be stressful. Adding a child with Philip's emotional baggage to the equation made it exponentially more difficult. A white family adding a black youngster to the family surely must have raised some eyebrows back in the late 1980s, but that was never even a consideration for the Leonards. They used to drop Derek off at the Boys Club in Springfield, where often he was the only white kid there playing basketball. "It was never a thing for me," Derek says. "I just wanted to play ball against the best players, and the best players were at the Boys Club. Sometimes I got picked to be on a team, sometimes I didn't. That's just the way it was. I just had to work on becoming a better player if I wanted to be picked."

Philip getting in trouble was a regular occurrence, so much so that it never elicited much more than a shrug from Derek or his younger brother Bradley. But it was a bit of a roller coaster for Ken and Liz. Ken recalls getting regular phone calls from Kris Glintborg, then the assistant principal at Grant Middle School. One time Philip got in trouble with a teacher, but by the time Ken arrived at the school, Philip somehow had convinced the teacher that he deserved a break. "I could tell she was kinda nervous saying anything," Ken says. "She goes on about Philip being a really a good kid who just made a mistake. I just stopped her right there. I said, 'Hold it. Philip is one of our children. You are the teacher. You are the authority. If he gets out of line and is not doing what he is supposed to do, don't let him sweet talk you into something.' That's how we treated all our kids, and it wasn't going to be different for Philip."

When he was a sophomore at SHG, Philip and some other sophomores on the football team got caught with alcohol on the team bus. One of the kids on the team had gotten hold of a couple of the small bottles of liquor often served on airplanes. During a stop at a McDonald's en route to Geneseo, some of the players were pouring small amounts into their drinks. Most of the players denied the accusation. In fact, only two of the players confessed, Philip and the assistant principal's nephew. The next step was a disciplinary hearing with some of the nuns and a priest from the school.

"Liz and I are in this big room at the hearing. I'm not sure the priest and nuns even knew Philip was our son," Ken recalls. "We're watching and Philip somehow has the nuns feeling sorry for him. I was like, 'Timeout! Timeout! Whoa, is this how it's going to be? Philip is a Christian, or he says he is. Do we want him to be the old Philip, or do we want him to be the new Philip? He should get the punishment anyone else would get. If he doesn't change, he won't go to school here until he shows that he can be the Philip we know he can be.' He probably got punished more than any player I've ever had. And Liz was right there with me, maybe even tougher than me. She would smell the breath of all three of our boys when they came home to make sure they had not been drinking or smoking."

Derek recalls the time he got caught walking to the high school gym without his coat and hat, a violation of team rules. Somehow, his mother found out and showed up at the gym after he had played in the junior varsity game. "Normally, the JV players would stay and watch at least a half of the varsity game, but she marched in and took me home. She wouldn't let me play the next game," Derek says. "It was just a short walk from our house to the gym, and I thought no one would see me. But someone did, and with my mom you did not break rules."

Liz's insistence on following the rules was one of the reasons Ken says a "real love-hate" relationship existed between Philip and Liz. "Philip was the ultimate manipulator, and he knew how to push Liz's buttons. He wouldn't talk back to me, and when things were good, no problem. But when things got tough, when he did something wrong – which was quite often – he would say something to Liz like, 'Well, you're not my mom anyway! My mom is in the women's prison in Dwight!'" Ken says. "It wasn't pretty, and I would get caught in the middle of it. There were times she would have all she could take and I would have to talk her back down and remind her that we were in this for better or worse."

With no father or mother for the first 10 years of his life and bouncing from foster home to foster home, it is not surprising that Philip had problems assimilating into the Leonard family. The older he got, the more he would bristle at the Leonard house rules, including the curfew that applied to all the boys. When a juvenile who has been in the state childcare system turns 18, they can make some of their own choices. Facing the ultimatum that he would have to abide by the rules if he were to continue to live with the Leonards, Philip decided to head to Peoria to a foster home where his older stepbrother Albert was staying. It seemed Albert could pretty much do whatever he wanted.

Ken and Liz tried to stay in touch, Ken checking in with the Peoria Richwoods High football coach only to find out that Philip had been skipping practices and was not going to be on the team. They even visited the group home in Peoria a couple of times, but the man who was the foster parent did not want the Leonards to visit. They left with some very bad vibes. About three months later, Philip called.

"He said, 'I want to come home. I was wrong,'" Ken says. "I was like, 'Whoa, what's going on?'" Ken says the man turned out to be someone who took in foster children primarily for the money. Ken says he learned the man allegedly abused some of the children. Because Philip was still in the state system, returning to the Leonards took some time. For a brief period, he was placed in a home in Peoria, where he lived with a minister and his wife. They took good care of him.

Eventually, Philip returned to the Leonard home, though they sent him to Springfield High instead of back to SHG. There, he came under the guidance of Jim Steinwart, the longtime baseball coach and special education teacher at Springfield High. Steinwart was among the top 20 most successful Illinois high school baseball coaches in history with 711 wins through 2023, including a state championship in 2021. During his 35-plus seasons of coaching, Steinwart routinely invited special needs students to be part of the team as batboys. In that setting, Philip started making the best grades he had ever achieved. After one semester, the Leonards re-enrolled him at SHG. He went on to do well in school and became a starting defensive back his senior year on the 1995 team that advanced to the state championship game. Derek was a sophomore quarterback on that team, playing behind senior Ryan Wells. Another player on that 1995 team was Christian Gripper.

The Other Brother

Christian Gripper got to know the Leonards when he began attending SHG as a freshman in 1991. It was there that he met and was drawn to Philip Pearson. Gripper would hang out at the Leonard home, sometimes sleeping over.

"Phil and I became best friends, inseparable. He had this air of confidence about him...he was great at everything, and such a people person. I was the opposite of him, but I gained confidence through being around him," Gripper says. "Derek was the golden boy, Bradley was the baby of the family, and Phil and I were the troublemakers. We used to drive Mama Leonard crazy, asking her to pull our fingers and stuff like that."

Gripper says he and Philip were two of about 10 black students at SHG at the time and were two of four black athletes on that 1995 football team. Though Gripper says he never experienced any racial issues with fellow students, he sometimes did with some parents and some outsiders. "I asked a girl I liked to Homecoming. She liked me, too," Gripper says. "I found out later the reason she couldn't go to the dance with me was because I was black and her parents were upset." He also remembers playing a baseball game in Lincoln his sophomore year. He caught a line drive to end the game for a Cyclones win. "Some of the Lincoln players were calling me the 'N' word, but my teammates were there in an instant taking up for me."

One of his fondest high school memories was participating in a "Jackson 5" skit at the school talent show. "Of course, Phil was

Michael Jackson," Gripper says. "Phil was a great dancer. The other four of us were just in the background trying to dance. He was the only one who could stay on the beat. The other students loved it!"

A bittersweet high school memory was of him and Philip as senior teammates on the 1995 Cyclones team that played in the state championship game – the first of Ken Leonard's teams ever to make it that far. They were heavy underdogs to a powerhouse Providence Catholic team that has been ranked among the state's all-time best teams. SHG led 17-7 with under four minutes to play and was on the verge of one of the biggest upset wins in state history. Providence Catholic cut the lead to 17-15 by scoring a touchdown and adding a two-point conversion with 3:35 to play. The Celtics had no timeouts left. SHG just needed one first down to run out the clock.

SHG's first two downs lost yardage. On a third-and-12 play, the Cyclones gave the ball to Gripper, a fullback who had not fumbled the ball all year. A video replay shows that Gripper slipped at the line of scrimmage, regained his balance and was fighting for yardage when one of the Celtics tacklers knocked the ball loose. Providence Catholic recovered the ball at the SHG 23-yard line. The Celtics scored the game-winning TD on a 4-yard run with just 46 seconds left.

"My best moment in sports was when we made it to the state football championship game…but it was also my lowest moment because my fumble cost us the championship," Gripper said years later. "I had not fumbled all year. Somebody just knocked the ball from under my arm. I thought my knee was already down before the ball came loose." But that was in the days before anyone used video to review calls.

Gripper would go on to be an assistant football coach at Conant High School in the Chicago suburbs of Hoffman Estates. He says the game and life lessons he learned from Ken Leonard have helped guide him.

Gripper still remembers what Leonard said to the Cyclones after that most devastating of losses. "You could see the disappointment on his face, but Coach Leonard was just so calm. He just told us, 'Lots of successful people at SHG ended their career with a loss, but then they went on to be winners in life. God has bigger plans for your life.'" Gripper says. "I'm still getting there, but I have a degree, I have a good job, and I am taking care of my family. I grew up without a father in the house, and I have gravitated toward some father figures. Papa Leonard is definitely one of them. He showed me what a father should be.

"Coach Leonard was a fiery guy back when I played for him. He and Coach (John) Sowinski both would tell us, 'Listen to what we say, not how we say it.' Those were different times. I can't coach kids today as hard as they coached me. If you want to talk about Coach Leonard's legacy…he used football as a tool to make us into great men. I try to live and coach like that."

Gripper witnessed Leonard living his faith even in the hardest of times. "He lives his faith every day, but I probably saw it best when Phil died. He fell back on his faith. I had a hard time doing that. In fact, I just told our Conant team the other day about losing Phil. I had experienced death when my great grandparents had died, but Phil was the first person close to my age that had died. He was my best friend. Derek and I both had been around (the guy who was driving) a couple of times when we had visited Phil. We had a bad feeling about him. He kind of scared us."

In early 2000, Derek and Christian were playing football at different colleges in Jacksonville, Illinois. Derek was at Illinois College and Christian at MacMurray College across town. Christian was playing a pickup basketball game when he saw Derek walk into the MacMurray Fieldhouse the morning of February 3. It wasn't unusual to see Derek there because he sometimes would come over to MacMurray to play in one of the pickup basketball games. But this day was different.

"He said, 'Gripp, you gotta get out of the game.' I was like, 'Why, I'm playing good?' Then I saw him just break down crying. He said Phil had been killed. I will never forget that moment," Gripper says. "The last time I talked to Phil, he told me he was going to be a millionaire. He said, 'It's coming!' I believe he would have been. He had that 'it' factor. I mean, he could sell a mouse a cat. He made me a better version of myself."

When the details of what happened the night Philip was killed came to light, Ken and Liz Leonard made an excruciating decision. Prior to the sentencing for the young man who had been driving – the only person of the four in the car who had survived the crash – Ken met with the state's attorney and expressed forgiveness for the driver responsible for Philip's death. He asked for leniency and mercy to be shown to the young man. "Liz and I prayed a lot about that. It wasn't an easy choice to make, and the parents of the other kids who lost their lives that night weren't very happy with us," Ken says. "But vengeance was not going to bring Philip back, and a really long sentence would just ruin another life. From the cross, Jesus forgave those who were crucifying him. It was what we felt God was commanding us to do."

McKenzie, who preached Philip's funeral, says he was not surprised that Ken and Liz asked for mercy for the driver. "That is the type of Christians Ken and Liz had become. As it says in Ephesians (4:32), *'Be kind and compassionate to one another, forgiving each other, just as in Christ, God forgave you...'* Ken has never been ashamed of his faith, and he's not going to back down from it."

For Christian Gripper, it was a demonstration of faith that left a lasting impression. "I mean, isn't that what we're called to do as Christians? I could see Papa Leonard and Mama Leonard doing that. I'm not sure I could," says Gripper, who still refers to Liz as "Mama" Leonard and Ken as "Papa" Leonard, although it was always "Coach" on the football field.

"The amount of love in the Leonard household was unbelievable. Growing up with a single mother and without a father in the house, I really hadn't ever seen a happy marriage. It was awesome to feel that and be part of that family where they were loving you and loving each other. That was my second home...sometimes my first home," Gripper says. "You know, after Phil died, I was really hurting. Mama Leonard told me, 'You're going to live with us.' Of course, she's also the one who kicked me out of Springfield!"

Just as it had been with Philip, the Leonards expected Gripper to follow the house rules, including a midnight curfew even though he was 22 years old. "One time I was at a bar and a guy comes up to me and says, 'Coach Leonard is here...to get you!' They didn't want anything bad to happen to me," Gripper says. "At that point in my life, I wasn't really doing anything productive, so one day Mama Leonard told me I had two choices: I could go live with my dad up in Chicago and get a job, or I could join the military. I chose Chicago."

Gripper got a job at Maryville Academy, a Catholic-sponsored home for boys. It was there that he met a coworker named Miranda, who would become his wife. The couple has two sons, Christian Gripper II and Braxton. From Maryville, Gripper went on to become a P.E. teacher and crisis intervention counselor at the School of Expressive Learning and Arts, a private school specializing in special education in Lombard. His coaching job at Conant High School was owed in part to references from both Ken and Derek Leonard. "I didn't know it at the time, but both Ken and Derek vouched for me to Coach Stortz (Conant head coach Bryan Stortz). They had met him at coaches' clinics, and they knew I always had wanted to coach," Gripper says.

In fact, he remembers as a kid talking with Derek about becoming a football coach, specifically an assistant coach for Derek, who is three years younger than Gripper. "Oh yeah, I always knew Derek would be a coach. You know, Bradley could have been a great coach, too, but he chose another path and has been successful in business. Derek talked about becoming a coach when we were kids. I told him I wanted to be his offensive coordinator," Gripper says. "But we would play this video football game, and he would always beat me using these unique plays. He finally told me, 'Gripp, I don't think you're going to be my offensive coordinator...but maybe a special teams coach.'"

In life, things sometime come full circle. In late 2022, Gripper informed Derek that he and his family were planning to move to Rochester so his youngest son could play for Derek. Derek planned to add Gripper to his football staff in some capacity and that he was looking forward to coaching Braxton Gripper, who as a fourth grader at the time already had demonstrated the same type of football ability as his father and older brother.

Both Derek and Bradley Leonard refer to Christian Gripper as their "other brother," and Gripper says to this day he feels like if he made a phone call, the Leonards would be there to help him, regardless of the time or place. On the other hand, he says he never envisioned life without Mama Leonard or Phil. "You know the song Fire and Rain," he says, referring to the James Taylor hit song. *"'I've seen fire and I've seen rain...I've seen sunny days that I thought would never end. I've seen lonely times when I could not find a friend. But I always thought I'd see you again...'* It was like that. I never thought there'd be a day when I couldn't reach out and call Mama Leonard or Phil."

Ken remembers Liz being almost inconsolable for days after Philip's death. Eventually, after Philip's body had been returned to Springfield, Ken and Liz went to the funeral home to make arrangements. Ken had spoken to Philip earlier the evening of the accident. Philip told him he had accepted Jesus as his savior.

"Remarkably, despite the horrible accident, his face was... well, it was Philip. That's when the Holy Spirit took over Liz. She became the consoler and I broke down. God used me at first, then He used her," Ken says. "But the most remarkable thing was when these people we didn't even know, people Philip knew from down around St. Louis, came up to us during visitation and told us how Philip led them to Jesus. He would be selling things in the mall, and he would have his Bible there and talk to them about Jesus. I can't count how many people went through that line who said, 'Philip led me to the Lord.'"

One of the people Philip had led to the Lord, in a roundabout way through something as simple as a haircut, was Ken Leonard.

Victorious!

A Haircut and Salvation

The Bible is full of stories about God using unlikely people to carry out His works. Consider Saul of Tarsus, who persecuted and killed Christians before his lightning-bolt-like conversion turned him into the Apostle Paul, who would be credited with writing almost half of the New Testament. Sarah was the 90-year-old childless wife of 99-year-old Abraham, who was selected by God to become the father of the Jewish nation. Despite her laughing at God's plan that she would bear a child at her age, Sarah would give birth to Isaac. Through Isaac and one of his sons, Jacob, the family tree of Abraham and Sarah eventually would produce Jesus of Nazareth.

Rick Braun might be another example of God using an unlikely person to help lead others to salvation. Braun was the owner of Rick's Place, a one-chair barber shop located near Springfield High School. It was where Ken Leonard ended up one spring morning in 1992 in search of something more than a haircut.

Ken awoke that morning with a feeling of emptiness. It was a different sort of hunger, one located more in his soul than in his stomach. The nagging ache didn't stem from a lack of football success. He already was the winningest coach in Griffin/SHG history with a 69-16 record after just eight seasons. Even before that morning, he had discussed his feelings of emptiness with the school principal Sister Mary Paul McCaughey before she left SHG. Sister Mary Paul suggested he talk with the bishop. She also counseled him that sometimes the spiritual answers a person is seeking are found outside the walls of the church. Ken heeded her advice and went to talk with Bishop Daniel Ryan. Ken then headed to confession at the cathedral. He didn't need a haircut, but sitting in his car in the parking lot after confession, Ken felt a strong urge to go to Rick's barber shop.

Rick Braun grew up in the Kankakee area and attended barber school in Texas. He eventually ended up back in the Chicago area, where he became licensed to be a barber in Illinois. He had an interest in the metaphysical, which included the supernatural as well as psychics. He got to know a teacher in Springfield who shared his interest in things beyond the laws of physics and nature. That connection is what led Braun to move to the capital city and set up his barber shop.

Braun also aired his own TV show titled "The World Beyond" on the Springfield community access channel. One of his regular guests was a self-described "parapsychologist" named Greta Alexander, who claimed to have supernatural connections. In one highly publicized case, it was reported that she helped law enforcement find the body of a kidnapped boy who was murdered. It is true that some of her clues turned out to be accurate, but upon further review many of them also turned out to be vague enough to loosely fit into almost any ending to the search. Braun also spent a lot of time preparing astrological charts for people, and he was into the idea of reincarnation.

The gap between the metaphysical and religion may be narrow in some respects. After all, one definition of faith is a belief in things unseen. Braun had been attending Catholic Masses off and on but says he would not have described himself as religious at that point in his life – let alone "a Godly man," which is how Leonard describes him. Braun met his future wife, Jann, in Springfield. Church had long been a part of Jann's life, thanks to the faith of her mother, Ruth. Jann decided to invite Rick to attend a service at her church in Auburn.

"I sat down with my best friend, Cheryl Harvey, and we made a list of things we hoped the preacher would not say Sunday because we were afraid it might freak Rick out if the preacher came on too strong," Jann says. "Cheryl and I prayed over that list." The small church was crowded by the time they arrived. They ended up sitting in the front row, Rick between the two women. The preacher's sermon included almost everything on the women's list of things to avoid. "It was like the preacher somehow had a copy of the list and was just checking every box," Jann says. "When the service was over, we very gingerly asked Rick if he would consider attending future services."

Turns out, the message resonated with Rick so much that he returned for a special Easter service. The speaker that day concluded his sermon by asking if anyone in the congregation wanted to be saved. Rick's hand was among the first to be raised. His life's path had changed. It wasn't long before he became a deacon in the church. "You can stick your toe in the water, or you can dive in," Rick says. "For me, it wasn't just about becoming a Christian. It was the beginning of a relationship with Jesus and walking hand in hand with Him. I was all in."

His first barber shop had burned, so he moved into a new space he dubbed Rick's Place. He cut hair and gave straight-razor shaves in an area of the shop with one barber chair. That area looked pretty much like any other small barber shop of the 1980s and early 1990s. The waiting area in the foyer didn't look anything like a barber shop. It had a couple of comfortable leather sofas and several plants. It also featured an open, oversized Bible on a wooden stand. A framed picture on the wall was of Jesus laughing uproariously. The depiction had first appeared in Playboy magazine.

"There are not many images of Jesus laughing or even smiling. Most times they showed him being somber," Rick says. "But I envision Jesus being forgiving, full of joy and having a sense of humor. Someone showed me that picture, so I got a copy of it for my barber shop."

The look and feel of Rick's Place were welcoming and so was

Rick. Standing around 6-foot-3, Rick towered over most of his customers, but he was soft spoken. Despite his commitment to Jesus, Rick says he never discussed his faith unless someone asked. The environment was so inviting that students from nearby Springfield High would drop in on their lunch breaks just to talk about life. So many students started hanging out at Rick's Place that the high school principal showed up there one day to investigate what was going on. He ended up coming back to get his hair cut for the rest of his tenure at the school.

Philip Pearson was only about 10 years old when Rick started cutting his hair at his first barber shop that later burned down. It was located near what was called an "attention home," where homeless youngsters like Philip were housed by the state. The kids, their ages ranging from about 8 to 12, started stopping by Rick's barber shop. He would give them free haircuts and a willing ear. They kept coming back. Rick says the reason was simple: "I listened to them, and I would answer their questions. They found out it was okay to talk about whatever was bothering them." He remembers Philip as "a sweet boy who had been through some really tough times." He continued to cut Philip's hair at his new barber shop, which is where he first met Ken after the Leonards adopted Philip. Pretty soon Philip, Derek, Bradley and Ken were all getting their hair cut at Rick's Place.

Rick Braun is not a football fan. In fact, he says he has never seen a game in person and has watched a game on TV only a couple of times when SHG or Rochester was playing for a state championship. Football was never the reason he sought to connect with the coach. "What I saw in Ken Leonard was a light that shines brighter than any light in the city," Rick says. "I knew that he had the ability to touch and shape the lives of thousands of young men. Our relationship seemed to center around the barber shop; I don't think I've ever been in Ken's house all the years I've known him. I never pushed Jesus on him or anyone else that ever came into my shop. But if they had any questions, I would try to answer them."

Neither Rick nor Ken remember the exact date in the spring of 1992 when Ken showed up at the barber shop looking for those answers. But the other memories of that day are vivid for both men. "He parked right in front of my shop," Rick says. "No one else was in the shop. He walked in and immediately said, 'I don't need a haircut and I don't know why I'm here. But there's something missing in my life and I'm struggling.' I told him what was missing in his life was Jesus Christ. I kept it simple. We prayed together, and we talked about John 3:16, *God so loved the world that he gave his only begotten Son, that whosoever believeth in Him should not perish, but have everlasting life.*"

The whole visit did not take long, but for Ken the impact was everlasting. He kept returning to the barber shop day after day with more questions. His sons, Derek and Bradley, noticed the difference immediately. Approaching their teen years, they thought he had gone way overboard and tried to talk him into toning down all the Jesus stuff, especially around their friends. Much like Rick the barber, Ken dove into the deep end headfirst.

"At first, I was just angry that no one had told me this before," Ken recalls. "I mean, I had been to church, heard some of the stuff, but no one had ever really talked to me about it or explained what it meant. I kept going back to ask Rick about things I read in the Scriptures. I wanted to immediately share the message with my wife and kids, my mom and dad, my siblings, with everyone in my family. I wanted them all to be saved, and I think most of them have been. I wanted to share it with anyone who would listen." Ken says he does not try to offend anyone with his beliefs. "But I won't compromise my faith. I'd rather offend people than offend God."

Ken's sister Sheila Easley also thought at first that her brother was kind of out there with his newfound religious zeal. "Ken just kept talking and talking about it," she says. "But he never was pushy. He didn't just talk the talk, he has also walked the walk." Sheila married Sam Easley, whose older brother Ed played high school ball with Ken in Chenoa. The Easleys were one of the families Ken lived with during his senior year in Chenoa. Sam says he was blown away hearing Ken speak at the funeral of the Leonards' adopted son Philip Pearson, who died in an auto accident in 2000. "It was like he had been touched and was speaking for someone higher."

In less than three years, the Easleys would mourn the death of their own son, Dustin, a 22-year-old senior at Purdue University who was killed in a car accident returning to his parents' home in New Milford, Connecticut, in the early morning hours of Thanksgiving Day in 2003. Like Philip, Dustin had been a passenger in a car driven by a friend. Sam and Sheila started the Dustin Easley Memorial Foundation, and until they moved to South Carolina years later, they delivered Thanksgiving meals to families and provided a community feast at a local church, sometimes going through as many as 180 turkeys. They said it was a way to honor Dustin, and it also was a way to stay busy on a day that for them held such sorrow.

Ken attended weekly Catholic Mass with his players his entire time at SHG. He never joined a church, instead attending various churches in the greater Springfield area, going where he felt he was being spiritually fed at the time. Jesus invited the fishermen he recruited to join his disciples to lay down their nets and become fishers of men. When it was suggested that Ken Leonard was a good catch for Rick, the barber shied away from that description. "When I was around Ken, I was thinking more like the fish. He probably drew me out more than I did him when he asked all those questions. We had some great talks. I just knew that being around him was going to be a good thing."

One of those good things to come from Ken's conversion was his connection to the Fellowship of Christian Athletes (FCA). He started an FCA Huddle at SHG in 1995, welcoming the school's athletes and coaches from all sports. He and Bryan McKenzie also began hosting a 6 a.m. Thursday morning Bible study for area coaches in Ken's office, a weekly gathering that was ongoing 28 years later. One reason Ken wanted the meetings to be held in his office was to make him accountable to attend. "If it's in my office, I have to be there to open the door," he explains. After his retirement at the end of the 2022 season, Ken joined the FCA staff as a part-time ambassador.

Kevin Elliott, the Central Illinois Area Director of FCA, attended most of those weekly meetings of coaches in Ken's office for almost three decades. He has witnessed much of Leonard's faith journey up close. "God wired Ken to be a football coach and a leader. He is probably the most competitive person I've ever been around," says Elliott, who played college baseball at Oakland City College in Indiana. "Sometimes your greatest strength can also be a weakness. There were times we'd be in that Thursday morning Bible study and he'd say, 'Hey guys, I need to say something here. I blew it in practice last night and said some things I shouldn't have said. I apologized to the players. I asked forgiveness from them, and I want to ask forgiveness from you.' He would be brutally honest. I saw his desire to grow stronger in his faith, and I also saw the consistency of someone who would show up at 6 a.m. every Thursday, even in the middle of the football season."

Elliott also saw how Ken lived his faith when he lost his adopted son Philip in a car crash and when he lost his wife Liz to cancer. Elliott's wife Jenny sang at Philip's funeral. "I will never forget Ken's sons Derek and Bradley saying to him in the days after Philip died, 'Dad, this is game time; it's why you have been teaching and preaching to us the importance of knowing Christ.' Ken would often say that it's easy when things are going well, but when you're tested, that's when you grow as a Christian."

Elliott and his wife were tested, suffering the loss of a child. Luke Thomas Elliott was perfectly healthy when he was born in 2003. A couple of days after they brought the baby home, they noticed he was not eating well and was kind of listless. The baby ended up being helicoptered to a children's hospital in St. Louis, where he and the family went through five days of a roller-coaster of prognoses. Luke died nine days after his birth. Doctors determined that he had contracted a common virus and that his body had not developed enough antibodies to fight it off. In addition to Luke, the Elliott family includes daughters Emma and Annie and three sons, Isaac and adopted brothers Titus and Jackson. "Your goal as a Christian parent is for all of your kids to have everlasting life in heaven," Elliott says. "The Bible teaches that children as young as Luke will be in heaven. We are thankful to know he is there."

Elliott says the experience of losing a child increased his urgency to spread the word of God to young athletes through FCA. "Because sports are so big in our culture, I'm not sure there's a better avenue to share the gospel with young people," he says.

He says Ken and Derek Leonard have been important to the growth of FCA in central Illinois and throughout the state. He met Ken at an FCA banquet in 1995, the first of what would become an annual fundraiser for the FCA in central Illinois. It was put together by Ron Michaelson, Jim Howard and Bob Cook. The list of speakers was quite impressive, headlined by Dallas Cowboys Hall of Fame coach Tom Landy and University of Illinois football coach Lou Tepper. Ken Leonard was on the list, too, representing the local coaches. "I went to hear Tom Landry and Lou Tepper, but I came away much more impacted by Ken, and that's not to downplay the other two. But here's a local coach in Ken, who had only known the Lord two or three years at that point, and he had such passion. He likes to joke that he wasn't the sharpest tool in the shed growing up. He kept the message simple and to the point about how God had saved him as a person and as a coach."

Derek's impact on FCA was illustrated when the organization began a multi-sport camp on the campus of Illinois College in Jacksonville, where Derek had been a quarterback. Elliott says every year there would be more kids from Rochester than from any other school. Derek never missed the camp, not even after another in his remarkable run of state championships. Elliott once asked Derek why he never missed a camp and why he brought so many of his players. "Derek said, 'I know this is what our kids need more than they need the X's and O's of football. They'll hear plenty about football from me, but the faith message at this camp is what I want them to hear first and foremost. This is what brings our team closer together.' Coaching really is a spiritual thing for both Ken and Derek. They care about reaching the hearts of their players."

Victorious!

The Heart Behind the Jersey

Considered by many to be the greatest basketball coach ever, former UCLA coach John Wooden once said, "A good coach can change a game. A great coach can change a life." The Rev. Billy Graham once observed that "a coach will impact more people in a year than the average person does in a lifetime."

That line of thinking is what drove former Florida State assistant football coach Jeff Duke to write a book titled "3D Coach: Capturing the Heart Behind the Jersey." Duke, who coached on the staff of legendary Florida State coach Bobby Bowden, has a doctorate in education and has studied the cultural influence coaches have on young people. He contends that coaches have become among the most authoritative figures in the lives of adolescents in our society. A statistic from the National Council of Youth Sports says that 60 million children and teens participate in organized sports each year. Concludes Duke: "...the question isn't whether coaches leave a legacy, but rather what will that legacy be?"

Duke is on staff as a lecturer at the University of Central Florida and is a National Coaches Trainer for the Fellowship of Christian Athletes (FCA). Bryan McKenzie, Director of FCA Football for the Midwest, also trains coaches in a 3D approach. McKenzie's football career was remarkable in that he became one of the few National Association of Intercollegiate Athletics (NAIA) players ever to be signed by the NFL. The NAIA serves mainly smaller colleges as opposed to the National Collegiate Athletic Association (NCAA).

75

The Atlanta Falcons signed McKenzie as a free agent linebacker in 1991 after he earned NAIA All-American honors at Georgetown College, a private Baptist school of about 1,500 students located in Georgetown, Kentucky. A shoulder injury in training camp derailed McKenzie's pro football chances. As deeply disappointing as that was to McKenzie, the injury redirected him to a career path that he already was predestined to follow.

McKenzie's father was a Baptist minister in Russell, Kentucky. "I not only heard the gospel but got to see it lived out in front of me on a daily basis," he says. "As a sixth grader, I felt a need for a savior in my life, and that's when I accepted Jesus Christ as my savior. I have tried to live out my faith as an athlete through the Fellowship of Christian Athletes."

McKenzie served as a pastor for 13 ½ years in Lake Jackson, Texas, before joining the FCA staff in Springfield, Illinois, in 1994. He describes coaches that take a 3D approach as being "transformational versus transactional." He breaks down the three dimensions this way:

> ➤ The first dimension is the purely physical approach to coaching – the bigger, faster, stronger goals and the X's and O's, or tactical side of coaching. "All coaches do those things," he says. "Ken and Derek are brilliant, better than most at those things. But those things are the easier parts of coaching."

> ➤ The second dimension he describes as the mental/emotional level. "How do you motivate kids and help give them confidence? How do you help them deal with their emotions? How do you achieve team cohesion?" McKenzie says a national survey of coaches showed that only about 25 percent said they felt like they had reached the second dimension.

> ➤ The third level, McKenzie says, is reaching the heart of the athlete. He says this dimension is about building character and giving youngsters a feeling of self-worth and purpose that goes beyond the field or court. He said the national survey showed that only about 3 percent of coaches felt that they had been able to reach this level.

"The word coach comes from the word stagecoach, taking someone of importance from where they are to where they want to go or need to be. That's what great coaches do," McKenzie says. According to the Online Etymology Dictionary, the word "coach" stems from the Hungarian word *kocsi* because most of the superior carriages used across Europe in the 15th Century were built in the Hungarian town of Kocs. The word was used in reference to tutors at the University of Oxford starting in the 1830s. By the 1860s, the term coach was being used in reference to sports, now the most common use of the word.

A pastor in Springfield often used sports analogies to illustrate points in his sermons. One was a football parable. He said a fan might observe two coaches yelling at his players during a game. In one case, the players ignored the coach. In the other case, the players responded. The difference? "In the first example, the players realized that all the coach cared about was how their performance reflected on him," said the pastor. "In the second example, the players knew the coach cared about them, and not just because of what they could do for him on the football field. That coach loved his players, and they would do anything for the coach."

Says McKenzie, "Thirty years ago, coaches used to say they had an open door. That doesn't work anymore. Coaches need to meet kids where they are. Screaming at a kid because they mess up or making them run as a punishment doesn't really motivate most people. To reach the heart of a kid, you have to invest the time to really get to know them. A kid messes up or acts up, how do you know that the kid's dad didn't show up drunk the night before and beat up mom?

"Love is the greatest motivator, not fear. Fear lasts only so long, and then a person just quits trying. If kids know you truly care about them, they will do almost anything to succeed. It sounds counter-intuitive, but when a coach gives his players the freedom to fail, it allows them to move beyond mistakes and maximize their ability. That's transformational."

Duke's book was published in 2014. McKenzie says he saw that deeper-level coaching from Ken Leonard almost two decades earlier. He first met the Sacred Heart-Griffin coach at an FCA event in the fall of 1994. Leonard was fairly new in his born-again Christian life and had started a weekly Bible study for coaches on Thursday mornings in his office. He asked McKenzie to lead the group. McKenzie was observing an SHG football practice in the fall of 2015 when Leonard lost his temper and used a few choice words. The coach gathered his team at the end of practice and apologized profusely.

"He said, 'That's not what a follower of Christ is supposed to do. Would you forgive me?'" McKenzie recalls. "I met with him after practice, and he was crushed at having snapped like that. He was still newer in his walk of faith, and I told him that he probably made a bigger impact on his players by handling the situation the way he did. He didn't make excuses. Being a Christian is an ongoing process, and we all sometimes fall short. The way he witnessed to his players showed them how serious he was about his faith. In Ken Leonard, I saw a man who was on fire for Jesus Christ and a man who had his priorities in order. He's a man who has never been ashamed of his faith and is never going to back down from his belief in Jesus."

Leonard credits the barber Rick Braun with leading him to Christ. He says McKenzie has become "the most influential Godly man in my life...someone who holds me accountable to this day. I know we all have sinful ways, and I have never quite finished taming my tongue. I still screw up; the difference is now the Holy Spirit convicts me and I know it instantly."

Over the years, Ken Leonard has implemented several things in his football program that to some might seem to have little to do with football. For example, several years ago he began asking his players to write letters to their mothers. The instructions were pretty simple... "speak from your heart, put thought into the letter, and don't hurry through it because your mom does so much for you." He also held a father-son jersey night, when jerseys were handed out the night before the first game. Players were to sit with their father or male role model, express their appreciation for all they had done for them, and then the player would hand them a replica jersey with the player's number on it to wear to games. If a player had neither a father nor a role model in attendance, a coach would fill that role. The fathers and role models were asked to then speak from their hearts to their sons.

Leonard established the position of Character Development Coach on his staff in 2020 and hired Charlie Brown, a former Cyclones player, to work with players. Brown would meet weekly with individual players to talk about things going on in their lives and to serve as a kind of spiritual coach. Cyclones players were required to perform acts of community service, ranging from helping clean up the state fairgrounds to visiting nursing homes. If school officials heard about someone in the community needing assistance with a project, those requests often were directed to the football team.

Leonard has invited Marines to work with the team in the off-season. He even has had ballet dancers in to work with players on drills and exercises related to flexibility and balance. Fittingly, Ken played the part of Uncle Drosselmeyer in the December 11, 2022, performance of *"The Nutcracker: Land of the Sweets"* ballet performed by the Springfield Youth Performance Group. Leonard performed with his 9-year-old granddaughter Julia Leonard.

Both Ken and Derek credit a lot of their success to a long list of assistant coaches, too many to list here. One name mentioned quite often by former Cyclones players was John Sowinski, who died in 2009 at the age of 78. Sowinski was head coach at Springfield High for 17 years and then was a member of Leonard's staff from 1987 until his death. Sowinski's specialty was coaching offensive linemen. A former Marine, he was known to be a taskmaster, demanding that players use proper blocking techniques and give maximum effort. One of his students at Springfield High was Bob Trumpy, who became an All-Pro player for the Cincinnati Bengals.

"John never changed. John had discipline. He was an authority figure that kids respected. The rules never changed with John. He wouldn't let the kids do anything but the right things. Was he tough? Was he stern? Yes…They learned so many life lessons from him," Ken Leonard said at the time of Sowinski's death. "Other than my father, John Sowinski was one of the most influential people in my life. I learned so much about football, life, everything, from John. I was blessed."

Another assistant who left a big impression on Ken was Jack "Teddy" Wise, who was on his staff for 15 years. Wise, who died in 2019 at the age of 65, played football at Southern Illinois University, where he won the Harry Bobbitt Spirit Award in the mid-1970s. "Teddy was just a special, special person for lots of our players," Leonard says. "He would oversee the team's overnight lock-ins before our Saturday games. He would do anything to help the team and the players loved him."

Relinquishing control of anything did not come easily for Ken Leonard. "It's one of the adjustments I made over the years," he says. "I listened to my father and to my brother, who is very successful in business. They both told me you need to realize your strengths and weaknesses. You need to get people smarter and better than you to help in those areas where you are not as strong. Loyalty is a big thing to me, and it is a two-way street. I have learned that if you treat people well, they perform."

Ken believes football is the ultimate team sport. He has never given out individual awards at the team's end-of-the-year football banquets. He and/or one of the assistant coaches introduce and talk about each senior player, focusing mainly on character traits rather than on-the-field accomplishments. The only honors routinely mentioned are for those players who earned all-academic certificates.

"How can you talk about football being a team sport – a sport where all 11 players have to do their jobs and depend on each other to succeed – and then start talking about one person being more valuable than everyone else?" he reasons. "I have great admiration for those players who were not stars but stuck it out for four years and maybe only got to play on the scout team in practice. For most of the all-state type of players, success came easily on the football field because they were so blessed with athletic ability. Those guys that didn't have that natural ability, for them to work hard and be good teammates...those are the type of young men who will have successful lives and be good husbands and fathers."

One of the Bible verses that Ken regularly shared with his players is from Philippians 2: 2-5: *Then make me truly happy by agreeing wholeheartedly with each other, loving one another, and working together with one mind and purpose. Don't be selfish; don't try to impress others. Be humble, thinking of others as better than yourselves. Don't look out only for your own interests, but take an interest in others, too.*

Ken also subscribed to the "Rule of 3" theory of teaching and coaching, which is 1) Tell them and they will forget, 2) Show them and they will remember more, and 3) Involve them and they will understand.

Ken was on the cutting edge of off-season football activities. His Gridley team began participating in summer 7-on-7 competition in 1981, something that was rare back then but had become commonplace by the early 2000s. His three-a-day summer workouts at Camp CILCA when he was hired at SHG have taken on mythical status. That survival-of-the-fittest approach has evolved over the years, but even in those early years the sessions were highly organized with specific football purposes in mind. He has implemented other activities, including:

> ➢ Running the "Eight Days in May" program for Cyclones players not participating in a spring sport. Players would report at 6 a.m. for each of those eight days. The workouts would last a little longer than an hour. Players would engage in speed, endurance and agility drills. There also would be team competition, such things as tug-of-war and relay races up and down hills.

➤ Teaming up with his son Derek to offer a spring camp designed to help quarterbacks and receivers from all over central Illinois become more fundamentally sound. The training also used some of the principles of the Don Beebe House of Speed Camp, a regimen designed by the Aurora University coach who was one of the fastest players and best route runners in the NFL when he was a wide receiver for the Buffalo Bills in the 1990s.

➤ Taking players to powerlifting meets and holding Lift-A-Thon weightlifting fund-raisers, where players would solicit donations based on the amount of weight they could lift.

Derek was a sophomore backup quarterback at SHG when McKenzie first met him, but McKenzie could already see the makings of an exceptional football coach. "Derek wasn't a great athlete in terms of pure physical gifts, but he made himself into a really good quarterback because he loved the game and he studied the game," McKenzie says. As of 2022, Derek Leonard is still ranked 10th all-time in SHG history with 3,128 career yards passing (1995-98) and fourth in Illinois College with 6,667 career yards passing (1999-2001). "The other thing that really stood out to me was that he valued his teammates. You can see the same things in him as a coach. He loves the game, still looks for new ways to give his team an advantage, and you can tell he values his players."

Derek has implemented many of the same types of off-season and non-football programs as his father regarding such things as community service, team-building drills and competitions, and enhancing individual players' strength, speed and skills. Like his father, Derek does not hand out individual awards. "A guy like Hank Beatty doesn't need another MVP award," he says. "I would rather talk about what type of person and teammate he is and the character traits that helped make him great."

The highlight of the Rochester postseason banquet is when Derek calls each senior up to sit in a chair while he talks about the player. Often, his longest orations are about players who saw relatively little game action but became team leaders in ways that don't show up on the stat sheet. Those sorts of things that don't show up on the stat sheet include positive attitudes, leadership qualities and a willingness to do the less glamorous things that are integral for championship teams – things like being on the "scout" team playing the role of that week's opponent in practice against the first team offense or defense.

One thing Derek adopted from McKenzie is the "Rocket Spotlight." After each practice, Derek gathers the players together and, starting with the seniors, has one player stand up in front of the team. That player's teammates then cite one positive thing – aside from football or athletic ability – about the player in the spotlight. The potential for building self-confidence and a feeling of worth beyond the football field are obvious goals. "Each day we might have a dozen or so players raise their hand and share something they are thankful for about that particular player. It is really a cool thing because players often don't know the kind of impression they have made on their teammates," Derek says.

Of course, it's hard to predict what is on the mind of a teenager at any given moment. Asked if the exercise ever veered off course, Derek recalled one of the practices during the 2022 season. After listening to other players share a lengthy list of great character traits about the player in the Rocket Spotlight, one of the sophomores raised his hand. He was, Derek noted, "one of the quieter, more reserved kids on the team. But he proceeds to say that he's really thankful for his teammate's mother…because she's sooo good-looking!"

Victorious!

Quarterback Whisperers

Ken and Derek are best known for their teams' explosive offenses and for their ability to develop top-notch quarterbacks to ignite those attacks. The physical traits they look for in a quarterback differ slightly in terms of priority, with Ken valuing athleticism the most and Derek placing passing accuracy at the top of his list of physical abilities. However, both cite quick decision-making as the main attribute, one that makes the difference between the good and the great quarterbacks. Ken notes that football IQ is not necessarily the same thing as being book smart.

"Guys who are great at taking tests and solving problems by taking a thorough, step-by-step logical approach may not be the best decision-makers as a quarterback because things happen so fast once the ball is snapped," he says. Ken's quarterback lineage at SHG featured 16 different All-State selections and 15 quarterbacks who went on to play in college, including the likes of his first quarterback Chris Ondrula (Illinois and Miami of Ohio), Bart Geiser (Northern Illinois), P.J. Becker (Illinois State), Scott Norris (Western Illinois), Ryan Wells (McKendree College), Derek Leonard (Illinois College), Brad Selinger (Lindenwood College), Eric Peterman (Northwestern), Bobby Brenneisen (Southern Illinois and Quincy College), Tim Dondanville (Princeton), Eric Williamson (St. Ambrose College), Pat Smith (St. Ambrose College), Gabe Green (Southern Mississippi), Tim Brenneisen (Missouri Baptist College) and Sam Sweetland (Wisconsin-Whitewater).

Derek quickly developed a reputation as an offensive guru at Rochester, taking the Rockets to scoring heights few high school teams could match. His younger brother Bradley lovingly refers to Derek as an "idiot savant" when it comes to running an offense. "Derek would tell you there are a lot of things he might not know how to do, but no one can design and run an offense better than him," Bradley says. "He gets calls from college and even NFL coaches who want to pick his brain about how to run a spread offense. I knew he was going to be a coach when he was about 10 years old because he was designing great plays back then."

Bradley thinks he knows exactly when the fuse was lit for Derek. He was sitting in the stands as part of a sellout crowd of about 1,500 at England Field on the campus of Illinois College in Jacksonville on November 10, 2001. It was a crisp, cool day, and the Blue Boys were taking on a St. Norbert team that had won 27 straight games. Illinois College was 4-4 and had never beaten the Green Knights of the Wisconsin-based school. The game against St. Norbert was supposed to have been the season finale, but the game scheduled for September 15 had been postponed until November 17 because of the attacks of 9/11. The IC head coach, Tom Rowland, was so convinced his team would lose that during the week leading up to the St. Norbert game he exhorted his squad to focus on winning the game the *following* week against Lawrence College so they could finish the season with a 5-5 record.

As the players were walking from the locker room to the field to face St. Norbert, Rowland sidled up next to Derek and told him he was turning the play-calling that day over to the senior quarterback.

What transpired was a preview of what Rochester fans would get to enjoy years later. Derek ran a no-huddle offense at warp speed, throwing the ball a school-record 68 times, completing a school-record 44 passes for a then-school record 461 yards. He threw three touchdown passes and ran for another TD. St. Norbert finally grabbed a 40-33 lead with just 1:17 left to play. Derek then drove the Blue Boys 71 yards in 72 seconds, throwing a 10-yard

TD pass with just five seconds left to draw the Blue Boys within a point. He didn't even give the coach a chance to think about kicking a game-tying extra point. Derek wanted to go for two points and the win, so he quickly got his team to the line of scrimmage and called another pass play. He hit future Rockets assistant Erik Kahrliker with a pass for a two-point conversion. The Blue Boys had pulled off the most stunning upset in Illinois College history, ending St. Norbert's streak by a 41-40 score. For the record, the Blue Boys also beat Lawrence the following week to finish the season at 6-4.

Says Derek, "It's probably a fair assessment that the St. Norbert game changed things for me. It's one of the days I look back on and understand it was part of God's plan for me. It was the beginning of the whole thing." He credits Jim Good with a lot of his success as a creative play-caller. Good grew up in the northwestern part of the country, and he brought some of the more west coast style of football with him when he arrived as the offensive coordinator at Illinois College for Derek's sophomore and junior years. Good left for a coaching job in Texas before Derek's senior season and ultimately was named head coach at the University of Redlands in California in 2021 after serving as offensive coordinator there for more than 10 years. His first year as head coach, Redlands went undefeated to win the conference championship and make the playoffs. The 2019 Redlands team scored a school record 445 points with Good calling the plays.

"I think Derek was destined to become a coach the day he was born," Good says. "I would joke with him that I wasn't sure he'd ever graduate from Illinois College because he was always in my office bringing me football plays he'd diagrammed during one of his classes. I'd say, "You know, you probably need to be paying more attention to what's going on in class.' He would be in my office more than any player I've ever coached. We'd talk about football, talk about life, watch game film and draw plays on the white board." For the record, Derek graduated from Illinois College with a bachelor's degree in education…and a doctorate in the spread offense.

Good recalls traveling with Ken Leonard to visit the football staffs at Northwestern and Purdue during the off-season between Derek's sophomore and junior seasons at IC. The Purdue coach was Joe Tiller, who brought some of the new no-huddle and spread-the-field offensive concepts with him from the University of Wyoming, and the Northwestern coach was Randy Walker, who had brought some fresh ideas with him from the University of Miami in Florida. "I learned a lot from those guys at Purdue and Northwestern on that road trip," Good says. "But I really got a football education just being in the car and talking with Ken. I remember thinking *'Holy smokes! This coach is legit!'* I also learned a lot about life and faith in that car."

Good's first impression of Derek as a quarterback was equally eye-opening. "He didn't really look the part because he's the first to tell you he wasn't super athletic," Good recalls. "But what I saw on the game film was that he could really play the position." In describing what made Derek such a good QB, Good resorted to intangibles, things like being a great competitor, a love for the game, and being a student of the game. Cumulatively, they add up the "it" factor that is part of the DNA of so many great players and coaches.

One play Derek made in practice really made an impression on Good. The Blue Boys were practicing a passing formation called "Empty," which meant receivers were spread all over the field and there were no running backs in the backfield, just the quarterback. To counter, the defense moved the middle linebacker to the edge of the line to go all out after the quarterback. But Derek did not attempt to pass. He took the snap and ran straight up the middle, attacking the space the linebacker had vacated. "He could just see things most quarterbacks couldn't see," Good says.

Good's first season at IC, the Blue Boys ran the ball a lot because they had a standout running back, Patrick Bowman, who owned the state's career rushing record by the time he finished playing for Greenfield High School in 1996 and was still 16th all-time as of 2023. Bowman also set IC's single-season rushing record in 1999 and still ranked third on the college's career rushing charts 24 years later.

The play Good called in one game was supposed to be a hand-off to Bowman. Derek noticed the defensive end had been focusing solely on Bowman. He faked a handoff to Bowman, kept the ball and took off while the defensive end was chasing Bowman. "Derek ran… not real fast, but he ran for about 20 yards before anyone touched him," Good says. "The end decided to go right at Derek the next play, so Derek flipped the ball to an open receiver, again in an area the defender had vacated. He was just so good at taking whatever the defense would give him. It's really hard to stop a quarterback who does that."

The thing about being a mad scientist is that to really be effective you can't worry about being called crazy. "Not only is Derek so creative in designing plays, but he also is fearless," Good says. "Most of us coaches aren't willing to try some of those things because if they don't work, fans, the media and maybe even your boss will be all over you. Derek doesn't care. If it doesn't work, he'll just go back to the drawing board." Good is such a fan of Derek's schemes on offense, he will hurry to his office after his college practice is over on Friday nights (most of his college games are on Saturday) to watch the Rochester games on the Rocket TV internet broadcasts. One problem is the two-hour time difference between Illinois and California. Often by the time Good wraps up his team's practice, the Rockets are so far ahead that Derek has toned down the offensive fireworks.

Perhaps the ultimate compliment the college head coach gives his former student is this: "Any time I need to fix something or add something to our offense, Derek is the first person I usually call," Good says. "A couple of years ago, I called him and asked, 'What's the craziest thing you're doing now?' Derek said, 'Take a look at this!'" What he showed Good was a formation where one of the receivers would line up 10-15 yards behind the line of scrimmage, way behind the quarterback, and take off sprinting toward the line when the ball was snapped. The quarterback could hit the receiver in full stride with a pass behind the line or fake a pass so the receiver could blow right past the defender and run a deep pass route. It looked like something straight out of the Canadian Football League or the Arena Football League, where their different rules allow offensive players to be running every which direction before the ball is snapped.

Naturally, Good could not wait to try it in his team's next game. When one of the Redlands receivers lined up way behind the line of scrimmage, the coaches' reactions on the opposite sideline were priceless. One of them whacked another on the arm with a clipboard and was gesturing at the weird formation with a quizzical expression on his face. The play went for a 20-yard TD.

Derek coached an All-State quarterback before he arrived in Rochester. His first season at Prairie Central in Fairbury was 2003. He was coaching the quarterbacks, and his senior quarterback Dylan Ward had one of the best seasons in state history, leading his team to a second-place finish. Ward completed 270 passes (6th) for 4,186 yards (4th) and 46 touchdowns (8th), to rank in the top 10 in state history for a single season in all three categories. Ward had great size for a quarterback at 6-foot-3 and a strong arm. The next season, Derek had a different sort of quarterback. Cody Freed was smaller and did not possess the arm strength of Ward, who went on to pitch at Southern Illinois University. Oddly enough, Derek says he may have learned more coaching Freed in his final season as an assistant before he was hired at Rochester. "I learned you have to adapt your offense to fit the type of quarterback you have. It was something that helped me later on at Rochester," he says. Freed also was a successful quarterback, good enough to lead Prairie Central to a 10-2 record and go on to play at North Central College.

Derek's reputation as a "quarterback whisperer" grew exponentially at Rochester with all 10 of his primary quarterbacks through the 2022 season earning All-State honors, nine going on to play in college. That list included brothers Wil (Western Illinois) and Wes Lunt (Oklahoma State and then Illinois), Sean Robinson (Purdue),

Robbie Kelley (Quincy College and Akron), Austin Green (Eastern Illinois), Dan Zeigler (Truman State), Hank Beatty (Illinois), Clay Bruno (Western Illinois), Nic Baker (Southern Illinois) and Keeton Reiss. All had some combination of passing accuracy, athleticism and arm strength, but it was the mental part of the game that allowed some of the quarterbacks to excel in Derek's offensive scheme.

"You have to want to learn, that's probably the most important thing," Derek says. "I've been lucky and blessed because I've had a whole line of kids who enjoy playing the quarterback position. It's not easy in this offense. There is a lot of film study and even more than film study, it comes down to repetition. You have to do it over and over to really get it. Then it becomes a 100-question test. Have you studied for it? Do you know it? Sometimes, the answers are built in. At the pace we run our offense, the quarterback has five, maybe 10 seconds to look at the defensive alignment and have an idea where to go with the ball before the ball is snapped."

Often in the Rockets offense, the play is predetermined by Derek. Other times, the quarterback will be given a run-pass option, or RPO in coaches' lingo. On those plays, after the ball is snapped, the quarterback must make split-second decisions to hand the ball off to the running back, throw to one of his receivers or take off with the ball. It all depends on what the QB diagnoses the defense doing. For the truly great ones, the game slows down in their minds, turning what looks like 22-person chaos to most fans into chess moves that result in open passing or running lanes to the eyes of the QB.

There is one final box a Rochester quarterback must check. It is intangible. "My quarterbacks have to be able to think like me," Derek says. "To do that, we need to spend a lot of time together, studying film and really getting to know each other. I tell all my quarterbacks, 'Don't do what I say, do what I'm thinking!' Those guys will tell you I sometimes blurt out stuff. The great ones know what I'm trying to say."

Victorious!

A Super Week…for Everyone Else

It's unclear how the father-son rivalry game between SHG and Rochester got dubbed the "Leonard Bowl." By any name, ever since the unforgettable inaugural game in 2010, it became the most anticipated high school football game of the season in central Illinois. At least for the fans. "For the community, it was the ultimate. It was great for football," SHG coach Ken Leonard says. "But it was not fun for the Leonards. We just wanted to get it over with each year."

The first Leonard Bowl on September 17, 2010, was an instant classic. It was Rochester's first year in the Central State Eight Conference, and the Rockets had the smallest enrollment in one of the premier high school football conferences in the state. They were a 4A team playing in a 5A/6A league. The Rockets came into the game 3-0 but had not yet really been tested. The Cyclones came into the game riding a 59-game conference winning streak that spanned almost 10 years.

Most neutral observers gave Rochester little chance. Ken knew better. He had seen the Rochester program starting to take off and had been at some of the Rockets practices the previous couple of years after his son Derek became the coach. He knew many of the players through summer ball, and he had been on the Rochester sideline the year before when the Rockets came up inches short of advancing to the state championship game.

"They had some dudes. I told my players, 'When you go out there tonight you are going to be looking yourselves in the eyes across the line of scrimmage. They are not going to be in awe of you,'" says Ken, referring to the intimidation advantage that his team's reputation often afforded even before the first ball was snapped. "Many of their coaches wore the gold helmet here playing for SHG. They were going to do a lot of the same things we do, but with some of Derek's brilliance thrown into the mix. I warned my team that the game would go all the way to the end."

The crowd at Memorial Stadium in Springfield that night was estimated to have been between 8,000 and 10,000, with the stands on both sides full and people standing three or four deep around the field. Some fans were even watching from the top rows of an adjacent baseball stadium. Despite having 14 state championships between them, both father and son say it was the most intense atmosphere of any game they have coached.

"We would always show up for those games at Memorial Stadium pretty late," Derek says. "When our bus pulled up, I remember thinking it was just insane. Imagine how many Griffin games I had been to there as a little kid and then as a player, including some really big games. But this atmosphere was stunning even to me. The cops had to open a path through the crowd for us to get from the bus to the field. I had never been involved in anything like this in terms of the crowd size and just the sheer intensity."

As Ken Leonard predicted, the game did not disappoint. Somewhat unexpectedly, the match between two coaches and teams known more for offensive fireworks ended up being a defensive battle. It came down to the final minute. To one play.

Rochester led 13-10 and SHG was facing a fourth-and-4 from the Rochester 18. Quarterback Pat Smith faded and threw the ball toward his favorite receiver, Jarrod Sergent, who was slanting toward the end zone and appeared to be breaking open. Seemingly from out of nowhere, Rockets linebacker Jon Gilson got his fingers – or the tip of one finger, to be precise – on the ball and deflected it away with 41 seconds left to secure the victory for Rochester.

Derek Leonard knew in that moment that he had witnessed

something special. "When we met at midfield, I told the team, 'You just beat a great team tonight! That means we can be a great team!'"

Gilson had given up football after his freshman season to concentrate on baseball, which was his best sport. Leonard invited him to rejoin the football team his senior year. Gilson described his game-saving play to reporters afterward. "I just saw that the quarterback was dropping back and throwing a slant. I saw that slant coming, and I just ran as fast as I could," he said. "I saw the ball in the air, jumped up and tried to hit it…and I barely did. It was the best feeling I've ever had in my life. I did that for everyone on this team because I love everyone on the team, all the coaches on the team."

A few months later, Gilson's life would take a tragic turn. He was set to become a pitcher for the Lincoln Land Community College team, good enough with a fastball clocked at 93 mph to have started attracting interest from Division 1 schools. In the wee hours of October 13, 2011, he lost control of his Ford Explorer and slid through a curve on a rain-slickened road in Springfield, ramming into a steel billboard post. He nearly died and was in a coma for two weeks. When he awoke, he had no movement below his shoulders. During the next two years, his father John suffered a stroke, and his mother Carol was diagnosed with cancer that would take her life in 2016 at the age of 52. Carol Gilson's obituary included a request that in lieu of flowers, memorials were to go to the family to help continue the level of care for Jonny that she had been providing.

In a 2014 interview with the Lincoln Land student online news site *The Lamp*, Gilson talked about the accident. He said he had been drinking at a party and that a friend unsuccessfully tried to keep him from driving home. The last thing he remembered was leaving the party, until he woke up in the hospital two weeks later. "Even when I turned 21, I didn't really have a desire to drink again. It's not worth ruining your life over," he said. "My whole life was baseball. It was my one true love, and not being able to do the one thing you truly love to do is probably the hardest thing to live with. Having suffered a traumatic brain injury, I'm thankful to have my head on my shoulders. One thing I keep in mind: There's always someone out there worse off than I am. I can think clearly and I have my memory."

Gilson's play is one of Derek Leonard's fondest football memories. But it is bittersweet when he thinks about the tragedies Jonny Gilson would encounter so soon after he had experienced the highest of highs on the football field. "No matter how many years I coach or how many championships we win, I will always remember that play. Jonny was in his first year playing outside linebacker and somehow managed to get the very tip of his finger on the ball to deflect it. I will never forget the roar of the crowd in that moment," Derek says. "But Jonny is in a wheelchair now. And then his father had a stroke and he lost his mother to cancer. It's just a sad story. He's such a great kid, and he was a helluva athlete. He was a big-time baseball player. He was all set to get that Division 1 scholarship...

"It's one of those things in life where you don't understand why it happens, and you just have to rely on your faith. We were at one of the players' weddings recently, and the guys still talk about that play Jonny made. To this day, that team might be the closest group I've ever had," Derek says. That 2010 team would go on to win the first of Rochester's many state championships.

Both teams would emerge from that first Leonard Bowl thriller primed for even better things. SHG would put together another 30-game conference win streak and win two more state titles (Nos. 4 and 5) in back-to-back unbeaten seasons in 2013 and 2014. Meanwhile, the Rockets would go on to win five straight state championships, eventually winning the crown eight times in 10 years.

The week leading up to each Leonard Bowl became a time of estrangement for father and son. Instead of speaking daily, often multiple times a day, they self-imposed a telephone blackout. For Derek, the reason was simple. "My mom and I would talk about a lot of things. When dad and I talk, 80 percent of the time it's about football. That week, we don't want to BS each other, and we don't want to fib," he says. "Dad's slick, and that week I want to keep the eye of the tiger. I don't want to get on the phone with him and get weak and share something I shouldn't."

Father and son have had their moments of confrontation in the heat of those Leonard Bowl games, but they both say the biggest confrontations came during the freshman-sophomore games even though neither was actually coaching. "For one thing, you usually can't even hear what each other is yelling during the varsity games with the crowd noise and all. The worst ones by far were at those frosh-soph games," Derek says. "A couple of years ago, dad was almost halfway onto the field yelling at the refs about us holding. I know what he's doing; he's just trying to get in the refs' heads and get a call or two. Just stop. We're not holding any more than they do."

Some Rochester assistant coaches, such as JC Clark, used to play at SHG for Ken Leonard. Their nerves sometimes got frayed in the heat of battle, too. "It's like one big family, and sometimes families clash," Ken says with a shrug. "The good thing is, when it's over it's over, and we're still family."

Ken and Derek got into a short, but fairly heated confrontation during a 2021 game when one after another SHG player stayed on the ground after a play in the fourth quarter, causing the referees to stop the clock and pause play while the downed player received attention. The stoppages prevented the Rockets from keeping the game going at the frenetic pace that is one of their main weapons. In many instances, the "injured" player would return after sitting out just one play. When it happened on the sideline near the Rochester bench, Ken came across the field to check on his player. Fans saw an animated Derek and Ken jawing at each other for a few seconds. In that particular case, Ken thought his player might have actually suffered a knee injury and took umbrage at Derek questioning the stoppage. Fortunately for the player, he was not seriously injured and soon was back in the game.

"I know all of his tricks…and he knows all of mine," Derek says. Ken denies any gamesmanship was involved – with this caveat: "It's not something we as coaches tell our kids to do. But our kids at SHG are smart players. They might have been doing that on their own sometimes. But, hey, it's the same thing Rochester is trying to do when they try to snap the ball before the defense is ready."

As difficult as the Leonard Bowl was for the two coaches, it was probably even more stressful for Liz Leonard watching her husband and her son do battle. "Oh, she didn't like it even a little bit," Ken says. "She tried to be down the middle. Truth be known, that first game she was probably pulling more for Derek than me because he was the son."

After one of the Leonard Bowl games, the local paper ran a photo of Derek pointing his finger at his father during the postgame handshake line. It was a photo that captured the intensity of the football rivalry. Liz was not pleased. "Mom told me to never ever point my finger at my dad like that again," Derek says, remembering the moment with a smile. "Then she turned to dad and said, 'Ken, what in the world did you do to make Derek so mad that he would point his finger at you like that?'"

In that 2012 finger-pointing game, SHG won 29-26 when Cyclones defender Eric Brydl forced two turnovers. With the Rockets leading 20-14 in the third quarter, Brydl stripped the ball from a Rochester running back one yard from the end zone. Then, as time was running out, Brydl intercepted a pass near midfield. SHG would go on to reach the Class 5A semifinals before losing to Morris 30-20 to finish at 11-2. The loss to SHG would be Rochester's only defeat as the Rockets rolled to a 13-1 record and their third straight Class 4A state championship, beating Rock Island Alleman 43-18.

The Leonard Bowl was a must-see event for fans of both teams as well as neutral fans who just wanted to witness the annual football spectacle. "Personally, it's been stressful and draining," said Derek a few days before what he thought was going to be the Leonard Bowl finale in the 2022 season-opener. "It's my dad. I've always wanted him to have success, but I'm loyal to these Rochester kids and our school. It's my job to beat his team. It's been a great 13 years of football. In that entire time, I don't think there has been one game that hasn't been for a conference championship or a playoff game."

In that 2022 season-opener, a veteran SHG team that had finished second in the state the year before rolled over Rochester 62-27. The Cyclones had returned most of their starters from the 2021 runner-up squad. The regularly scheduled Leonard Bowls were tough enough, but both coaches said meeting in the playoffs multiplied the intensity because the loser's season would come to an abrupt end. Going into 2022, they had met twice in the playoffs, splitting those games.

"When they beat us in 2019, that really stung. In reality, it was for the state championship even though it was in the quarterfinals because they went on to clobber the next two teams," says Ken, referring to a 49-35 Rochester win over SHG. The game was tied at 35 in the fourth quarter before Hank Beatty broke loose for an 81-yard TD run and Justin DuRocher added an 8-yard scoring run. Rochester then destroyed Mascoutah 56-34 in the semifinals and handled Chicago St. Rita 42-28 for its first Class 5A championship to go along with seven 4A titles.

Those playoff fortunes reversed in 2021 when SHG eliminated Rochester 49-42 in a semifinal game that the Rockets once led 25-7. They still led 39-35 going into the final quarter before Cyclones quarterback Ty Lott threw a 21-yard TD pass to grab a 42-39 lead. Lott threw for 437 yards and five TDs to help the Cyclones avenge a regular-season Leonard Bowl loss 49-42 and advance to the championship game before losing to Joliet Catholic.

The Cyclones returned with most of their star players for 2022, Ken Leonard's final season. Rochester, having lost Beatty and a host of other key players to graduation, was in a bit of a reloading phase. The 2022 season-opener was billed as the Leonard Bowl finale, and the veteran Cyclones raced to a 62-27 win. Little did Ken and Derek know that they would meet one more time with more on the line than in any of the previous father-son contests.

Competitiveness is just part of the Leonard family DNA. The

competition between Ken and Derek Leonard began when Derek was a little boy. And it was not limited to football. There were take-no-prisoner Whiffle ball games, hotly contested basketball games of H-O-R-S-E, and even card games that might end with the loser's cards being tossed in the air. The main combatants were not only Ken and Derek. Bradley might have been the most competitive of all the Leonards, according to witnesses, some of whom say they were chased by the Whiffle-ball-bat-wielding younger brother.

"It's true, I wouldn't cut the boys any slack whether it was Whiffle ball or H-O-R-S-E," Ken says. "That's how I was raised. Losing teaches you humility, and it makes you work to get better. When Derek didn't win, he sometimes would get mad and go crying to mom. Liz was his defender, but she was competitive, too, when it came to cards and different things. Bradley would go off sometimes; being the younger brother, he had a pretty low threshold. With Derek, it took longer to get there, but he could lose it, too. You had to watch Derek because he was not afraid to cheat to win when he was little."

Ring-Gate

The 2013 Leonard Bowl game would go into the history books with an asterisk. Rochester overcame an incredible performance by SHG quarterback Gabe Green, who threw for 444 yards and two touchdowns to lead the Cyclones to a furious comeback from a 17-point deficit in the final nine minutes. Rockets defensive end Matt Swaine staved off the rally by sacking Green four times and forcing a fumble to preserve a 38-33 win in Week Two. That action was on the field.

Off the field, unbeknownst to Rochester coaches and administrators, a problem was brewing. It would make headlines a few weeks later and eventually wipe out that Week Two victory. A non-school-sanctioned group known as Football Moms had paid for 2012 championship rings for three Rochester players whose families could not afford the $457 price tag. In the No Good Deed Goes Unpunished category, the Football Moms thought they were doing something helpful by providing keepsakes for the players. They were unaware of Illinois High School Association (IHSA) Bylaw 3.080, a guideline that limits ring contributions to $200. The violation was discovered during the school district's routine annual audit of the Football Moms' books.

It was Wednesday of Week Nine, the last week of the regular football season, and Derek had run across town to Subway to grab a sandwich during his lunch break. He had taken about two bites of his sandwich when his cell phone rang. It was Rochester High School principal Dennis Canny telling him he needed to get back to school, that something had come up that needed immediate attention. He walked into a meeting room to find Canny and superintendent Tom Bertrand. They told him about the audit discovery.

"I was stunned. I knew that the families of three of the players had not been able to purchase the rings, and I knew that the Football Moms had stepped up to make sure those three kids would get rings like everyone else. I guess you could call it ignorance on my part, but I didn't know anything about that dollar limit. Neither did Jostens," Derek says, referring to one of the leading companies that sells class rings, championship rings and other memorabilia to schools throughout the country.

The championship ring design was selected by a group of four or five seniors, the process Derek had followed ever since that first championship in 2010. "We always had let the seniors pick out the ring design," he says. "The first one was a pretty simple ring. But every year those seniors wanted to make that year's ring a little different and no one thought much about the price, which had gone up each year."

Derek initially pushed back against the idea of self-reporting. He argued that no one knew what the IHSA might do in terms of punishment and that it would not be fair if all the players on the team – none of whom had ever heard of Bylaw 3.080 or done anything wrong – might be banned from the playoffs. The final decision rested with the school administration. Bertrand and Canny, the two men who had hired Derek for his first head coaching job, decided to report the issue to the IHSA and issue a press release. "Unfortunately, the representatives of Football Moms unknowingly jeopardized the eligibility of three Rochester High School football players who had no knowledge of or involvement in a violation of the by-law," Canny said in the press release.

Reporters cited as precedent an old case regarding Kewanee Wethersfield. That 2002 team was stripped of all 11 of its wins and had to return the Class 1A semifinal plaque from the 2002 season when it was discovered that a booster had paid half of the cost of 2001 championship rings for the entire team. Because the amounts the booster had contributed were in excess of the IHSA limits, all of the players who had received the rings and were on the 2002 team were ruled to be ineligible. For an anxious 24 hours, Rochester school administrators, coaches, players and fans held their collective breath. If the IHSA made the Rockets forfeit all eight games up to that point, they would not qualify for the playoffs and there would be no shot at a record-breaking fourth straight state title.

"We know they (the Football Moms) mean well, and they're there to support the kids and the school," IHSA assistant executive director Matt Troha told reporters before the final ruling came down. "But because they're not inside the school, they're not always up to speed on what the rules are. There really needs to be a good relationship between the schools and these outside organizations to make sure everybody is on the same page."

The IHSA decision was handed down on Thursday afternoon. The Rockets would be forced to forfeit only one game, the Leonard Bowl win over SHG. In addition, the three players who received the rings and Derek had to sit out the Week Nine game, a 49-24 win over Jacksonville. In announcing its decision, the IHSA noted that the SHG game was the only margin of victory small enough that the participation of the three ineligible players could have made a difference. The other narrowest wins were by at least three touchdowns. Rocket Nation exhaled. The Rockets would be eligible for the playoffs, albeit with an 8-1 rather than a 9-0 record. The only real impacts being that it cost Rochester a conference championship, and the Rockets would be seeded lower in the playoff bracket.

"We followed past precedent for these types of situations," IHSA Executive Director Marty Hickman said in a news release at the time. "While it may be difficult to judge a defensive player's impact on a game, upon reviewing information related to the Rochester/Sacred Heart-Griffin game, it was apparent that one of the players had a significant influence on the game's outcome. Based on the margins of victory, the Sacred Heart-Griffin game was the only contest where I felt the outcome could have been different had those players not participated." Hickman commended Rochester school administrators for self-reporting the violations and noted that was a factor that led to a less-severe punishment.

In hindsight, Derek says the decision made by Canny and Bertrand was the right thing to do. Still, he compares the whole episode to jaywalking. "Would you self-report jaywalking? Even the one-game forfeit to me is like getting a 60-day jail sentence for jaywalking." While the forfeit officially goes in the record books as a 1-0 victory for SHG, Cyclones coach Ken Leonard does not count the win among his career totals even though the IHSA does.

"Look, we got our butts kicked. They beat us on the field," says Ken, who went so far as to call the IHSA to say SHG did not want to accept the forfeit win. "They told me we had no choice. But we never put anything up in the school about being conference champions or being 'unbeaten' that year. We just celebrated the state championship."

The forfeit loss would be the only blemish on the Rockets' record as they cruised into the 4A state championship game to meet Geneseo. Likewise, SHG rolled into the 5A title game, where they would meet Lombard Montini. If both Rochester and SHG won, it would be the first time in state history for a father and son to win state football championships on the same weekend.

Revealing the Best of Sports

All arrows were pointing up for both the SHG and Rochester football teams going into that 2013 season. The Cyclones were in the midst of one of the most dominant runs in Illinois history, a stretch from 2002-2012 that included three state championships, two state runner-up finishes and a 125-12 record in that period. Meanwhile, the Rockets had gone 51-4 in the previous four seasons and were gunning for their fourth straight state championship, something no public school in Illinois had ever accomplished.

Both teams were loaded. In fact, both teams would go undefeated. Sort of. The only "loss" for SHG would come at the hands of Rochester, 38-33, in Week Two of the season. But that was the game that was ultimately declared a forfeit win by the Cyclones because of the ring debacle. The "asterisk game" aside, both teams simply overpowered their opponents during the regular season. SHG won its other eight regular-season games by an average score of 69-11, the closest game being a 49-27 win over Memphis Whitehaven High School, the defending Class 6A state champs from Tennessee. Rochester's average victory was 41-13, the closest game being a 28-7 win over Chatham Glenwood, whose only other two losses were both to SHG, including a second-round playoff loss.

SHG rolled through the playoffs with scores of 45-7 over Peoria Richwoods, 55-7 over Glenwood, and 42-8 over Highland to advance to the semifinals against unbeaten Washington, the team that twice ousted highly touted Cyclones teams on last-second desperation TD passes 33 years apart. Washington defeated Normal's University High 41-7 on Saturday, November 16, 2013, to advance to the semifinals with a perfect 12-0 record. It was a night of celebration for the community of some 15,000 people. The celebration would be short-lived, but not because of anything football related.

Temperatures had been unseasonably warm for mid-November, reaching as high as 70 degrees in the days leading up to Sunday. The Storm Prediction Center had begun forecasting a moderate risk of severe weather for a wide swath of the Midwest, including west central Illinois, as early as that Thursday. As midnight approached on Saturday, the forecast worsened, placing central Illinois at high risk for severe weather. At 8:40 a.m. Sunday, the National Weather Service issued a tornado watch for all of Illinois, and the Storm Prediction Center issued a PDS (Particularly Dangerous Situation) alert.

Though late fall is not usually associated with tornadoes, environmental winds tend to be much stronger in November than in the spring or summer months, creating greater wind shear. However, the other elements necessary to form tornadoes, warmer temperatures and high dew points, are typically missing that time of year. But on November 17, 2013, the air was warmer than usual, and moisture had been carried up from the Gulf. In a meteorological sense, it had all the makings of a perfect storm.

At around 8:30 a.m., Ken Leonard phoned Washington coach Darrell Crouch to congratulate him on his team's victory as well as to finalize the kickoff time for the semifinal game and the logistics of exchanging game film. The two had known each other since the 1980s, when Crouch was a student teacher at Chenoa High School, where Leonard was a teacher and assistant football coach.

At around 10:57 that Sunday morning, an EF-2 tornado (wind speeds reaching 120 mph) touched down in Pekin, about 15 miles southwest of Washington. It stayed on the ground for only about two and a half miles and was about 100 yards wide. However, another tornado touched down eight minutes later, about 11:05 a.m., in

Washington. This one had grown into an EF-4, with winds reaching as high as 190 mph. In a matter of moments that must have seemed like an eternity for the residents of Washington, the tornado roared through, destroying most everything in its now half-mile-wide path.

All totaled, more than 1,200 homes were damaged or destroyed, with final damage estimates close to $1 billion. But that was just the property toll. More than 125 people were injured, and three people died in Washington that morning. The death toll likely would have been much higher if not for the fact many residents were attending church services that morning, and remarkably – some might say miraculously – most of the churches were spared serious damage.

Players and coaches were among those who lost their homes less than 12 hours after they had ridden through town in a victory parade celebrating the Panthers' first 12-0 season and their first return to the semifinals since 1985. That was the year Washington won its only state football championship, eliminating SHG in the semifinals on one of those last-second TD passes. Washington senior quarterback Colton Marshall rushed home from his job that Sunday morning after the tornado had ripped through the town. His family survived by taking shelter in the basement. But the house was gone. "It took my house down. Me and about eight or nine other guys on the team…it took our houses completely away," Marshall told reporters. "It was devastating to us and the rest of the community."

The Washington team returned to practice on Tuesday, accepting an offer by Illinois State University officials to use their college field about 40 miles away in Bloomington. The Washington players and other high school students had spent all day Monday helping residents clear away debris, a process that would take more than a month. Football practice is not usually described as a relief, but this time it was. "Just the fact that we were able to get them together and get some normalcy back as far as routine-wise – you saw some kids laugh, smile, have some fun today," Crouch, the head coach, told ABC news.

After returning home from Mass that Sunday morning, Ken

Leonard heard about what had happened in Washington. About eight hours after the tornado struck, Leonard dialed Crouch's number again. This time he said only one thing: "What can we do?"

A few months later, being interviewed for a story the IHSA would publish regarding the tornado relief efforts undertaken by SHG, Crouch explained why Leonard's call was so meaningful to him. "It would have been easy to simply make a courtesy call and then go ahead with his preparation for the game," Crouch said. "Ken did all in his power to help us out spiritually, emotionally and financially." Crouch said neither he nor Washington administrators ever considered cancelling the game, viewing it instead as a welcome distraction and respite for the team and for the community that had backed the team all season.

Leonard and assistant principal/assistant coach Bob Brenneisen met the next day to plan how SHG could help Washington players and fans with their most pressing needs surrounding the game: transportation, food and water for the team and its fans. Brenneisen and two mothers, Anne Dondanville and Michele Reavy, who had freshmen sons playing in the SHG program, organized the relief effort. Help came from everywhere, including other Central State Eight schools such as Chatham Glenwood, Jacksonville and Rochester. Three semitrailers of water were obtained. The goal of a sandwich and chips for 300 people turned into full pre- and postgame meals for 1,500 people. The damage to vehicles in Washington was so extensive that SHG and others ended up paying for seven charter buses to take the team and fans on the 75-mile trip to Springfield for the game and then back home after the postgame meal.

"The media made a big deal out of it, but I don't think it was a story," Leonard told reporters. "In the Midwest, in Illinois, in central Illinois, this is how we were brought up. When someone needs help, everyone does what they can." Those in attendance that day donated more than $75,000 for tornado relief for the Washington community. The IHSA record book shows that the Cyclones won the game that day 44-14. But that's not the lasting memory from the game.

"This game felt different," Leonard said afterward. "It felt like high school sports should. No hostility or anger between the teams or the fans. It was a game, and then it was over, and both sides were supporting each other." When it was over, both teams gathered at midfield and Leonard led the players and coaches in prayer. He ended by telling the Washington players that the SHG team would represent them well and carry their banner into the championship game. Fans from Washington stayed for hours after the game enjoying the postgame meal and fellowship.

"They hugged and they ate," Brenneisen recalled. "They hugged and they cried. Then they hugged some more. The one thing we had failed to realize was that because of the inability to get around their town, many of these folks were seeing each other for the first time since the tornado. They could finally see that their friends and neighbors were okay."

SHG not only figuratively carried the Washington banner to the campus of Northern Illinois University in DeKalb the next week for the title game, but also literally carried the Panthers' footballs with them. "The Monday after the game, Gabe Green, our quarterback, found one of Washington's footballs in our bag. He loved the feel of it and asked if he could use it in the championship game," Leonard recalls. He called Crouch to see if that would be okay. The next day five or six more balls from Washington showed up in Leonard's office.

Anne Dondanville, one of the SHG mothers who helped organize the outreach, captured the essence of the day when she wrote: *"If you were there, you saw a public-school principal present a Catholic school principal with a homemade quilt of thanks. If you were there, you saw two groups of football players play their hearts out. Some of them in new equipment because a tornado had scattered theirs days before. If you were there, you saw courage and commitment and sportsmanship and spirit. If you were there, you saw the best of sports and the best of people on display in a high school stadium and a high school cafeteria. We are grateful for all of you who were there."*

Carrying the memories of that day as well as the borrowed Washington footballs he liked the feel of so much, quarterback Gabe Green led his Cyclones into that Class 5A championship game the next week with a laser-like focus.

A Son's Date with Destiny

Once "Ring-Gate" was in the rear-view mirror, Rochester's path through the playoffs in 2013 did not have the same type of compelling human drama that SHG experienced in the semifinal against Washington. The Rockets rolled past Taylorville 42-7, Breese Mater Dei 56-28, and Belleville Althoff 50-21 in the first of what would become an epic series of playoff games between the two teams. They then defeated Rock Island Alleman 46-21 to reach the Class 4A finals.

The Leonard family gathered for Thanksgiving at Ken and Liz's house as was the family tradition. Even though Ken and Derek would both be playing for state championships during the next two days, Liz's "Thanksgiving Rule" stayed in place: No talking football around the table. Watching the football games on TV after the Thanksgiving meal was part of the day for the Leonards, as it is for many American households on Thanksgiving. But discussing Ken's and Derek's accomplishments – even with the historic implications of becoming the first father-son duo to win titles on the same weekend – was out of bounds. She did not want other family members to feel left out or less important. For Ken and Derek, it also was a brief respite from the pressure of the tasks facing them in the next 48 hours.

Derek's team was first up, with the Class 4A championship game against a 12-1 Geneseo team set for 7 p.m. Friday at Northern Illinois University in DeKalb. Ken was in the stands watching his son because the IHSA had instituted a rule that allowed only coaches of the playing team to be on the sidelines. The state finals were being played at NIU for the first time, but the Rochester team had been on the university's field that summer. Derek Leonard had his Rockets attend a 7-on-7 passing camp, setting the tone to begin the hunt for a fourth straight title on the same field he hoped to return to later in the fall. The Rockets made it back to Huskie Stadium, as many expected them to do, but how that title game unfolded was different than anyone anticipated.

It was a cold, breezy night, and the Rockets' vaunted aerial attack was pretty much shut down by Geneseo's defense and the wind in their faces every other quarter. Robbie Kelley, the latest in a line of exceptional Rochester quarterbacks, had thrown for more than 3,000 yards and 33 TDs with just five interceptions coming into the game. But on this night, Geneseo limited Kelley to 11 of 22 passing for just 110 yards and intercepted three passes, all of them on throws into the wind.

Rochester turned to the ground game with senior running back Drake Berberet rushing for 146 yards on 24 carries. Berberet scored both touchdowns. The first came on a 9-yard run with 7:38 left in the first half and was set up by a roughing-the-kicker penalty on Geneseo. Berberet followed key blocks by David Gunter, Colton Piper and Drew Hill and rumbled into the end zone. With the kicker Grant Fitzsimons having been injured on the running-into-the-kicker foul, the Rockets went for two points, and Berberet ran into the end zone for an 8-0 lead.

Geneseo had its best drive of the game in the third quarter, using its ground attack to move to the Rochester 22-yard line, but Evan Sembell forced a fumble and teammate Eric Yakle recovered the ball to snuff out the Geneseo threat. The Rockets added a second touchdown midway through the fourth quarter when Berberet powered the ball into the end zone from two yards out with 8:25 to play. The TD was Berberet's 38th of the season, tying the single-season school record set by running back Colten Glazebrook in 2010. Kelley ran the ball in for another two-point conversion and a seemingly safe 16-0 lead on a night when the defenses ruled.

Geneseo would attempt only eight passes in the game, completing only three. But one of those was a 50-yarder that moved the ball all the way to the Rochester 2-yard line. The Maple Leafs scored on a run and then converted a two-pointer on a pass to cut the lead in half, 16-8 with 5:44 left to play. The Rockets then faced a critical third-and-7 with just over three minutes to play. Berberet was met at the line of scrimmage but refused to go down, bouncing the run outside for 21 yards and a new set of downs. He sealed the win three downs later with another run for a first down, this one gaining six yards on a third-and-5 play. The Rockets then went into their victory formation, kneeling on two snaps to run out the clock.

Evan McMinn suffered an ankle injury in the SHG game in Week Two and was unable to play the rest of season. Because the victory formation would include little to no contact, Derek inserted McMinn for those last two plays. It was a fitting end to McMinn's fine high school football career. McMinn had been, in Leonard's words, "the heart and soul of our team on defense." McMinn's senior class also included the likes of Berberet, Kelley, Gunter, Piper and Matt Swaine. In their four years at Rochester, the only game that class lost was the "Ring-Gate" forfeit.

Leonard said he told McMinn he wanted him to suit up for the championship game even though he could not absorb any contact. Once Berberet got the game-clinching first down, Leonard turned to McMinn and told him to go into the game. "I remember that he was excited and a little emotional," Leonard says. McMinn's older brother, Riley, had been a standout player on the Rockets' first championship team in 2010 and was a linebacker at the University of Iowa. A younger brother would also go on to win a championship ring. The Gunter family, close friends with the McMinns, also had three brothers win rings. In addition to David, Mike had been a free safety and linebacker on that 2010 team and played at Eastern Illinois University. Younger brother Jacob was a member of four state championship teams through his senior season in 2019.

The tough win over a Geneseo team that would not back down made Rochester the first public school to win four straight football championships. It also kind of destroyed the myth that the high-octane Rockets were built only on speed, offensive schemes and great quarterbacks, and lacked physicality.

"It's not probably the way we'd write our script to win a football game, but at this level it doesn't matter. It's a great way for us to win...probably nobody would've predicted we could win a game like this," Derek Leonard said in the press conference afterward. "Sometimes it's hard to keep coming back motivated, but we wanted to be the first public school in Illinois to win four straight championships. That was our talk from Day One of our summer workouts." Carthage (1998-2000), East St. Louis (1983-85) and Park Ridge Maine South (2008-2010) each had won three consecutive titles, but on this night in DeKalb, the Rockets were alone on the summit.

The game marked the first time the Rockets had been held under 40 points in a playoff game since the title run started in 2010. Kelley, the quarterback, took it personally. Minutes after clutching the record-breaking state championship trophy, he told reporters, "Give credit to their defense, but I sucked. We kept battling though, and we played great at the end." Leonard takes exception with Kelley's harsh self-evaluation. "It probably was his worst game of the year, but to grit it out like that and make some big runs and throws...he showed his leadership and showed what Robbie Kelley is all about. I couldn't be prouder of a kid than I am of him," Derek says. "He and Drake Berberet ran the ball against a team that doesn't allow the run." Leonard and Kelley have remained close friends, a relationship Leonard enjoys with many of his former players.

To win championships, a team must be good. Sometimes, it also must be lucky, and it has to be able to win in a variety of ways. It's not that the Rockets hadn't played good defense during the title streak. It's just that the offense garnered the headlines. Another factor is that when a team scores as quickly as the Rockets typically do, it means the defense is right back on the field.

On this night, defensive coordinator Steve Buecker's players matched Geneseo's toughness man-for-man, led by players like Dalton Handlin (11 tackles), Gunter (10 tackles), Sembell (eight tackles and a forced fumble), Swaine (five tackles) and Austin Staton (four tackles). "The defenses on both sides were absolutely huge," Buecker said afterward. "It was a physical war out there. I'm just so proud of our kids. Everyone talks about our offense, which usually allows us to play with no pressure, just fast and free. But the teams from up north are so disciplined with their option run games that you have to be just as disciplined on your side of the ball. All 11 players have an assignment, and everyone has to tackle their assignment."

Swaine, one of the seniors on defense, put it in perspective when he told reporters, "I love that our offense gets all of the attention. Then the teams we play underestimate our defense. Tonight, we shut them down for the most part. It's an unbelievable feeling to go out and play the best game of our lives on defense in this situation."

Watching the game unfold, Ken Leonard says he felt more nervous for his son and the Rockets than he was about his own team's monumental challenge the next morning. SHG would be taking on an unbeaten and No. 1-ranked Lombard Montini, a Catholic league team gunning for its fifth straight state championship. As he drove the 40 minutes back to his team's hotel, Ken's confidence grew. Most of the pressure would be on Montini because most observers gave SHG little chance. However, the Cyclones had fared quite well against the Broncos, winning seven of nine regular season games since Montini coach Chris Andriano turned down the SHG job, opening the door for Leonard. More importantly, Leonard had seen his offensive line steadily improve its play since the loss to Rochester, when quarterback Gabe Green had been sacked several times.

Following that loss, practice was rugged for the Cyclones, especially for the offensive line. "We realized we could be an average team, or we could be a great team," senior right guard Keegan Hamilton told reporters. "I think that week made us a team that could go to the state championship." For junior right tackle Quinn Oseland, it was more personal. "I'm pretty close friends with (quarterback) Gabe (Green)," he said. "I don't ever want him to get hit."

Derek Leonard had time to ponder the father-son attempt to make history after his team's championship celebration ended Friday night. Normally, Leonard would ride the bus back to Rochester with his team after a game, but this time he was staying over to watch his father go for his title the next morning. He had not booked a hotel room, waiting until both teams had punched their tickets to the state finals. Derek's wife Lindsey finally found a room in Aurora, about 40 minutes away from DeKalb. Derek says he had a gut feeling during that drive that his father's team had a better chance than most observers thought.

"My dad always says he feels good about his team's chances; that's just my father. But I could tell he felt pretty dang good. SHG had a smart team that had improved since we had played them, and he told me about their game plan, which sounded solid," he says. "Dad likes being the underdog, but it's a role he hasn't experienced much. In a way, being the underdog is relaxing because you're supposed to lose. I just had a weird feeling that the game would be closer than many people thought."

A Family Football Coronation

Saturday morning at Huskie Stadium in DeKalb broke clear, crisp and cool. The way SHG began the 10 a.m. Class 5A title game was not very crisp, and it definitely was not cool for Cyclones fans. Montini scored on its first two possessions to go up 14-0. Watching from high up in the stands, Derek wondered if the game might get away from the Cyclones, noting "When you get a couple of scores behind a good team, it just seems like you could end up chasing them the whole game."

On SHG's third possession, quarterback Gabe Green, using one of those borrowed footballs from Washington, found standout receiver Malik Turner for a 43-yard pass play that seemed to awaken the Cyclones. Turner later starred at the University of Illinois and played more than five years in the NFL for the Seattle Seahawks, Dallas Cowboys and San Francisco 49ers. Following his big catch, the Cyclones cut the lead to 14-7 when running back Anthony Di-Nello scored on a 2-yard run. That good feeling lasted precisely 10 seconds on the game clock because Montini's Derrick Curry ran the kickoff back 82 yards to again put his team on top by two TDs.

The SHG defense finally stiffened in the second quarter, forcing Montini to punt for the first time in the game. Two plays later, Green kept the ball and dashed 56 yards to make the score 21-14. Late in the second quarter, Montini threatened to score again, driving the ball all the way to the SHG 4-yard line with under a minute to play in the half. As Ken Leonard noted from his game preparation

117

study of Montini, "They always scored when they got inside the 10-yard line." Another score would have shoved the Cyclones back into that perpetual chase mode that had worried Derek.

After a short gain, an incomplete pass and the clock under 30 seconds, Montini lined up for its third down try. It would turn out to be the most pivotal play in the game.

Even at the high school level, a big part of game preparation is film study of the upcoming opponent. Hours are spent looking for strengths and weaknesses, or tendencies that indicate what type of play a team might run in certain situations, anything to give your team an edge. Most of the game preparation falls to the coaches, but players also pore over game film. In doing so, SHG linebacker Chris Overton had noticed something unusual. It was subtle, but the more film he watched, the more certain he was. Overton had detected a slight difference in how Montini quarterback Alex Wills stood when he lined up in the shotgun formation. When his feet were even, Montini always ran the ball. When Wills lined up with his right foot slightly behind his left, it was always a pass.

That Montini might throw the ball on this third-down play from the 3-yard line was likely because the clock would run out if a running play did not reach the end zone. Confirmation came when Wills lined up with his right foot slightly behind the left. The Cyclones called for a blitz. Overton sacked Wills for a 12-yard loss…and the clock ran out before Montini could try for a field goal or run another play.

Celebrating the crucial stop, Ken ran across the field toward the locker room, fist-pumping and urging on his players. To get to the locker room, Leonard and the Cyclones had to run by the Montini sideline and then into a tunnel underneath a whole section of Montini fans. The two coaching staffs jawed at each other, and the Montini fans unleased a verbal barrage on Leonard and his players. Derek had a bird's-eye view of the episode. "I remember giggling and thinking, 'Oh, boy! Here we go!' Even a bishop on the Montini side was giving dad heck! Dad doesn't mind that stuff. He wanted his players to know he wasn't going to back down."

"I was pretty animated, I felt like I was 35 again. Then their fans got rowdy, like they were kinda saying to us, 'Don't you dare bark at the bully!' I'm shaking my fists back at them. It was my job to fire up our kids," says Ken, still not ready to back down almost a decade later. "That play turned the whole game around. And their fans' reaction united us. We had a belief now that we could win."

Andriano, the Montini coach, shrugged off the episode, which included some of his assistant coaches and players yelling back at the SHG players. "When we don't execute, we get frustrated, and that's the competitiveness of my coaches and my kids, me included," he told reporters. "They rode that momentum at the start of the third quarter."

The halftime break included another important exchange. One of SHG's offensive linemen approached Leonard. "Coach, I can't block that guy," the player said. That "guy" was Montini defensive end Dylan Thompson, a 6-foot-5, 275-pound specimen and a four-year starter who had set the Montini record with 17 quarterback sacks during the season. One scouting service rated him the 16th best defensive end among all high school seniors in the country. He was recruited to Ohio State University to play college football. Not many high school players could have handled Thompson one-on-one.

But for a player to admit that to the head coach, the player must trust the coach, and/or the player cares more about team than self. "A player who says that has to know that one possible consequence of being that truthful is that he might get benched in the championship game," says Derek. "That player has to know the coach cares about him and that he's not going to get benched or told to just buck up and do better. That trust factor is one of the things that makes Dad such a good coach."

Ken appreciated the honest appraisal. He and his assistant coaches adjusted the offensive scheme during the halftime break. Thompson had been breathing down Green's neck any time the quarterback went back to pass. He was too strong for the Cyclones to run right at him, and fast enough that they couldn't just run away from him to the other side of the field. "I just said, 'OK, we're gonna put him on an island,'" Ken says, explaining that he wanted to make Thompson have to decide whether to pursue the running back or the quarterback on option plays. Green would determine whether to keep the ball based on what Thompson did.

John Allison, the SHG offensive coordinator, explained that to place Thompson on that "island," whichever side the Montini star defensive end lined up on, the Cyclones would use a formation that overloaded the other side with offensive players. That forced the Montini linebackers to shift to that side of the field so as not to be outnumbered, leaving Thompson, the defensive end, pretty much isolated.

When the SHG offense lines up, the quarterback scans the defensive alignment and makes a pre-snap "read" of where he thinks the defense would be most susceptible. Once the ball is snapped, the quarterback then has three options: hand the ball to a running back, run the ball himself, or throw a pass. That choice must be made in a split second. With a championship on the line, Green would choose an option based on how Thompson reacted. The hunter became the hunted. Leonard did not hesitate to put the game in the hands of Green. "When it came to decision-making," Leonard says, "Gabe was off-the-charts good."

The revised strategy helped neutralize the Montini star, and SHG dominated the second half against the four-time defending champions. The Cyclones scored 24 straight points, with Kenny Rowe kicking a 39-yard field goal, Green running for two touchdowns and DiNello adding a TD run after a fumble recovery by Cameron Murphy. Montini eventually got a TD to cut the margin to 38-28, but an interception by linebacker Chris Smith midway through the final period ended Montini's chances for a fifth straight championship.

"My brother (Jake Smith) got an interception in the championship game in 2008," Smith said afterward. "That was going through my head. I had dropped a few in the playoffs, but when I finally caught one, I thought, *'Wow! This is awesome!'* "

With the second half adjustment to the offense, Green was unstoppable. For the game, he passed for 110 yards and ran for 145 yards and three TDs. "We picked that one guy (Thompson) out on defense, and we 'read' him," said Green, who would earn a football scholarship to Southern Mississippi, Brett Favre's old school. "It started to work, so we just kept doing it."

With the 38-28 Cyclones win, Ken and Derek had become the first father-son duo in Illinois to win state football championships on the same weekend. "The Leonard family had a good weekend," Ken told reporters after the SHG victory. "This one is a sweet one. We wanted to show everybody that there is good football played south of Interstate 80."

In the stands, Derek watched his father and the Cyclones players celebrate. He did not attempt to join them. "Actually, I was still kind of ticked at the IHSA…for a couple of reasons," he says, referring to the forfeit loss and the rule preventing him from being on the SHG sideline with his father for the history-making achievement. "On the drive back to Rochester, I called my dad to congratulate him. We just said, 'This is pretty neat.'"

The two would attempt to repeat the father-son state championship weekend sweep in 2014.

Victorious!

Another Leonard Family Reunion at State

It was with great fanfare in 2013 that Ken and Derek Leonard became the first father and son to win Illinois state football championships on the same weekend. Repeating that family feat in 2014 would barely cause a stir. Probably because no one was surprised.

Rochester had proven it could reload by winning a public-school record four straight championships with three different quarterbacks and a revolving door of great running backs, receivers and linemen. SHG had a host of players returning to defend its title, including quarterback Gabe Green, who would end his career as the all-time leading passer as well as the No. 9 rusher in Cyclones history, amassing more than 10,000 yards of offense in three years as a starter.

Both teams got off to fast starts, achieving the mercy-rule running clocks in their first four games. SHG kept piling up the blowout wins throughout the regular season, but Rochester was tested in a surprisingly close 23-16 win over Springfield Southeast High School and a 54-46 slugfest with Jacksonville before being upset 38-33 by an athletic Decatur MacArthur team. The Leonard Bowl was the last game of the regular season that year, and SHG pounded the Rockets 56-13 behind three TD runs apiece by Sam Sergent and Anthony DiNello and two TD passes by Green.

That meant the Rockets would be coming off two straight losses entering the playoffs. "You never want to lose, but SHG had a championship caliber team, and MacArthur had some great athletes," Derek says. "Those games got us battle tested for the play-offs." Playing against schools its size in the 4A playoffs, Rochester blew past Mt. Zion (65-35), Quincy Notre Dame (35-14), Bloomington Central Catholic (56-21) and Herrin (28-9) to punch its fifth straight ticket to the finals. The championship game opponent would be a speedy and athletic Chicago Phillips team that reminded Derek and defensive coordinator Steve Buecker of Decatur MacArthur. Buecker told his players the week leading up to the title game that the MacArthur loss "would not be in vain."

Many in the Chicago press figured the 12-1 Phillips team, hardened by playing larger-enrollment teams from the Chicago area, would be just too much for Rochester to handle. Not that they necessarily were wrong about Phillips, a school that accumulated enough talent to go unbeaten in 2015 to win the 4A title and go undefeated again in 2017 to win the 5A title. Perhaps overlooked was the fact that Rochester routinely played 5A and 6A schools in the Central State Eight Conference.

Phillips proved to be a stern test, at least for most of the first half, trailing Rochester only 17-12 before junior Dan Zeigler – heir to the Wil Lunt-Sean Robinson-Wes Lunt-Austin Green-Robbie Kelley quarterback mantle – threw a 34-yard TD pass to Collin Etherton with about a minute left in the first half for a 25-12 halftime lead.

The end came quickly for Chicago Phillips in the third quarter as the Rockets scored three touchdowns in five minutes. Taking the second-half kickoff, it took the Rockets less than 90 seconds to score, the big play being a 48-yard strike to Jeremy Bivens, which led to a 10-yard TD run by Evan Sembell. The ensuing kickoff was fumbled, and Rochester's Colin Whitson fell on the ball at the Phillips 30-yard line. After a 7-yard sack, Collin Stallworth got behind the defense, and Zeigler hit him with a 37-yard TD pass. After a Phillips punt, the Rockets quickly scored again as Zeigler found Bivens for 13- and 31-yard passes before Colten Shadis ran the ball in from five yards out. In a span of about five minutes, the Rockets had scored 21 unanswered points to open an insurmountable 46-12 lead. Tyler Schlecht added a 21-yard field goal to go with his first half 20-yard field goal for the final margin of 49-28.

So much for the Rockets not being able to hang with the team from the big city. Their 49 points set a 4A title game record at the time. Derek had sidled up to his quarterback during the pregame warmups and told Zeigler, "You're going to become a legend after this game." Zeigler threw for more than 300 yards and three TDs. Bivens, who caught eight passes for 163 yards, told reporters, "A lot of the passes, Dan threw perfectly. Our timing has gotten a lot better throughout the season."

Eric Yakle led the Rochester defense with seven tackles, including a sack. Bivens had six tackles and an interception, and Whitson recovered two fumbles. All in all, a dominating effort. Sembell carried the ball 30 times for 180 yards and two TDs. Playing against Rochester is a pick-your-poison dilemma for opponents. The Rockets are best known for their ability to throw the ball, but their running game can cause just as much damage to defenses. Sembell may not have been as flashy as some Rockets running backs, but he was one of the best ever at the school. In fact, Sembell's 2,412 yards rushing in 2014 was a single-season school record and was second in Central State Eight history, only 32 yards shy of SHG's Kenni Burns' record set in 2002.

Phillips coach Troy McAllister summed up the game succinctly in his press conference, saying, "We lost to a really good opponent tonight in Rochester. We got out-played, out-coached, whatever you want to say."

The win marked Rochester's 25th straight playoff victory. The fifth straight state championship broke the Rockets' own record of four straight by a public school. It also set the table for Derek's father to complete another Leonard family sweep the next morning. SHG had cruised past playoff foes Jerseyville 49-7, Marion 42-6, Taylorville 63-14 and Peoria 49-21 to earn a 5A title rematch with Lombard Montini.

A year earlier, Gabe Green had run the SHG run-pass option (RPO) plays so effectively that Montini could not contain him. In leading the Cyclones to that 38-28 championship win in 2013, Green ran wild for 145 yards and three touchdowns. With a year to prepare, Andriano was not going to let the SHG quarterback repeat that performance. "Last year, we really didn't do a good job against their quarterback running," Andriano told reporters. "If your defensive front gets too far up field against these guys, they move you… and you end up opening up the running lanes."

This time, the Broncos defense limited Green to 72 yards rushing, about half of what he gained in the previous meeting. "A lot of things we were able to do last year, we couldn't do this year," Green told reporters afterward. "They were very hard-nosed and they stopped our run a lot." Ken Leonard looked for new ways to probe and counter Montini's defensive focus on Green. The answer was an almost even complement of runs (231 yards) and passes (205 yards) featuring a variety of players.

Montini broke on top 7-0 with a long TD pass in the first quarter. SHG answered halfway through the second quarter with an 81-yard drive that was sustained when Green hit Brendan Stannard with a 20-yard pass to convert a third-down play. Sam Sergent ran around end for 8 yards on another third-down play to give the Cyclones a first down at the 1-yard line. DiNello punched the ball into the end zone, but SHG still trailed 7-6 when the extra point kick was blocked.

The Cyclones moved the ball 83 yards in the final three minutes of the first half and took a 12-7 lead into halftime when Sergent plowed into the end zone with just 16 seconds left in the half. That drive was keyed by big-yardage runs around the ends of the line of scrimmage by Sergent and DiNello, who followed key blocks by guards John Fisher and Nick Martin. Those sweeps around end were plays the Cyclones would turn to repeatedly, with DiNello gaining 98 yards and two TDs and Sergent 56 yards and a score. The Cyclones grinded out 26 first downs against the tough Montini defense.

"Our run defense was excellent today," Montini's Andriano said in his post-game press conference. "But they found a weakness. They found a running lane with that stretch play that they were using, and we couldn't seem to get off blocks and get to them. They were able to control the ball and move the chains with that play."

SHG broke the tight game open in the third quarter by shutting out Montini and putting 17 points on the scoreboard to lead 29-7 heading into the fourth quarter. Green hit 6-foot-6, 250-pound end Albert Okwuegbunam with a 28-yard TD pass, Sergent scored on a 6-yard run, and Cody Bowman kicked a 37-yard field goal. Known as "Albert O" for phonetic reasons, Okwuegbunam would earn second-team All-Southeastern Conference honors at the University of Missouri in both 2017 and 2019. In April of 2020, he became the first Central State Eight Conference player to be drafted into the NFL when the Denver Broncos selected him in the fourth round.

The Cyclones offense gets so much attention, sometimes it's easy to overlook their defense. But it was a bend-but-not-break SHG defense that decided the 2014 championship game. The Cyclones gave up 234 yards passing but intercepted the Montini quarterback four times. Cole Hillestad intercepted a pass at his own goal line to thwart Montini on its first drive of the game. Interceptions on Montini's first two drives of the third quarter determined the outcome. Sean Mason not only led the team with eight tackles, but his interception at the Montini 40 set up the "Albert O" touchdown catch. On the very next possession, Bowman picked off a pass and returned it 21 yards to the Montini 20 to set up Sergent's TD run. Mason's second interception of the game at his own 8-yard line with three minutes left allowed SHG to run out the clock for the 29-14 victory.

During his career at SHG, Leonard often remarked that the Cyclones were their own toughest foes. Just stick to the game plan, do your individual jobs on offense and defense and trust the process, he told two generations of players. "That's the big thing and I've just pounded it into their heads," Leonard says. "Montini was a tremendous opponent and so was Rochester or whoever we're playing. But whether it's high school, college or the NFL, if you don't beat yourself, you've got a tremendous chance to win. As good as we were, that's what we talked about the most."

Summing up the unbeaten 2014 SHG championship team, Leonard says, "My goal was for them to be the greatest team to ever play high school football in the state of Illinois. Now, I don't know if we actually were, or even where that team ranks with the other state champions we've had at SHG, but I challenged them to be the best team ever. That really helped them to keep challenging themselves. They wanted to be great."

Where the 2014 SHG team ranks among Leonard's six championship squads is up for debate. In fact, the coach thinks the 2020 team that never got the chance to play for a title because of the COVID season might have been his best team. The 2014 Cyclones beat every opponent, most of them by running-clock margins. And they capped another Leonard family celebration at the state finals as father and son again won state titles on the same weekend.

A Portrait of Courage and Grace

Despite their football reputations, neither Ken, nor Derek, nor Bradley is the toughest member of their family. That title probably belongs to WWII combat veteran John Leonard, Ken's father. But no one in the Leonard family ever displayed more courage and grace than Elizabeth "Liz" Leonard.

Even before she battled the cancer that eventually took her life, Liz lived most of her adult years dealing with a condition known as agoraphobia, an anxiety disorder that can include an intense fear of crowds of people and unfamiliar places. Some affected by the condition seldom step foot outside their homes. Agoraphobia can manifest itself in a variety of ways for people, including panic attacks, rapid heartbeat, hyperventilation, headaches, dizziness, blurred vision and elevated blood pressure. Some 200,000 people per year are diagnosed with agoraphobia in the United States. Many have no idea what is wrong or that help is available.

When it was suggested that Liz living with agoraphobia was like telling someone with a fear of heights that they must climb a mountain, Ken interrupted. "No," he said. "It's like telling someone they have to live on the side of that mountain. It was not easy for her. Finally, when she was in her 40s, she was diagnosed and got some help. With the medication, things got better for her. But at times it was a real struggle."

Ken says he first became aware of Liz's condition while he was away working on the Alaskan Pipeline, before they were married.

"I called back home to talk with Liz and she was telling me about having a panic attack as she was entering one of the buildings at Illinois State University. She said it was almost a paralyzing feeling," Ken recalls. "I didn't know what to make of it. Being an athlete and a coach, my first reaction was to tell her that she needed to tough it out, to just keep going and she would be okay. I didn't understand it. Thank God, she finally found some help."

Derek says he knew his mother felt most at ease when she was in her home, welcoming anyone and everyone. He also remembers that she would never drive when they went to Chicago to visit her family. But he was not aware of her battles with agoraphobia. "Probably the biggest compliment I can give her in that regard is that growing up I had never heard the word, couldn't spell it and didn't know what it meant," Derek says. "She never ever complained about it."

His younger brother Bradley witnessed one of his mother's panic attacks. "Mom was driving to the mall one day when I was about 12. All of a sudden, she just couldn't drive any more. I drove us home that day," Bradley says. "The agoraphobia was horrible for her. There were just a few places where she felt really comfortable – our home, her parents' home, Dad's office and in the classroom at her school. Even dealing with all that she went through, she was the best mother ever...not only for Derek and me, but for every kid that ever came into our home."

Despite having a teaching degree, Liz Leonard remained a kindergarten teacher's aide in the Springfield school district for more than a quarter century. Bradley thinks that was so she could remain in the background and just help kids, the thing she most loved to do. She thrived in that position, helping teachers and hundreds of kids. Her teaching ability altered the course of Bradley's life.

"I had severe dyslexia as a kid. I was not dumb, but I was scared to be called on to read in class. She would work with me night after night to learn how to read better," he says. "Without her, I don't know how things would have turned out for me." Bradley went on to become a very successful businessman in banking and insurance. Ken and Derek both thought Bradley would have been a successful football coach, and he did assist Derek for seven years at Rochester. However, Bradley opted for the business route because, he says, "I wanted to make money."

Ken marveled at his wife's patience and endurance in helping Bradley overcome dyslexia. "It was unbelievable to watch Liz work with him…they would go on for hours. It was painstaking to watch them go over it word by word," he says. "The amazing thing is that Derek and I could read something quickly, but we might not be able to tell you what we just read. It would take Bradley three or four times as long to read the same thing, but he could tell you every detail."

Watching Bradley conquer dyslexia reinforced Ken's belief that overcoming obstacles prepares youngsters for life. "When I talk about my teams at the end of the season, I talk more about those other guys than I do about the all-staters," Ken says. "I try to tell the guys who have been so blessed athletically that football was so easy for them in high school, 'Guess what? It's not always going to be that way in life.'"

Victorious!

The First Lady of SHG Football

When Ken Leonard announced his retirement, Sacred Heart-Griffin President Katherine O'Connor said, "For a lot of people, Coach Leonard is Mr. SHG." That meant Liz Leonard was the First Lady of football at the school, another role that forced her to face her fears and go to some public places she preferred to avoid. Like attending football games.

Her role was ironic given that she didn't even like football. She loved the players and considered them extended members of her family, but she didn't care for the rough-and-tumble game itself. She sometimes would sit in her car outside the stadium and listen to the game on the radio. Other times, she would show up after the game had started and find a spot away from the more congested seating areas, sitting alone or with a friend.

Elizabeth "Liz" Brown was born on July 24, 1953, in Highland Park, Illinois, to Claude and Elinor (Zimmer) Brown. She met Ken Leonard while he was attending school and playing football at Harper College in the Chicago suburb of Palatine. She and Ken both graduated from Illinois State University. They were married on July 30, 1977, in Highland Park. Marriage can be both the blessing and challenge of a lifetime. And that is without complications like Liz's struggles with agoraphobia and Ken's often all-consuming focus on coaching football. The couple lost their first baby when Liz was six months pregnant and later lost adopted son Philip in a car accident. Through all the ups and downs, they remained married for 40 years, until Liz's death at the end of 2017.

"Liz got pregnant about a year after we were married. She was pretty far along when we lost the baby. It was a girl, and we were going to name her Lisa. We had never heard about people losing a baby like that. We just thought you got pregnant, you had the baby," Ken says. "The same day we lost her, some good friends of ours had a baby girl. We ran into them as we were leaving the hospital. You want to be so happy for them, but we had just lost our baby girl. It was so devastating, even more so for Liz because she was carrying the child. I think it probably also made the other issue even worse."

Two years later, on April 2, 1980, the couple had their first child, Derek. "That pregnancy was not easy for Liz, either. She was in the hospital and bed-ridden for several weeks before he was born," Ken recalls. Bradley was born on July 22, 1983.

Liz found out that she had breast cancer about two weeks before Christmas in 2015. The cancer was discovered through a routine mammogram. She decided to postpone the beginning of treatment until after the holidays. The family traveled to the Chicago area to spend Christmas with Liz's family, including siblings, children and grandchildren. Her mother, Grandma Ellie, had passed in 2008, and her father, Claude Brown, had preceded her in death. The Christmas celebration was not easy for Liz.

"She started to feel pretty bad on Christmas Eve," Derek recalls. "The soldier she was, she got up on Christmas morning and made sure nothing was going to spoil Christmas for the kids or any of us. We headed home the next day and by that night she was in the emergency room." Fluid had built up around her heart, a complication of the cancer that had been growing. She was rushed into surgery.

"The doctors told us there was a chance she would not survive the surgery that night," Ken says. "But Liz was tough, and she made it through that surgery. She fought all the way through everything that happened in the next two years. The entire time, what mattered to her the most was how everyone else in the family was doing. That was just Liz; that's how she had lived her whole life.

"I know it sounds strange, but those last two years were some of the best years of our marriage. She had taken care of everything in our home, which allowed me to pursue my passion for coaching football. Those last two years, the roles got reversed and I got to take care of her. I am so thankful for that. I am also grateful for how the school allowed me to do what I needed to do to take care of her, and how my coaches and players stepped up to help me."

Liz's cancer was in remission for a while, but by early 2017 tests revealed it was spreading. She knew she wasn't going to survive. She seemed at peace with that and she wanted the rest of the family to go on with their lives. She wanted Ken to put aside any talk of retirement because she knew that coaching would be his best refuge.

Sacred Heart-Griffin officials surprised Ken in late September of 2017 by naming the football field in his honor. "Ken Leonard Field" was dedicated on September 29, before the Cyclones were to play Springfield Southeast. Liz's immune system was compromised, and Liz had not been strong enough to attend any games that season. But on that night, even though she would succumb to the cancer just three months later, she showed up and slowly made her way to the center of the field for the ceremony honoring her husband.

"I knew something was up when the players didn't leave the field the normal way after the pregame warmups. Then I saw Liz," Ken says. "I thought they were going to honor Liz. In a way they did, because any time anyone honored me, they were honoring her."

SHG assistant principal Bob Brenneisen confirmed that the night was designed to honor Liz as well as Ken. "It was probably as much for Liz as it was for Ken that night. Seeing her, in the pain she was in, coming out to be with her husband and coming out there to be with her boys – she considered the 70-some kids on the football team to be part of her family – just to make that sacrifice to come out there in her ill health was special," Brenneisen told reporters. Brenneisen had served several years as an assistant on Ken's football staff, and his sons Bobby, Tim and Matt all played for the Cyclones. Upon Ken's retirement, Brenneisen would succeed him as the director of athletics at SHG.

Sam Madonia, the longtime radio voice of the Cyclones, said Liz's appearance that night is one of his most enduring memories of SHG football. He shared that memory with *The State Journal-Register* sportswriter Ryan Mahan when Liz died. "There wasn't a dry eye in the house when she came out onto the field that night. It was an incredible moment. People loved her," Madonia said. "I remember when we'd have postgame shows, she'd walk in humbly and go around and talk to everybody in the place and said 'hello' and 'thanks' and 'congratulations.' She cared about the players. She cared about their parents."

That caring was reciprocated, and the outpouring of love for Liz was not confined to the SHG football community. Signs saying "Play for Liz" could be spotted at away games after her cancer diagnosis became public.

Derek describes his mother by saying, "She just had that special 'it.' No matter who you were, she made you feel special and loved. I've never met anyone like her. She was the best mom a kid could hope for, and she was great with the kids in her classroom. She really reached out to kids who needed it the most, like Philip. We were all lucky to have her in our lives."

Just as Liz knew Ken needed to keep coaching during her illness, she also knew that he would not do well alone in the long term after she was gone. In the last year of her life, she had difficult discussions with Ken and her younger son Bradley. Her talks with Derek focused more on her continuing to battle cancer, her unwavering faith and praying for a miracle. "Through it all, Mom knew how to talk to Dad, Bradley and me in different ways," Derek says. "She knew what each of us could handle."

In a sermon about miracles, a pastor in the Portland, Oregon, area addressed why some people get healed and others don't. The sermon was titled "Does God Still Perform Miracles?" The gist of the pastor's message was that God does heal people miraculously. In other cases, the healing takes place over time. God ultimately heals all believers with eternal life in heaven, the pastor concluded. The screen saver on Derek's phone is a picture of a blonde woman being held in the arms of Jesus.

Liz told Ken she wanted him to get remarried if he ever found the right person. "I didn't want to even think about anything like that," Ken says. "But that was another case of Liz thinking about everyone else." She said the same thing to Bradley. "Mom talked to me about a lot of things in those final few months. She knew that she was going to die, and she wanted all of us in the family to be prepared and taken care of," Bradley says. "She told me that she wanted Dad to get remarried, that he was not the sort of person who would do well living alone." There was a caveat. "She had a 'No Way' list of women she shared with me." Bradley adds, smiling at his mother's sense of humor even during her battle with cancer. "But she said if he ever found the right woman, she wanted him to be happy."

Elizabeth (Brown) Leonard passed away in the early morning hours of December 31, 2017, at her home surrounded by family. She was 64 years old. She was survived by Ken, Derek and Bradley; grandchildren Savannah Williams, and John Patrick (JP), Blake, Julia and Austin Leonard; her siblings Barbara Brown of Highland Park, Claudia Brown of Honaunau, Hawaii, Dorothy Gross of Boise, Idaho, and Claude Brown of Highland Park. She had touched the lives of so many people that her visitation was held in the gymnasium on the SHG campus. Memorial contributions went to the Leonard Grandchildren Education Fund at the Bank of Springfield, where Bradley eventually became a vice president. She was laid to rest in Oak Hill Cemetery near Springfield.

In the online tributes to Elizabeth Leonard on the Butler Funeral Home website, people mentioned her smile, beauty, energy, kindness, teaching ability, sweet spirit, love of family and her faith. One noted the high moral character displayed by her sons Derek and

Bradley. Another referred to her as having been an "angel." Then there was one written by the Lantz family, Mike and Paula and their sons Ryan and John. John led the Cyclones to the 2008 state championship and ended up being the all-time leading receiver at SHG. As strong as the football ties were for the Lantz family, Liz Leonard made the connection go way deeper than any on-the-field accomplishments.

"Liz brought the true meaning of FAMILY to the sport of football," wrote the Lantz family. "Faith, Family and Football!"

Twice Blessed

Many never find that special someone to love them and go through life with them. Ken Leonard realizes he has been twice blessed.

Liz Leonard was the perfect counterbalance to Ken's career in coaching for their 40 years of marriage. She took care of everything having to do with the household, giving Ken the freedom to pursue his coaching career in a way that sometimes bordered on obsession and always with a work ethic that few coaches could match. She also created a loving home for Ken, Derek, Bradley and countless boys that migrated to their house on South Park Street, about the length of three football fields from the Sacred Heart-Griffin west campus. In the months leading up to her death in December of 2017, she had shared with Ken and Bradley that she wanted Ken to remarry if he ever found the right person. She told them she knew better than anyone that Ken was not designed to live alone.

The first time Ken saw Angie Madison was when he attended the visitation for her husband, Michael "Mickey" Madison, in January of 2018, about three weeks after Liz had died. Mick Madison was 14 years older than Ken, but their paths had crossed in the Springfield sports world. Madison was inducted into the Springfield Sports Hall of Fame in 1999 for his basketball, baseball, softball, and golf prowess. He did not take up golf until age 32, yet he finished in the top 10 of the Springfield Men's City Golf Tournament five times. Having earned All-American honors in amateur baseball, he later signed with the Houston Colt 45's (the original name of the Astros). His slugging power in slow-pitch softball was well enough known in Springfield softball circles that most pitchers chose to walk him.

Madison's second marriage was to Angela Dorks in 1993. Mick was 25 years older than Angie, and the couple had no children, though Madison had a son and daughter from a previous marriage. Angie was an elementary school teacher for 35 years in Virden and Auburn, where for a short time she coached basketball and track. Ken remembers seeing her for the first time at Madison's wake. "I was like, 'That's Mick's wife?' He outkicked his coverage!'" invoking a football coaching term that translates into Ken thinking Madison outdid himself marrying Angie.

He exchanged condolences with her that night at West Side Christian Church in Springfield. Having followed the Springfield sports scene, Angie recognized the coach. She thanked him for coming and remembers later thinking, *"Gosh, I forgot he's just gone through this himself."* They would not meet again until several weeks later at a grief counseling class at West Side Christian Church. The loneliness had hit Ken hard a few days after Liz's death, when family and friends went back to their own lives.

"I remember when that last person left the house and I shut the door, it all just came crashing down," Ken says. "The deathly silence was so hard. I kept the TV or radio on all the time just so there would be some sound. I was 'Coach,' the guy who should be able to suck it up and keep going. I'm thinking, *'What am I going to do? How am I going to get through this?'"*

Ken called some friends who had lost spouses to seek their advice. One of those calls was to Tammie Rockford, whose husband Steve had died a few months earlier at the age of 47 after a five-year battle with amyotrophic lateral sclerosis (ALS), commonly known as Lou Gehrig's Disease. Steve Rockford had been one of Ken's assistant coaches for two years at SHG and later was football and wrestling coach at Southeast High School in Springfield. Rockford was awarded the Medal of Courage by the National Wrestling Hall of Fame in 2014. Despite the calls and his other efforts to stay busy, Ken was still struggling.

Angie was, too. "When Mick was alive, the TV was always on and blaring. I don't watch much TV. The silence was suffocating," she says. "I went everywhere I could, to as many home Auburn games as I could find."

Ken and Angie both say their meeting at the grief class was a God thing. A member of West Side Christian Church, Angie started attending the grief-sharing class there, but only because of a promise she made to accompany a friend. Ken had tried a different grief group a couple of months after Liz's death but says it was probably too soon, and that he found himself feeling worse when he left the meetings. He ended up at the West Side Christian group because a teacher at SHG suggested it to him.

God was not done just getting the two of them to the class. The last night of the class, attendees were asked to write prayers and then read them to the group. When it was Ken's turn, he said, "God, what do you have for me?" Reflecting on that plaintive prayer some four years later, he said, "I had no idea that the answer was a lady sitting three seats down to my left. But that's how God can work." When the meeting ended, Ken approached Angie and asked if she might like to get together for dinner sometime. Mutual friends had previously tried to get the two together. One of them had given Angie's phone number to Ken. "I lost the number," Ken says. "That wasn't God, that was just typical me. I had to call the guy back and get it again." He says it took two months to work up the courage to call Angie.

Coaches will tell you it is never easy to follow a legendary coach because the bar is set so high – something John Allison will have to deal with at SHG in replacing the winningest coach in state history. Angie stepped into a similar situation when she married Ken. Liz Leonard's reputation had grown large, and for good reason considering what she had meant to her children, grandchildren, other family members and the countless kids who hung out at the Leonard home.

"For the most part, it has been good," Angie says. "I have struggled with it some because of everything Liz meant to so many people. I didn't really know Liz, so you can't emulate someone you didn't really know. I always wanted a family, but I have never tried to take over Liz's role as a mother and grandmother." That approach is something Derek and Bradley both noticed and appreciated. During the height of COVID, when most public schools had gone to remote learning, Angie used her teaching background to help Blake and Austin, Derek and Lindsey's boys, navigate through that year of learning.

Angie first met Derek and Bradley in the late summer of 2018. Ken's parents, John and Iona Leonard, had moved to Plymouth, Indiana, when Ken was a senior at Chenoa High School. Even as they got older, they would make the four-hour drive to Springfield most Friday nights each fall to watch Ken coach the Cyclones. John Leonard died in 2007. Iona had suffered a stroke several years earlier, but she was still living in Plymouth. She was 94 and Ken wanted to make sure his mother got to meet Angie, so the family planned a trip to Indiana.

Bradley was driving when he and Ken arrived to pick up Angie. "Bradley just immediately hugs me and tells me how happy he is to meet me. That's just Bradley," Angie recalls. They next picked up Derek. He rode in the front seat with his brother. "Derek pretty much worked on football plays for the four-hour drive," Angie says. "But he was very nice to me, too."

They had not yet told the boys about their plans to get married early in 2019, so Ken waited until Derek and Bradley had left the room before he told his mother. "Mom, I want you to meet the woman I'm going to marry," he said. Problem was, Iona was kind of hard of hearing, so Ken had to speak in a rather loud voice. "He said it so loudly...and the boys had just left the room," recalls Angie. "I thought, *'Oh, my God!'*" Ken's mother could hardly speak because of the stroke, but over the years Ken had learned how to read his mother's eyes. He saw a tear roll down one cheek. "She was happy. She knew that I was going to be okay," he says. The visit was the last time Ken would see his mother. She died the following week.

Angie says the first person deeply connected to SHG football that she met after she started dating Ken was Jim Reavy. His son, Alex, was an outstanding receiver on Ken's 2005 championship team. "Jim Reavy made me feel so loved and welcomed," Angie says. "He was genuinely happy for Ken, for us." Reavy's wife, Michele, was coordinator of alumni activities for SHG and active in the Cyclones football booster group. Ken says Michele was one of the few adult people outside of the immediate family that Liz allowed into her inner circle. The first time they met, Angie says Michele teared up, hugged her and said, "Liz would have picked you for Ken."

Angie says the Madison family was very supportive when she started dating Ken. The Leonard family also welcomed Angie, but she could tell that Derek was having a hard time with the relationship. "I was worried about Derek because I knew how close he was to his mother," Angie says. "Derek's wife Lindsey said that Derek told her he loved me and he wanted me to be with his dad, but that it was just too soon."

Ken says the couple knew soon after they began dating that they wanted to marry, but they agreed to wait until at least a year had passed after the deaths of their spouses. "Life was going on, and I wasn't getting any younger," says Ken, who was 65 when they got married. "How long should I wait? What's the right time? Well, there isn't a right time." Because of the terminal nature of Liz's illness, Ken says he had been going through the grieving process for almost two years before she died. "Liz got on me a couple of times during that last year. She told me to get on with life and to quit being stuck on death," Ken says. "She always worried about everyone else, even when she was so sick."

Bryan McKenzie, whom Ken had met through the Fellowship

of Christian Athletes (FCA), had for many years gone alongside Ken on his faith journey. A former Baptist minister, he had delivered remarks at Liz's funeral and before that at the funeral of the Leonards' adopted son, Philip Pearson. He also officiated at Ken and Angie's wedding. "I was concerned for Ken after Liz died," McKenzie says. "Because he was such a high-profile person in Springfield, I worried that some women might try to get close to him for the wrong reasons. When I got to know Angie, I had no more concerns. She loves Ken for the person he is, not for anything else. She always wanted a family, and she loves Ken's family. All I saw were two people who needed one another, and they both loved the Lord."

The couple was married at a family wedding ceremony on February 16, 2019, at the Lake Springfield home of Ken's longtime friends Todd and Chris Green, whose son Gabe played for Ken. Derek struggled through the ceremony. "It was never anything about Angie," Derek says. "She's been nothing short of great to me and my kids. I just missed my mom, and I always will."

Ken and Angie live in the same house on South Park Street that Ken and Liz bought in 1984, when he was hired to be the football coach at then-Griffin High School. Derek and Bradley were raised there, and Philip for a while. Upon Ken's retirement at the end of 2022, he and Angie began to travel to different parts of the country, something he could not do when he was always preparing for the next football season. Because they had spent several weeks in Florida, there were rumors that the couple planned to move there. They both shot down that speculation. "This is home," Ken says. "My kids and grandkids are here. It's always been my home, and I think it always will be."

Ken and Angie both say that they were attracted to each other on many levels, but first among them was their mutual love of God. "People ask me how I knew," Ken says. "You just know that you know. God didn't shout, 'Hey, she's the one!' It was more of a gentle whisper." Ken's reputation as a man who unabashedly proclaims Jesus Christ as his Savior preceded him with Angie. "Sure, I knew about his reputation as a Godly man. That was at the top of my list," she says. "I was not looking to get married again. I didn't even want to date again. To have a Godly husband who is understanding…I did not know marriage could be this good. I did not know life could be this good."

Victorious!

(Leonard family photo)

The parents: Ken Leonard (center) and his mother, Iona (left), and his father, John Leonard, at a Hall of Fame induction ceremony for Ken.

(Leonard family photo)

Alaskan Pipeline: Ken at work on the Alaskan Pipeline.

(Leonard family photo)

The kids: Ken with his children Derek (left), Philip Pearson (back) and Bradley (right).

(Leonard family photo)

Leonard family: From left, Philip Pearson, Ken, Derek, Elizabeth "Liz," and Bradley Leonard.

(Leonard family photo)

The ball boy: Derek Leonard serving as a ball boy for his dad's Griffin Cyclones.

(Leonard family photo)

Gridley celebration: Ken celebrates a win during his first head coaching job at Gridley High School.

(Leonard family photo)

Ken the quarterback: Ken Leonard as quarterback at Dakota State University.

147

Victorious!

Derek and mom at IC: Record-breaking Illinois College quarter-back Derek Leonard (right) and his mom "Liz" on Senior Day.

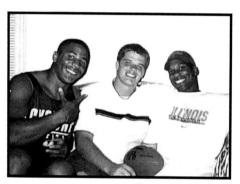

Cyclone brothers: Christian Gripper (left), Derek Leonard (center) and Philip Pearson. The three played on the 1995 Griffin team that finished second at state. Philip was the adopted brother of Derek and Bradley Leonard and they all referred to Christian as their "other brother."

The Nutcracker: Ken (left) played Uncle Drosselmeyer in a 2022 performance of Tchaikovsky's ballet "The Nutcracker." He appeared with his granddaughter Julia Leonard (center). Ken's wife Angie Leonard is on the right.

(Leonard family photo)

Grandma Liz: From left, JP, Austin, Grandma Liz, Julia and Blake Leonard.

(Leonard family photo)

The Leonard boys: From left, brother Phillip, father John, brother Curt and Ken Leonard.

149

Victorious!

Ken arrives at Griffin: Griffin High School Principal Father Robert Erickson (left) introduces Ken Leonard as the new Griffin High School football coach at a press conference on May 17, 1984.

Prayers for Washington: Sacred Heart-Griffin football coach Ken Leonard (right) leads a team prayer along with Washington coach Darrell Crouch (left) after the Cyclones beat Washington 44-14 in a Class 5A semifinal playoff game on November 23, 2013, at the SHG Sports Complex in Springfield. The game was played six days after a tornado had torn through Washington. SHG and surrounding schools provided transportation, water and food for the Washington players, parents and fans.

(Photo by Steve Sanders, Kansas City Chiefs)

Five-time Super Bowl champ: Chiefs assistant coach Brendan Daly (center) goes over in-game adjustments with his players. Daly has five Super Bowl rings, including three with Bill Belichick and the New England Patriots and two with Andy Reid and the Kansas City Chiefs.

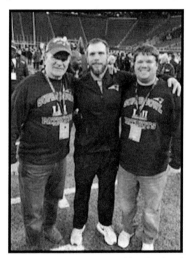

(Leonard family photo)

(Leonard family photo)

Super Bowl LII: Ken (left) and Derek (right) were guests of Patriots assistant coach Brendan Daly at the Super Bowl in Minneapolis in February of 2018, just weeks after Liz Leonard had died.

Derek's family: From left, Lindsey, Austin, Derek and Blake Leonard.

Victorious!

The wedding family: From left, Philip's daughter Savannah Pacha, Becky, Bradley, Blake, Austin, Ken, Julia, John Patrick (JP), Angie, Lindsey and Derek Leonard.

Leonard family: From left, JP, Ken, Julia, Liz, Blake, Savannah and Austin.

(© Photo by Justin L. Fowler, USA Today Network)

Coin Toss: Rochester coach Derek Leonard (left) and SHG coach Ken Leonard (right) watch along with the officials as Derek's son Austin Leonard tosses the coin before the two teams played at Rocket Booster Stadium in Rochester on September 27, 2019.

(© Photo by Justin L. Fowler, USA Today Network)

Try for two!: Rochester quarterback Sean Robinson is met by a host of Metamora tacklers just shy of the goal line on a two-point conversion attempt in the final seconds of the Class 4A semifinal game at Metamora on November 21, 2009. Metamora won 41-40 and a week later won the state championship in a blowout. Rochester would go on to win eight state titles in the next 10 years.

Victorious!

(© Photo by Justin L. Fowler, USA Today Network)

400th win!: SHG coach Ken Leonard celebrates his 400th win with grandson JP Leonard and the Cyclones players after they defeated Normal High School 49-6 on October 15, 2021, at SHG's Ken Leonard Field in Springfield. Ken would finish his career with 419 wins, making him the winningest high school football coach in Illinois history.

(© Photo by Justin L. Fowler, USA Today Network)

Competitive fire: Rochester coach Derek Leonard (left) and his father, SHG coach Ken Leonard, are both known to be intense competitors at everything ranging from cards to basketball games of H-O-R-S-E to the "Leonard Bowl" games. The photo was in the Springfield paper the morning after the Cyclones defeated Rochester in a 29-26 thriller on August 31, 2012. The two laughed it off as a misunderstanding in the heat of the moment, but when "Liz" Leonard saw it, she told her husband and son to rein in their competitiveness.

(© Photo by Justin L. Fowler, USA Today Network)

Ken and sons: Cyclone football coach Ken Leonard (center) with sons Derek (left), the head football coach at Rochester, and Bradley, then an assistant coach at Rochester who later went into a career in insurance and banking. The photo was taken on November 26, 2013, just a few days before Ken and Derek became the first father and son head coaches to win Illinois state football championships on the same weekend.

(Leonard family photo)

Ken and Angie's wedding: From left, Bryan and Jonell McKenzie, and Angie and Ken Leonard. Bryan McKenzie performed the marriage ceremony for Ken and Angie on February 16, 2019, at the home of Todd and Chris Green.

(Leonard family photo)

Ken and Angie: Ken and Angie Leonard

(Leonard family photo taken by Justin L. Fowler)

The Leonard family: A family photo taken at Ken Leonard Field in 2022. From left, Becky, John Patrick (JP), Bradley, Angie, Julia, Ken, Austin, Blake, Derek and Lindsey Leonard.

(Braun family photo)

The barber: Rick Braun, the barber Ken turned to on the day of Ken's born-again conversion.

Victorious!

The "Leonard Bowl" finale: From left, Julia, Bradley, JP, Angie and Ken Leonard walk to the center of the field along with SHG captains Ty Lott (16), Jake Hamilton (4), Keshon Singleton (5) and Madixx Morris (6) for the coin toss before the 16th and final "Leonard Bowl" game against Rochester and Derek Leonard in 2022.

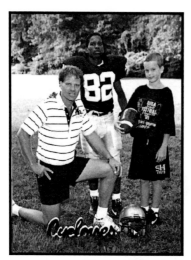

Philip and Bradley: Ken (left), Philip (center) and Bradley Leonard.

QB and the coach: Ken talks over an SHG game situation with quarterback Derek.

(© Photo by Thomas J. Turney, USA Today Network)

Final victory!: SHG coach Ken Leonard celebrates with his team after the Cyclones won the Class 4A state football championship 44-20 over Providence Catholic on November 25, 2022, at Memorial Stadium on the campus of the University of Illinois. It was Ken's sixth state championship and it was the 500th and final game of his career.

(Leonard family photo taken by Justin L. Fowler)

The hardware collection: Derek (left) and Ken Leonard pose with the 14 state championship trophies the father and son had won between them. Ken finished his career with six state titles and Derek had eight as of the end of the 2022 season.

(© Photo by Justin L. Fowler, USA Today Network)

The Coach: Sacred Heart-Griffin's legendary coach Ken Leonard finished his career with a 419-81 record.

Victorious!

A Very Heavy Monkey

Some trace the phrase "a monkey on your back" to one of Aesop's fables in which a dolphin carries a monkey through a raging sea only to drown it later when it discovers the monkey had tricked the dolphin. Others point to medieval transcripts in which a monkey represented the devil, or when an ape-like creature jumped on the back of Sinbad the Sailor in one of the tales of the fictional mariner. In the late 1800s, the term referred to owing a mortgage. By the 1960s, it meant having a drug addiction. It later became part of sports lexicon to refer to a player, coach or team that repeatedly failed to win the big game.

Wherever it came from, that monkey had started to feel like King Kong on Ken Leonard's back as the 1980s turned into the '90s, and the calendar then flipped to Y2K and a whole new century. Leonard had many great players and teams during his first 21 years as coach of the Cyclones. Those teams compiled a 187-49 record and earned 17 playoff berths. Despite winning at that 80-percent rate, a state championship remained elusive.

The origins of football can be traced back to Ancient Greece, where men played a game called *episkyros,* the objective being to throw the ball over a line while avoiding being tackled. By the late 1700s, a game closely resembling rugby was played throughout Europe with neighboring towns fielding teams of unlimited numbers of men competing to drag an inflated pig bladder across a marker placed at each end of the town. The pig bladder could be advanced by any means possible other than manslaughter or murder. The popularity of those games faded when the United Kingdom's Parliament passed the Highway Act of 1835, banning that form of football from being played on public roads.

There are some mentions of Native Americans playing a football-like game, but most football historians trace the game back to a hybrid soccer/rugby game brought by European settlers to the east coast. Students at Princeton University in New Jersey began playing a game called *ballown* in the 1820s, and students at Harvard University began a tradition called Bloody Monday in 1827. That annual event involved a mass game between the freshman and sophomore classes in an open area known as the Delta located in the middle of the campus. A poem titled "The Battle of the Delta" included a reference to "shins unnumbered bruised." In 1860, police and campus officials in Cambridge, Massachusetts, agreed to put a halt to "Bloody Monday." The ban on the mob style of football at Harvard would last 12 years.

At the same time, officials in New Haven, Connecticut, banned all forms of football at Yale University. The game began to return to college campuses later in the 1860s. The first intercollegiate game was played on November 6, 1869, in Brunswick, New Jersey, the home of Rutgers University. Rutgers beat Princeton 6 goals to 4 goals. The game more closely resembled rugby as the ball was round and throwing it was not allowed.

Walter Camp is considered by many to be "The Father of Football" in the United States. Camp enrolled at Yale University in 1876 and earned varsity letters in every sport the school offered, including the rugby-like version of football. Camp is credited with rule changes such as limiting the number of players to 11 to reduce chaos, the center hike of the ball to the quarterback, establishing a line of scrimmage that neither team could cross until the ball was snapped, and the legalization of interference or blocking, which was not allowed in rugby.

By the mid-1880s, many major universities were playing

Camp's version of football. The sport grew among high schools through the late 1880s and into the 1890s, one reason being that many of the college players became teachers upon graduation and started spreading and coaching the game at high schools. Illinois was a bit ahead of the football curve. The first recorded high school football game in Illinois was played on November 1, 1879, when Evanston High defeated Northwestern Academy.

The Cyclones started playing football in 1933 as Cathedral High School. Earl Reavy coached the team to a 3-3-1 record in his only season. Don Anderson, Charles Dirksen, Greg Sloan, Jack Fabri, John Corcoran, John Hendricks, Al Lewis and Joe Beja had coaching stints ranging from one to three seasons with middling results. The most successful teams during those early years were during World War II, as Fabri's 1941 team went a perfect 7-0 and Hendrick's teams posted a 16-7 record from 1943 through 1945. Luke Gleason coached eight years with a 29-33-2 cumulative record. James Weithman went 24-15-4 in three seasons, including the undefeated 1956 team that went 6-0-2. Bob Astroth had a 10-8 record in two years, and Bob Teater went 62-41-3 over the next 12 years.

The all-boys Cathedral High was renamed Griffin High in 1959 in honor of Bishop James Griffin, the first bishop to oversee the Catholic Diocese of Springfield, serving from 1924 to 1948. Griffin merged with the all-girls Sacred Heart Academy in 1988 to form Sacred Heart-Griffin. The school colors morphed from Purple/Gold to Black/Gold. Still, no football state championships.

The Illinois High School Association (IHSA) implemented statewide football playoffs in 1974, but Griffin failed to qualify for postseason play that first year. Enter George Fleischli, who took over in 1975 and began to turn Cyclones football into a perennial powerhouse. Fleischli's first team made it all the way to the state championship game after qualifying for the playoffs in a most unusual manner.

For the first several years of the playoffs, only conference champions were eligible. Griffin ended the regular season in a three-way tie with Champaign Centennial and Normal Community atop the Capitol Conference. Griffin had beaten Normal but lost to Centennial, which had lost to Normal, resulting in a three-way tie. In addition to the tri-champions, the Capitol Conference at that time included Decatur's Eisenhower and MacArthur, Jacksonville, and Springfield's Lanphier and Southeast. In a special meeting of the conference's athletic directors, Griffin was voted to be the conference's playoff representative, a decision that proved prescient when the Cyclones advanced to the finals.

Griffin's first step along that playoff trail was the toughest. Playing in front of one of the largest crowds at Memorial Stadium until the Leonard Bowl games came along, the Cyclones eked past Lincoln by a matter of inches. The Cyclones trailed Lincoln 8-7 late in the second quarter when the Railers tried to run a reverse handoff inside their own 5-yard line. The Lincoln ball carrier was tackled in the end zone – though some in attendance swore he had escaped the end zone before his knee hit the ground. The two-point safety put Griffin ahead 9-8, and the margin stood up because neither team would score in the second half. The Cyclones then defeated Carbondale and LaSalle-Peru to make their first title game appearance. In that 1975 championship game, Griffin took an early 7-6 lead over Joliet Catholic when Stu Scheller scored on a 4-yard run and Greg Baxa kicked the extra point. That lead was short-lived, though, and Joliet Catholic won 34-14.

The 1975 Cyclones were quarterbacked by Kevin Martin, whose father served as an assistant coach at Griffin from 1965-1982. Martin would finish his Griffin High School career with more than 2,200 yards passing, which 45 years later still ranked No. 12 at the school, two spots behind Derek Leonard. Martin received Division I scholarship offers, including one from the Air Force Academy. Martin eventually ended up at Illinois College, where he was a four-year starter and broke virtually all the school's passing records...until Derek came along a few years later to eclipse those records. Martin was inducted into the Illinois College Hall of Fame in 1983. He succeeded in business, too, becoming the longtime Executive Director of the statewide Illinois Insurance Association. He was among those wondering what school officials at Griffin were thinking when they hired a relatively inexperienced coach from one of the smallest schools in Illinois to take over its burgeoning football program in 1984.

"I was probably like everybody else who followed Cyclone football when I heard they were hiring this young guy from Gridley. Who was this Ken Leonard guy?" Martin says. He quickly became a believer. "Football was starting to evolve with the 'Air Coryell' style of passing offenses and getting the ball to your best athletes in open space. Ken started doing that before anyone else around here. Some people questioned it, but I would have loved to play for Coach Leonard in that wide-open offense."

In 1982, Robin Cooper's team rolled to a 9-0 record with a strong defense that allowed only 62 points. The Cyclones steamrolled Mt. Zion, Champaign Central and Roxana by a combined 75-17 score to reach the championship game. There, Griffin ran into three-time defending state champion Geneseo. The Maple Leafs built a 44-14 lead before Cyclones quarterback Kelly Ryan threw for three touchdowns in the final five minutes. Time simply ran out, and the comeback fell short, 44-36. Ryan earned All-State honors that year and, as of 2023, still ranked No. 8 in career passing yardage at Griffin/SHG. He went on to play football and graduated from Yale University, where he broke the school records for most passing yards in a game, season and for a career. Yale football records date back to 1872. As of 2023, Ryan still ranked No. 5 for yardage in a single game (426 yards against Army in 1986) and No. 6 in career passing yards.

Victorious!

Near Misses of All Types

All championship teams need a little luck to go along with talent. For Ken Leonard's first 21 years as coach of the Cyclones, the ball always seemed to bounce the wrong way. There was the usual assortment of dropped passes, fumbles and penalties that all teams experience. There were also unbelievable late-game heroics by opponents, and games where the Cyclones snatched defeat from the jaws of victory.

"It got to the point," Leonard says, "that it began to feel like we might never win a championship."

A recap of some of the most memorable playoff disappointments includes:

Air Attack Grounded (1984)

Leonard admits his first Cyclones team surprised even him by winning eight of their first nine games before losing 10-6 to Lincoln in the first round of the playoffs. Griffin was led by junior quarterback Chris Ondrula, who would earn All-State honors and go on to play at the University of Illinois and Miami of Ohio. "We relied on passing the ball, and I just remember how windy it was that night," Leonard says. "Lincoln was really good. It might have been their best team in my years coaching against them."

Defeat from the Jaws of Victory, Part I (1985)

Ondrula was named the Illinois Player of the Year his senior season. The Cyclones were 10-0 going into the second-round game against Washington. A Houdini-like fourth-down escape by the Washington quarterback resulted in a last-second 12-yard TD pass that turned an 18-14 Griffin lead into a devastating 21-18 loss. The Panthers would go on to win the state championship.

Part II:

Fast forward 33 years to 2018 and the Panthers would eerily repeat the last-ditch heroics.– this time for a 45-yard TD pass to the very same corner of the very same Washington end zone for a 23-21 shocking win over the Cyclones.

The One Rantoul Will Never Forget (1987)

The Cyclones won their first 12 games in 1986 before losing 15-6 to eventual state champion Rock Island Alleman in the quarterfinals. Griffin returned with many of its starters in 1987, including such stars as Doug Hembrough, who would go on to play at the University of Missouri; Dan Dee, who earned All-American honors as a defensive lineman at Eastern Illinois University in 1992; and Chris Stapleton, who was one of the Big Ten's top punters at the University of Michigan and went on to a movie and TV acting career. Stapleton appeared alongside Jack Nicholson and Morgan Freeman in the movie "The Bucket List" and appeared on the TV series "NCIS" and "Suddenly Susan."

The Cyclones featured a strong-armed junior quarterback Leonard nicknamed Bart "Starr" Geiser, a reference to Green Bay Packers Hall of Fame quarterback Bart Starr. Geiser's father was a Packers fan and wanted to name his son Bart Starr Geiser when he was born in November of 1970, but his wife was not into naming her kid after a sports star, so she changed the name on the birth certificate to Bart Joseph Geiser. Nevertheless, Geiser turned out to be a high school version of the Packers quarterback, and he had outstanding receivers in Joe Bonansinga and Bruce Sommer. The Cyclones won their first 10 games and were ranked No. 1 in the state heading into a second-round playoff game at unranked Rantoul.

It was, Leonard would say later, "a nightmare of a game. Anything that could go wrong for us did." Geiser had returned to action after recovering from a concussion and incurred another blow to the helmet that sidelined him for a while, this coming decades before concussion protocols were put in place in football. Lead running back Greg Steil was unable to play because of a toe injury suffered three days earlier in the first-round win over Mt. Zion.

Griffin took a 7-0 lead before a 47-yard field goal attempt by Rantoul kicker Mike Pond hit the crossbar…bounced in the air… hit the bar a second time…and fell through for three points. A Griffin fumble set Rantoul up to take a 10-7 lead on a TD pass that somehow got through a maze of defenders to the receiver. "It was a sprint-out pass I don't think I ever threw successfully even once in practice," Rantoul quarterback Deron Jones told a reporter from the *Champaign News-Gazette* in a 2012 story that celebrated the 25th anniversary of the Eagles' most memorable football victory. "I can remember throwing the ball and seeing three different people crisscross right in between (the receivers). To this day, I still don't know how in the hell that ball got there."

Griffin regained the lead 14-10 just before halftime, but those would be the last points the Cyclones would score. Pond kicked two more field goals in the second half, and a safety made the final score Rantoul 18, Griffin 14. People who drove through Rantoul in the days following the game were reminded of that score because the school left the scoreboard on for an entire week.

Geiser and his teammates were crushed. More than 35 years later, he still remembers the pain of that loss and not being able to compete at his best because of the injury he suffered. He also remembers what Leonard told the team afterward. "He told us that as much as that loss hurt, that God had bigger plans for our lives and that the game was just part of the journey," says Geiser, who went on to have a successful career in financial management in the Dallas-Fort Worth area. "At that point in my life, I couldn't even spell

Bible. I didn't really understand what he was saying, what he was teaching me. All I could think about was that we lost to a team we should have beat, and I wasn't able to help enough. But those words and how he demonstrated his faith, the way he handled the death of Liz, have stayed with me and helped guide me."

Putting sports wins and losses into perspective, two of the star players from that 1987 Griffin team died prematurely. Dee died in a car accident soon after college, and Hembrough succumbed to brain cancer at the age of 35.

Geiser's Finale (1988)

The following year was the first season under the banner of Sacred Heart-Griffin. It was also Geiser's senior season, and he led the Cyclones back to the second round of the playoffs before state runner-up Peoria ended SHG's playoff hopes 13-9.

Geiser threw for 2,441 yards and 27 TDs in 1988. Through the 2022 season, he still ranked eighth in most yards passing for a season and fifth in Cyclones history with 4,001 career yards passing. He was a consensus first-team All-Stater, and the Atlanta Touchdown Club named him the Illinois Back of the Year. He earned a football scholarship to Northern Illinois University, choosing NIU because of the reputation of its business school and the recruiting promise that the Huskies were going to start throwing the ball more. He earned a valuable degree in business management, but his college football career never really took off because the Huskies went with a running quarterback his freshman year and then Geiser suffered a torn rotator cuff injury.

He became a student assistant coach after reconstructive surgery on his shoulder. When the starting quarterback got hurt in mid-October of 1993, the coaches turned to Geiser because he knew the offense better than any of the backup QBs. "The offensive coordinator asked me if I wanted to come back. I said, 'That's not even funny. Don't be playing games with me,'" Geiser recalls. After four frustrating seasons, he made his first collegiate appearance late in a 33-19 loss to Southwestern Louisiana the next week, completing a pass on the final play of the game. He started the following week and almost led the Huskies to a win over Louisiana Tech, except the normally reliable NIU kicker missed a chip-shot field goal and the Huskies lost 17-16.

"For a guy who had never played in a (college) game, I think he performed admirably," offensive coordinator Joe Dickinson told reporters. "I admire him big-time for what he did. He looked like a quarterback. He got us in position to win the game."

A Future Five-Time Super Bowl Champion in Their Midst (the early 1990s)

The Cyclones missed the playoffs in 1989 but then rolled to 10 straight wins in 1990. They had Jeff Fleischli at quarterback along with such talented players as receiver Mike Ferega and the Stapleton twins, Brian and Tony. They were eliminated 28-21 in the second round of the playoffs by Mascoutah. They were ousted by Washington 29-13 in a snowstorm in the first round in 1991, missed the playoffs in 1992, and made it to the quarterfinals in 1993 before losing to eventual runner-up Geneseo 20-3.

That 1993 team was ranked No. 1 in the state for much of the season and featured junior standout tight end and defensive lineman Mike McGee. During his senior season in 1994, McGee had an incredible 34 tackles for loss. That performance would earn him Honorable Mention on the USA Today All-American team. It would also net him several big-time college football offers, including from Notre Dame and Penn State. He chose Illinois, where he had a good enough career to get a free-agent contract from the Carolina Panthers of the NFL. A hamstring injury, which had plagued him in college, cut his pro career short.

The 1989-92 Cyclones teams included a lineman by the name of Brendan Daly, who would go on to play tight end at Drake University. Daly is more well-known for having five Super Bowl rings, serving as an assistant coach under two legendary NFL coaches, Bill

Belichick of the New England Patriots and Andy Reid of the Kansas City Chiefs.

In describing Belichick, with whom he won Super Bowl rings in 2015 (28-24 over Seattle), 2017 (34-28 over Atlanta), and 2019 (13-3 over the Los Angeles Rams), Daly says: "He challenges every person in the organization every day. He is demanding but fair and one of the best football minds I've ever been around. He was always open to listening and interested in ways to get even better."

Daly was hired by Reid to be the Chiefs defensive line coach after the Patriots Super Bowl win in 2019. The Chiefs beat the San Francisco 49ers 31-20 to win Super Bowl LIV the next year. They also beat the Philadelphia Eagles 38-35 in Super Bowl LVII in 2023. "Coach Reid is just a brilliant offensive mind, and he's one of the most likeable people I've ever been around," Daly says. "He has great rapport with coaches and players, and he's incredibly good at changing as the game evolves."

Being on the staff of two of the greatest coaches in NFL history and playing for the winningest coach in Illinois high school history are not lost on Daly. "Man, I've been so fortunate to get to work with really good players and coaches. Having Coach Leonard's name in that mix is not a stretch," he says. "Much like Coach Reid, Coach Leonard has shown the ability to evolve. He's often even ahead of football's evolution. Like Coach Reid, he has a tremendous ability to connect with his players. I remember we had to sign a contract with Coach Leonard stating we would not use drugs or alcohol. He did some other off-the-field things that made an impression on a kid from Springfield, like having us share a meal with players from Chicago Marshall and room overnight with players from Palatine on a summer football trip."

In addition to Leonard's influence, Daly says his football career was impacted by assistant coaches Marty Lomelino and John Sowinski, who coached the offensive line. "Coach Sowinski was a no-nonsense guy who could really drive you to be better. If Coach Sowinski had asked me to run through a wall, I might have tried to do it because we would do anything for him."

Daly's journey to becoming an NFL assistant coach included many stops and lots of miles driven with all his belongings in the back of his red pickup truck. He played college football as an under-sized tight end at Drake University in Des Moines, Iowa, where he developed a reputation as a tenacious blocker. After being an assistant coach for a winless high school team in Florida for one year, he was hired back at Drake to coach the tight ends. He supplemented his income by cleaning carpets for Stanley Steemer. From Drake, he had one-year stops as an assistant coach at Villanova and Maryland and then a three-year stop at Oklahoma State. There, he met assistant coach Karl Dunbar, a former NFL player who eventually would recommend Daly for his first NFL job. After Oklahoma State, Daly coached at Illinois State, then back to Villanova.

"He moved a lot. Every year, he'd take his little red truck and throw everything in the back of it. That's how he fought his way up," his mother, Anne, told reporters on the eve of his fifth Super Bowl victory. According to Google maps, Daly drove that pickup truck more than 10,000 miles just going from coaching stop to coaching stop.

Dunbar had been an all-Southeastern Conference defensive tackle at Louisiana State University (LSU) and then played three years in the NFL for the New Orleans Saints and Arizona Cardinals. At LSU, Dunbar played for Pete Jenkins, considered by many to be one of the top defensive line coaches in college football. After his NFL days ended, Dunbar was hired to coach the defensive line at Oklahoma State. He brought with him a box full of VHS tapes containing the practice drills Jenkins used at LSU. Dunbar and Daly dug deep into those tapes, spending countless hours studying Jenkins' drills. When Dunbar eventually became defensive line coach with the Minnesota Vikings, he recommended Daly to be his assistant defensive line coach. Daly was hired by the Vikings in 2006.

Daly spent three years with the Vikings before moving to the St. Louis Rams staff under head coach Steve Spagnuolo for three years. He returned to the Vikings staff in 2012 before the Vikings made wholesale coaching changes a year later. His hiring by Belichick bordered on the bizarre. Or fate, depending on your point of view. Daly was at the college Senior Bowl in Mobile, Alabama, where he had just concluded a four-hour interview with the Bears. He received a text message from Belichick, who was on his way to Mobile and wanted to meet with Daly. The two sat in the stands during the next day's Senior Bowl practice and talked for a couple of hours.

"Belichick asked me what was next for me," Daly recalls. "I told him I was headed back to Minneapolis to clean out my office. He asked me if I would instead go to Boston to meet with his defensive coaching staff." Daly was hired by the Patriots and helped them to three Super Bowl championships.

He left the Patriots to join the Chiefs after that third Super Bowl title, a 13-3 win over the Rams in Super Bowl LIII in 2019. There was speculation Daly might be named defensive coordinator of the Patriots when Brian Flores left the Patriots to become head coach of the Miami Dolphins after that Super Bowl win in 2019. With several staff changes taking place with the Patriots and his contract due for renewal, Daly received an intriguing offer to become defensive line coach for the Chiefs. Weighing on his decision was the fact that Spagnuolo, with whom Daly had worked in St. Louis, had become the Chiefs' defensive coordinator. Spagnuolo at one point called Daly "the best defensive line coach in the NFL." The offer from the Chiefs included a promotion in that he also would serve as the run defense coordinator.

Daly helped the Chiefs win the Super Bowl 31-20 over the 49ers the very next season. In fact, he was the only one in Super Bowl LIV to have participated in a fourth straight Super Bowl. He addressed his move to the Chiefs in one of the press conferences leading up to the win over the 49ers. "There were a number of factors," Daly told reporters. "It was a very difficult decision for me. My time there was so special, and my respect for Coach (Bill) Belichick and the organization and the people there is second to none. There were a lot of factors and a lot of things that kind of happened at the right time in the right situation, and here I am. I'm happy to be here. I'm excited about the opportunity to be in this game again, for sure."

Daly has maintained his ties to Springfield and with the Leonards. The Super Bowl is one of the most widely viewed events in the world. The days leading up to the game are pressure-packed for the players and coaches involved, including off-the-field demands for interviews and ticket requests. Daly is nicknamed "Captain Intensity" by family members because of his focus and work ethic. Despite the demands of coaching in a Super Bowl, Daly invited Ken and Derek Leonard to join him in Minneapolis the week leading up to Super Bowl LII in February of 2018, when the Patriots were preparing to play the Eagles. It had been just a little over a month since Liz Leonard had died.

"Liz Leonard was a phenomenal human being," Daly says. "She was the mother of SHG football. I remember her with a dustpan at 10 o'clock at night when we were cleaning out the grandstand at the State Fairgrounds after the motorcycle races as a football fund-raiser."

Daly says he made a concerted effort to stay in touch with Ken after he learned about Liz's battle with cancer. "I could feel the strain they were under and the emotional and physical toll it was taking. I was incredibly impressed how he dropped everything to be there for her because that's not always how we are wired as coaches. I was not able to attend her funeral services, and I was worried about Coach Leonard because I knew what a big void her death had left. I was thankful Ken and Derek could come to the Super Bowl. My only regret is that we lost the game (the Eagles won 41-33)."

Daly says the five Super Bowl rings are great, but his greatest football fulfillment comes down to family, especially his wife Keely, their son Liam and daughters Ciara and Avelin. The kids were spotted making snow angels in the confetti that fell from the rafters after one of the Super Bowl wins. Says Daly, "There is no better feeling than seeing my wife and kids run to me after a Super Bowl win."

Injury Intervenes (1994)

The Cyclones made a run all the way to the semifinals before losing 14-6 to eventual state champion Belvidere in 1994. Quarterback Scott Norris, who would go on to play at Western Illinois University, threw for more than 2,000 yards during the season. Mike Pilger was on the receiving end of 1,241 of those yards, a single-season mark that as of 2022 still ranked third in Cyclones history. When Pilger suffered a lacerated kidney early in the semifinal game against Belvidere, the Cyclones suddenly were without the player who had accounted for more than 60 percent of their receiving yardage.

The Best Upset Win Ever...Well, Almost (1995)

In a timeline filled with tough Cyclones losses, the 1995 championship game probably stands as the most devastating. The Providence Catholic Celtics had won 27 games in a row, a streak that ultimately reached 50 games – second in state history only behind Pittsfield's 64-game winning streak. Pittsfield's streak lasted from 1966 to 1973, all but the last two seasons under coach Donald "Deek" Pollard, who would go on to become an assistant coach for several NFL teams. The Saukees' streak featured an incredible 46 shutouts. In fact, the only points they gave up in one two-year stretch came on an interception return in 1969; the 1970 team went the entire season without giving up a point. The only asterisk to that Pittsfield streak is that it came before the statewide playoffs were implemented. Providence Catholic's reign included four straight state championships going against the best teams from all over the state.

The 1995 Celtics were ranked as the ninth-best team in the country by USA Today, and the Chicago Tribune named them one of the best 32 teams in Illinois high school history. The Cyclones led that heavily favored team by 10 points with less than four minutes to play before Providence Catholic staged a dramatic rally to escape

22-17.

The Cleansing (1998)

The only losing season in Ken Leonard's 43-year career came in 1998. The Cyclones didn't just lose, they lost convincingly. Their only wins that year came against a 1-8 Springfield Southeast team and a winless Lincoln team. Some of the losing could be explained by attrition. The core group of players that had posted a 10-2 record in 1996 and an 8-3 mark in 1997 had graduated, including quarterback Derek Leonard, receivers Ryan O'Malley and Mark Rechner, and running backs Brad Svoboda, Dan Maurer and John Bohan. Ricky Davis, the top returning running back, suffered a season-ending leg injury in the first game. The SHG kicker Peter Christofilakos was named to the All-State soccer and football teams, and offensive lineman Eric Schulenburg went on to play for Central Michigan University. They had some good players, just not enough of them. The fact that their best player was a kicker is telling.

As of 2023, Christofilakos still ranked No. 15 in the SHG record book for career points with 180, quite a feat for a high school kicker. In that 2-7 season, his kicking accounted for 49 of the 120 points the Cyclones scored. He went on to kick for the University of Illinois football team, choosing the Illini over offers from Ohio State and Indiana. He then kicked professionally for the Arizona Rattlers of the Arena Football League. Soccer was his first love, and 25 years after he graduated from SHG, he still held the school record with 123 goals. Leonard plucked him off the soccer pitch late in Christofilakos' freshman year because the kicker on the freshman team had gotten injured.

"Coach Leonard came to soccer practice and said, 'Hey, Pete, how would you like to kick some footballs?'" There were only three games left that year," Christofilakos recalls. "I won the varsity job the next year." The Cyclones won 18 games during his sophomore and junior seasons. He was as surprised as anyone at the team's struggles his senior season. "I wish I had an answer," he says. "I know that the air seemed to go out of the balloon when Ricky (Davis) had his leg snap during the first game." Davis was one of Christofilakos' best friends on the team, and Christofilakos wore Davis' uniform number 24 instead of his usual number 22 for the rest of the season.

Christofilakos was impressed with how Leonard handled his only losing season. "He was the same Coach Leonard as he was my first two years on the varsity. He stayed positive and kept pushing us to get better even through that last game."

One of Christofilakos' enduring memories is of Leonard approaching him during a 35-0 loss at Taylorville on a night when there were gale-force winds. The coach approached the kicker and asked him if he thought he could make a 70-yard field goal. "I said, 'Are you serious? I'll try if you want me to.' The wind was at my back, and I hit the ball really well...and the wind caried it so far. It ended up bouncing off the crossbar." A few more inches and it would have set the record for the longest field goal ever. That record is a 69-yarder by Ove Johansson of Abilene Christian University in 1976. The national high school record is a 68-yarder by Dirk Borgognone of Reno (Nevada) High in 1985. According to news reports, Borgognone specialized only in long-distance field goals for Reno High and never made another field goal in high school. The NFL record is a 66-yarder by Justin Tucker of the Baltimore Ravens playing indoors at Detroit in 2021.

The 1998 season was a humbling experience for Leonard, and it wasn't just the losing that took its toll. "There were some issues, and we had to let a few kids go," Leonard recalls. "It was just a tough year all the way around. It caused me to take a hard look at how I was doing some things as a coach. I called it a cleansing." The cleansing was not just in terms of how Leonard would reimagine his approach to coaching. The rooms the Cyclones used for weightlifting and meetings had been adorned with murals. One day during the off-season, Leonard had his players and assistant coaches meet him at his office. There they found Leonard with paintbrushes, rollers and gallons of white paint. They whitewashed all the walls in the football rooms. It symbolized a fresh start. Personally, for Leonard it also meant letting go of some things, including his obsession with winning a championship, and turning them over to God.

"It made me think of the story about the Buttermilk Prayer," he says, recounting a story about a Sunday morning at a small southern church when a new pastor called on one of the older deacons to lead an opening prayer. The deacon stood up, bowed his head and said, "Lord, I hate buttermilk. I hate lard, too." At this point, the pastor had opened one eye and was wondering where the prayer was going. The deacon continued: "And, Lord, I ain't too crazy about plain flour either. But after you mix 'em all together and bake 'em in a hot oven, I just love biscuits. Lord, help us realize when life gets hard, when things come up that we don't like, whenever we don't understand what You are doing, that we need to see what You are making. After You get through mixing and baking, it'll probably be something even better than biscuits. Amen."

When Kenni Burns was "The Man"

What the Lord was creating in Ken Leonard's life and career was a work in progress, as was what Leonard was doing with the Cyclones football program. Following "The Cleansing," Leonard decided to spread the field and open his offense up even more, but going to an all-out aerial attack would have to wait. That's because Kenni Burns, a running back like no Cyclone who had come before, stepped onto the SHG campus in 1999.

"Our philosophy on offense has always been to get the ball to 'The Man' in open space," Leonard says. "Kenni Burns was the 'The Man' for us. We still used the spread offense, but spreading the field also opens up more space for running lanes, and we gave it to Kenni a lot. He was a good-sized running back and he was quick, had good speed and really great balance. His vision, the way he saw what was happening on the field during his runs, made him special."

The Cyclones improved to a 5-4 record in 1999, the first year after "The Cleansing," but the real story was the emergence of

Burns, who caught Leonard's eye even as a freshman who primarily returned kicks that year. As a sophomore in 2000, Burns ran for a school-record 1,601 yards, and the Cyclones won their first 11 games before being eliminated by eventual state champion Joliet Catholic. Burns missed a large chunk of his junior season of 2001 because of injury, and SHG posted a 9-3 record. Healthy for his senior season of 2002, Burns would shatter the school record he set as a sophomore by running for 2,444 yards, not only a school record but also a Central State Eight record still standing 21 years later. The Cyclones won their first 11 games before being eliminated 35-31 by Belleville Althoff when Matt Lauber caught a late touchdown pass for the Crusaders. Lauber later would become the head coach at Southeast High School in Springfield before stepping down and joining Derek Leonard's staff at Rochester after the 2022 season.

Burns ended his career without a state title, but his 4,584 yards rushing (more than 2.6 miles) remained the SHG and Central State Eight career record ahead of Tremayne Lee, who gained 4,335 yards for SHG from 2014-2017. Burns played in the Big Ten for the Indiana Hoosiers and then went into coaching. Included among his college assistant coaching stops was one at North Dakota State, where the team won three straight national championships, and one at the University of Minnesota, where the Golden Gophers went to four straight bowl games. He was named head football coach at Kent State University in Ohio in December of 2022. Indiana coach Tom Allen described Burns as "one of the bright young minds in our game…a leader of men and a tremendous man of character."

Knocking at the Door

In the nine-year period from 2000 through the 2008 season, the Cyclones would post a cumulative record of 103-10. There would still be disappointments, such as an excruciating 24-21 loss to Joliet Catholic in the 2003 state title game. In that game, the Cyclones fell behind 24-7 before Eric Peterman hit J.C. Bland with two fourth-quarter TD passes to cut the lead to just three points. However, Joliet Catholic recovered an onside kick and was able to run out the clock.

"When I turned my life over to the Lord, I thought that a state championship would be the perfect platform for me to glorify Him. Standing on the sidelines in the final moments of that 1995 championship game against Providence Catholic, I thought that winning that title surely was part of my destiny," Leonard says. "But that's not how God works. That's probably the toughest loss I've ever been a part of. But as I walked across the field after the game, I just felt the peace of Jesus Christ come over me. I realized I needed to glorify Him in that situation and in all situations. I also knew I needed to be better in all areas of my life, including coaching. In Romans 8:28 the Bible says, '*We know that all things work together for good to them that love God, to them who are the called according to his purpose.*'"

The Bible also speaks to perseverance, such as Galatians 6:9, which says "*And let us not grow weary of doing good, for in due season we will reap, if we do not give up.*" The Apostle Paul's letter to the Galatians most assuredly was not referring to football. But Paul's words apply to all facets of life. Ken Leonard would continue to persevere in his quest to lead the Cyclones to a state championship.

Victorious!

Sometimes When You Least Expect It...

It was a junior-dominated SHG team that finished second in the state in 2003. That strong and deep class full of experienced players would be returning for their senior season, including Eric Peterman, one of the best quarterbacks in Cyclones history. To say that Ken Leonard was optimistic entering that next season is to put it mildly. He thought 2004 might be *"the"* year to finally achieve the school's elusive first state championship. A season-opening 47-3 thrashing of eventual state champion Lombard Montini only served to fuel that belief.

The 2004 Cyclones won their first 10 games, all by blowout scores of an average margin of 50-7, including a 42-14 romp over Jacksonville in Week Four. The SHG defense achieved three shut-outs. The most points it had given up was 15 to Chatham Glenwood in a 40-point victory. The offense was never held under 40 points. Until a second-round playoff rematch with Jacksonville. "Anything that could go wrong did," Leonard says. "We had three touchdowns called back and a couple more touchdown passes dropped. Peterman got dinged up a little bit but never told anybody. He wasn't really at 100 percent after that though. And Jacksonville played great."

In the first meeting, the Cyclones had unveiled a new "Lone-some Polecat" twist for their offense, a strange-looking formation that moved all five offensive linemen, the tight end and running back way over on one side of the field. They put two receivers on the opposite side of the field. In the middle of the field were just two players, the center and "Lonesome Polecat" quarterback, who had no other blockers. The center was an eligible receiver in that alignment, and the Cyclones used one of their top receivers and blockers, Jeff Sanders, in that role. It looked like something from a backyard pickup game of touch football. It put lots of strain on the defense to figure out how to defend the different run/pass options without being outnumbered on either side of the field or being left one-on-one with a quarterback like Peterman who could run or pass with equal ability.

It worked magnificently in the first meeting with Jacksonville. The Cyclones scored early and often. But the Crimsons had done their homework in preparing for the rematch, and with the element of surprise gone, Leonard didn't want to leave Peterman too exposed. Jacksonville stifled the SHG offense, holding it some 40 points below its scoring average. The Crimsons stayed even with the Cyclones and took a 21-14 lead late in the third quarter when running back J.R. Manker busted loose for a 73-yard touchdown run.

That seven-point lead stood as the game entered its final minutes. Peterman then led SHG on a last-ditch drive that reached the Jacksonville 10-yard line. Two potential game-tying touchdowns were wiped out because of penalties on that final drive. One of them was a 90-yard TD that was called back when sophomore receiver Bobby Brenneisen was flagged for a clipping penalty. The game ended on an incomplete pass by Peterman.

"At halftime I remember thinking it was a close game, but I was also thinking there was no way were going to lose," Peterman recalled six years later in an interview with Todd Engle of *The State Journal-Register.* "We had the ball on our last play...I had the thought in my head that I don't know what miracle is going to happen, but some way, somehow, we're going to win this game. That might have been my toughest loss in high school. In my junior year, we lost in the state championship game and we came back with a lot of seniors who played hard and had experience. Our goal was nothing less than to win (a state championship)."

The loss not only ended what many thought was the Cyclones' best chance yet to win a state championship, it also ended the high school careers of that strong senior class of players that filled 14 of the team's 22 starting positions. Their graduation left many holes to fill – including replacing one of the all-time greats at quarterback – when Leonard greeted the Cyclones at the start of camp in 2005. An encouraging note was that the incoming junior class led by quarterback Bobby Brenneisen had not lost a game in freshmen football and had also produced a perfect record on the SHG sophomore team.

Brenneisen never viewed his role as having to fill Peterman's shoes as quarterback. "Eric and I were two different quarterbacks. He could run two 40-yard dashes in the time it took me to run one. I was never going to amount to what Eric accomplished in football," he says. "Eric was also a great leader, and I really tried to follow in his footsteps in that way."

Weighing heavier on Brenneisen's mind was being called for that key penalty in the upset loss to Jacksonville in 2004. "I can remember that play to this day," he said 19 years later. "Curtis Robinson caught a screen pass and ran 90 yards for a touchdown that would have tied the game, but the ref threw a flag on me for clipping. I honestly don't think I hit anyone from behind, but as a sophomore I felt so bad for those seniors."

The 2005 Cyclones had only 12 seniors, the smallest senior class Leonard had coached since his days at tiny Gridley. Despite that, Brenneisen says the Cyclones always believed they were capable of doing something special. "Every time we would end practice or break the huddle, we all would yell 'State Champs!' That is a Cyclone tradition and that is always the goal. No one else expected much from us at the start of that year, but we believed we could be state champs."

They served early notice that they might come of age more quickly than expected by winning their opener against Montini 40-15.

Perhaps experiencing Post Traumatic Football Stress Disorder from some of the previous 21 title-less seasons, Leonard remained in a wait-and-see mode. What Brenneisen and the Cyclones showed him were eight more wins to roll through the regular season unbeaten.

In the playoffs, SHG's first opponent was Chatham Glenwood. Like Jacksonville the year before, the game would be a rematch against a conference foe the Cyclones had beaten during the regular season. The way the game unfolded, it looked like it might be "Deja vu all over again," as Yogi Berra once famously said. The two teams went back and forth, Glenwood never falling more than a touchdown behind the heavily favored Cyclones. SHG survived 28-21 when Alex Reavy intercepted a pass at his own 35-yard line with seven seconds left. Running back Chris Peterson, who at one point was the fifth string running back because of a hand injury, led the way for the Cyclones by rushing for 137 yards and a touchdown.

SHG steamrolled Morton 55-7 in Round 2 before running into a tough Kankakee Bishop McNamara squad. It was another nail-biter that the Cyclones managed to win 34-28. The 29-19 margin of victory in the semifinals against North Chicago was a bit deceiving. "North Chicago might have been the most talented team we played that year," Leonard says. "They had a couple of guys that ended up playing in the NFL. The few seniors we had got better, and the juniors progressed throughout the year. We also caught a few breaks after years of the ball not bouncing our way. The main thing was that we didn't beat ourselves." For the fifth time in school history and the fourth time under Leonard, the Cyclones were back in the championship game. Standing in the way was that "Green Team" from Rock Island Alleman.

Alleman had an antidote to counter the fast-paced style of game that Leonard and the Cyclones preferred. Brenneisen had put together the best season of passing in school history. He would finish the year with 3,284 yards passing, still the school record 22 years later. He had two explosive receivers in Reavy and Sanders. Polar opposites, the Pioneers seldom threw the ball, relying instead on a triple-option running game based on deception and power. If Alleman could churn out first downs that way, it could keep the ball away from SHG and effectively shorten the game by draining the clock.

Leonard remembers that game at Champaign drawing one of the biggest crowds of any Cyclones title game because the school had a larger enrollment back then (782 students in 2005 compared to fewer than 500 in 2022). The Cyclones got the ball first but appeared to have a case of jitters. Reavy caught a pass on the first play from scrimmage but fumbled. SHG recovered the ball, but six plays later Brenneisen lost the ball at the Alleman 23-yard line.

Leonard met his quarterback when he came off the field following the fumble. "I was wearing a long sleeve Under Armour shirt underneath my jersey because it was so cold," Brenneisen recalls. "The first thing Coach Leonard did after the fumble was to take scissors and cut off my long sleeves. I guess he thought they were too slick and might have caused the fumble. Then he told me to stop trying to do so much, to settle down and trust the game plan."

Whether it was the pep talk or the removal of the sleeves, Brenneisen and the Cyclones started clicking the next time they got the ball. They used a mix of runs and passes to move 70 yards in nine plays. Brenneisen hit his tight end Sanders with a 15-yard touchdown pass. However, Alleman answered four plays later using one of its few passes to tie the score 7-7.

After Alleman missed a 40-yard field goal try that would have given the Pioneers the lead, it took SHG only three plays to make them pay. Leonard signaled in a play called "Money." The play was designed for Brenneisen to take the snap under center instead of several yards behind the snapper in the shotgun formation the Cyclones normally used. "We almost always ran the ball when I was under center," he says. This time, he faked the handoff and found Reavy streaking behind the defense. "I knew it was either going to be a touchdown or incompletion because Alex was so open." Brenneisen put the ball on target for a 60-yard TD and a 14-7 lead.

Reavy was the leading receiver in the game with 12 catches for

149 yards, and Sanders caught 10 balls for 134 yards. Reavy and Sanders were two of only eight seniors who started for the Cyclones. Sanders had started for two years, but 2005 was the only season Reavy played football as he had been concentrating on baseball, basketball and golf, a sport in which he would earn All-State honors. "At 6-foot-5, Jeff was a big target, and I looked for him any time I was in trouble. I can't remember him ever dropping a pass. He bailed me out lots of times," Brenneisen says. "Alex was 6-foot-3 and so athletic. I kind of think Jeff had a lot to do with Alex playing football his senior year, and the two of them caused headaches for any defense."

The advantage grew to 17-7 on a 33-yard field goal by Mike Edwards that was set up when Bobby Rakers forced a fumble that was recovered at the Alleman 16-yard line by Andrew Collings. Collings, who played in three state title games, tied Mike Stieren for a team-high nine tackles. Leonard says Collings was one of the smartest Cyclones ever, having missed just one question on his college ACT and earning a top-of-the-scale score of 36. Leonard says, "One day at practice, I told him, 'That's nothing, Coach Wise, Coach McMann and I had a 36, too…if you add our scores together.' Coach McMann said, 'I don't think so coach.'"

Rakers forced another fumble and recovered it himself at the Alleman 22-yard line early in the third quarter. Edwards again kicked a field goal, this one from 37 yards, and SHG led 20-7. An interception by Alleman led to a TD that allowed the Pioneers to close to within 20-14. The Pioneers would get no closer. Brenneisen again led SHG on a long drive covering 73 yards in 13 plays. The TD came on a 7-yard run by Andre' Pendergrass, who two plays earlier converted a fourth-and-1 play into a first down by gaining six yards. The Cyclones carried a 28-14 lead into the final quarter.

A couple of penalties against SHG helped Alleman sustain a late drive for a touchdown to draw within 28-21, but the score came with only 30 seconds left in the game. As the Pioneers lined up for an obvious onside kick, Leonard had flashbacks to other times the

Cyclones had been so close to a championship but came up short. "That's when bad thoughts started to come into my head. *'Is this gonna be another Providence Catholic or Joliet Catholic kind of ending?"* Leonard says.

Adding to the coach's angst was the fact that the onside kick rules for high school football back in 2005 allowed for rugby-like scrums, which is where the term "onside kick" emanated. For safety reasons, the high school onside kick rules have evolved over the years so that players from the kicking team no longer can make contact with players from the receiving team until the ball travels a minimum of 10 yards or a member of the return team touches the ball. Also, the kicking team now must have five players on each side of the kicker as opposed to loading most of the players on one side of the field.

Sure enough, the onside kick resulted in a huge pileup of players scrambling to get the ball. Watching from the sidelines, neither Brenneisen nor anyone else knew who had the ball until the officials unstacked the players. Those several seconds seemed like minutes. The player at the bottom of the pile holding onto the ball for dear life was Rakers, the same guy who had forced two fumbles and recovered one.

"It meant we'd get to do what we all dreamed about, lining up in the 'Victory Formation' at the end of a game for the state championship," Brenneisen says, referring to taking a knee on the final snap to run out the clock. "I thought about finally accomplishing what every player who wore the gold Cyclone helmet had wanted to do. We all wanted to give Coach Leonard his first championship. I also thought about my dad, who had been with Coach Leonard longer than I had been alive. I also remembered being a water boy for the team in 1995 when I was 6 years old and the feeling when we lost that championship game."

Ken Leonard's reaction was not what he had anticipated. "Honestly," Leonard said, reflecting on it 18 years later, "it was more a feeling of relief to get that monkey off our backs. Of all the years it took, and all the guys that had come before, that 2005 team was one of the least expected to win one. I told the team how proud I was of them for believing in themselves. That championship also was for the players from the past and the Cyclones tradition they established."

The Class that Wouldn't Be Beat

Investment companies include this caveat for investors: *"Past performance may not be indicative of future results."* The same could be said about sports teams. Ken Leonard had every reason to believe that his 2006 Cyclones had all the ingredients to repeat as state champions. The junior class had powered SHG to its first state football title in 2005, and Leonard was welcoming back nine starters on offense and eight on defense.

"That senior class was talented and deep. They were also a bunch of hard-nosed football guys, and we had a few good juniors to mix in," Leonard says. "We had a great team with no real weaknesses."

Seniors Nick Thoele (defensive end/offensive tackle), Mike Edwards (linebacker/wide receiver), David Kavish and Keenan Gilpin (wide receivers/defensive backs) were two-way starters as seniors. Edwards (Villanova), Kavish (South Dakota State) and offensive lineman Matt Mast (Missouri Science and Technology) would go on to play college football. Three out of the four junior starters also would play college football, including linebacker Leonard Hubbard (Wisconsin), wide receiver Robby Mosher (McKendree University) and defensive back Josh Gossard (Lindenwood University).

The defending state champions got a rude awakening in their season opener against a Montini team that would finish with only a 5-5 record. The Broncos gave SHG all they could handle before the Cyclones prevailed 32-25, in large part because Gilpin returned the second half kickoff for a touchdown. "In hindsight, that Montini game might have been a blessing," Leonard says. "They hit us in the mouth and got our attention, that's for sure."

Bobby Brenneisen says a lot of his teammates think the lack-luster performance was because they didn't wear their tall socks. "I hated wearing those long socks, so I convinced everyone to wear low-riders," the quarterback says. "I'm not superstitious, but after that game everyone wanted to go back to the long socks, and I really had no argument."

What followed was a week of tough practices intended to re-mind the Cyclones that their 2005 championship rings were worth nothing on the scoreboard in 2006. The Cyclones were refocused and back to wearing long socks. They absolutely dominated the remaining eight regular-season games and the first-round playoff game. During that nine-game tear, SHG allowed a grand total of just 42 points while scoring 397. To put that in perspective, the Cyclones' offensive average for a single game (44 points) was more than their opponents' points for the nine games combined.

It was hard to find any holes in the SHG defense. While Thoele manned one defensive end, the other end was held down by Mike Stieren, who would go on to earn college all-conference honors at Western Illinois University. Seniors Jason Moore and Sean Johnson plugged up the middle of the line. The linebacking corps of Edwards, Hubbard and Collings covered sideline to sideline, and defensive backs Gilpin, Kavish, Gossard and junior Joe Marrin allowed fewer than 70 yards per game passing.

The offense was led by returning All-State quarterback Brenneisen, who again would throw for more than 3,000 yards and would come close to breaking his own single-season school record for passing. Some 17 years later, Brenneisen still ranked second at the school in career passing behind only Gabe Green. Most amazing is that during his four years of high school, Brenneisen's teams never lost a game in which he was the starting quarterback. His freshman and sophomore teams were unbeaten, and so were the varsity teams he quarterbacked his junior and senior seasons.

"Bobby had such a good feel for the game. In that way, he reminded me a lot of my son Derek. Bobby was a coach's son, too," Ken says, alluding to his longtime assistant Bob Brenneisen. "Bobby had good size for a quarterback (6-foot-1 and 200 pounds), and he was a good athlete." Bobby Brenneisen earned a football scholarship at Southern Illinois University and later played at Quincy College. His younger brother, Tim Brenneisen, would come along nine years later to throw for almost 3,000 yards, the sixth best year ever for a Cyclones quarterback.

Bobby was the first of seven Brenneisen children to star in multiple sports at SHG for an 18-year stretch from 2003 through 2021. He was followed by sisters Becky, Jenny and Laura, quarterback Tim, linebacker Matt and sister Emily. The Brenneisen kids obviously benefitted from good bloodlines, given the fact that their father Bob and their mother Jane both were accomplished athletes and both were coaches. "My mom was head girls basketball coach at Lanphier (High School in Springfield). She was pretty hard-nosed, too" says Bobby. Asked who was the best athlete in the family, Bobby says, "Probably my youngest sister Emily, who was good at everything and plays basketball at Millikin University. But I'm the only one who can say they never lost a game in high school."

Bobby was protected in 2006 by an offensive line consisting of Thoele and Mast at the tackles, Moore and Matt Israel at the guards and junior Kelby Jasmon at center. The running back was senior Chris Peterson, and the wide receivers included Kavish, Gilpin, Edwards and Mosher. The unit was talented and versatile with the ability to run or pass depending on the other team's defensive alignment and/or weakness.

The Cyclones breezed past Mattoon 49-0 in the first round of their playoff title defense. They would receive a stiffer test on a sloppy, muddy field in Kankakee. The weather made it difficult to pass, so the Cyclones leaned on running backs Peterson and Gossard and fullback Hubbard to grind out a 22-8 win. They then blasted Cahokia 42-6 in the quarterfinals and beat Metamora 19-6 in the semifinals to get back to the title game.

This time, SHG would face an unbeaten Woodstock Marian Central Catholic team in the 5A championship game in Champaign. The Spartans were a loaded team with no fewer than three future Big Ten players, including Bryan Bulaga, who played at Iowa and was a starting offensive tackle for the Green Bay Packers when they won the Super Bowl over the Pittsburgh Steelers in 2011.

Marian Catholic and SHG felt each other out in a scoreless first quarter before the Cyclones began to exploit the Spartans' defense on their first drive of the second quarter. Brenneisen hit Gilpin on back-to-back passes for 32 and 8 yards. The quarterback then pitched the ball to Gilpin on a sweep around end for 10 more yards and a first down at the Marian 24-yard line. Gossard covered the final 24 yards on runs of 18 and 6 yards for a 7-0 lead.

Gossard scored again moments later, this time on a 4-yard run to cap a quick 51-yard drive highlighted by a 28-yard pass to Mosher and a 20-yard scramble by Brenneisen. Marian Catholic put together an 80-yard drive at the end of the first half to cut the margin to 14-7. The Spartans received the second-half kickoff and drove across midfield looking for a tying touchdown, but Kavish intercepted a long pass at the Cyclones' 14-yard line.

"David read that pass play really well," Leonard said after reviewing the game film years later. "He made a nice play on the ball, but our dudes up front caused the interception by getting so much pressure on the quarterback. He had to throw the ball before he wanted to a few times." SHG's defensive line sacked Marian Catholic quarterback Jon Budmayr three times, and three of his hurried throws were picked off. It's not like Budmayr got rattled easily. He became the starting quarterback at Wisconsin his sophomore year in college.

Two plays later, Brenneisen found Kavish behind the Marian Catholic defense and hit him with a 52-yard pass to the Spartans' 17-yard line. Brenneisen and Kavish lived near each other, had attended school together since first grade, played youth football together and both were water boys for the Cyclones. "Bobby's probably thrown that pass to David a million times in the back yard or at practice," Leonard says. On the next play, Gilpin took another pitchout around end for a 17-yard TD run and a 21-7 lead.

Marian Catholic had a chance to get back into the game when the Spartans recovered a fumble at the SHG 34-yard line, but three plays later, Kavish came up with his second interception of the game. Brenneisen then led the Cyclones on a 14-play, 87-yard march, mixing short passes and runs. Brenneisen scored on a 3-yard quarterback sneak, and the Cyclones led 28-7 near the end of the third quarter.

Marian Catholic would not go away, cutting the lead to 28-14 and then driving deep into SHG territory later in the fourth quarter. The Cyclones came up with their third interception, this one by Gilpin at his own 3-yard line. Brenneisen led the Cyclones on a decisive drive the length of the field. The knockout punch came on a short inside screen pass that Gilpin turned into a 46-yard TD. "It was just a quick pass to Keenan at the line of scrimmage and he had a couple of blockers in front of him," Brenneisen says. "As soon as he caught it and I saw where the defenders were, I knew he was gone. He just split the defense."

The TD pass clinched a second straight state championship, this one by a 35-14 score. It also ensured that Brenneisen and his senior teammates would never lose a high school football game, a goal he says they began fixating on even as freshmen. "We were aware and it drove us to take nothing for granted, no matter who we played," Brenneisen says.

Leonard felt a whole new wave of emotions with the second title. "It was just a feeling of joy. There was joy the year before for sure, but it was more sheer relief to finally get that monkey off your back," he says. "Now you win one and you become the hunted instead of the hunter. That's different, and it can be tough. Twenty-eight and zero for the two years...what can I say? Those boys were just winners."

One Tough Dude

The Cyclones' bid for a "three-peat" as state champions ended in the first round of the 2007 playoffs with a 28-20 loss to Providence Catholic. Key players from the state championship teams the previous two years were gone, and there were not a lot of experienced players returning that year. However, with a bevy of talented juniors returning in 2008, the Cyclones looked to be back as title contenders. The playoff challenge would be daunting, though, because the IHSA formula for private/parochial schools resulted in SHG being bumped up to 6A.

"In addition to the enrollment multiplier, the success factor had just been put in by the IHSA," Ken Leonard says. "It had an impact on all private and parochial schools, but really it was aimed at us and two or three other schools up north that had been having success. They moved us up so we would have to go against bigger schools."

Tim Dondanville and John Lantz were two of the key returnees. They had developed a great connection the year before as juniors when Dondanville passed for more than 2,200 yards, Lantz being on the receiving end of almost 900 of them. Other than the fact that he was a left-handed passer, Dondanville was similar to so many others in Ken Leonard's line of prolific quarterbacks. In addition to the physical skills required to operate Leonard's offense, Dondanville had next-level intelligence. He would play some at Princeton, but more importantly, he got a degree from the Ivy League school and later a law degree from Notre Dame. Lantz described Dondanville as a quarterback who "knows his reads and very seldom makes a mistake."

Lantz's good junior year was just a preview of his explosive abilities. During his senior season of 2008, he would catch passes for 1,257 yards, the second-most productive season for a receiver in SHG history behind only future NFL player Malik Turner. Lantz's yardage accounted for 49 percent of Dondanville's 2,540 passing yards, the seventh-most single-season passing total in school history. "John was just a special player," Leonard says. "He was so smooth and fast, and his hand-eye coordination was off the charts. He played a little as a sophomore on that 2006 championship team, and he was good his junior year, but his senior year he was really special for us. Other coaches said it seemed to John like the game was unfolding in slow motion but he was going really fast."

In addition to his exploits as a wide receiver, Lantz also patrolled the middle of the field on defense as a ball-hawking free safety who had 12 interceptions in two years. He also was a threat to go all the way returning punts and kickoffs. He returned the first kickoff of 2008 for a touchdown. Before the season was over, he had returned four kicks, three punts and an interception for touchdowns. "I took a lot of pride in being a threat on special teams," Lantz would say later. "I think it helped us make that run to the championship."

The Cyclones opened the season against Montini, as they had been doing for years. They led 31-14 with just over nine minutes to play but collapsed to lose 34-31 to a junior-dominated Montini team that would win the 5A state championship a year later. Leonard vowed that the SHG defense would bounce back with "the biggest turnaround in history."

The coach's bold prediction wasn't far off. The Cyclones rebounded in Week Two to demolish Jacksonville 62-16, a game in which Lantz scored five touchdowns and had two interceptions before being pulled early in the second half. Over the course of the next six regular-season games, SHG's defense held opponents to 21 points, an average of just 3 ½ points per game. When the 6A playoffs began, they dispatched Chatham Glenwood 35-21 as Adrian Cave caught a 79-yard TD pass. They then beat Peoria Richwoods 48-21, with Lantz catching 3 TD passes and returning a kick 89 yards for a score. They defeated Bloomington 32-12 as Lantz returned a kick 99 yards for a TD.

That win set up a semifinal showdown with Providence Catholic, the team that had ended the Cyclones' bid for a third straight championship in 2007. The motivator he was, Leonard played the lack-of-respect card with his team heading into the rematch. "Back in the day, there wasn't a lot of respect for downstate football," he says. "Some in the Chicago area kind of looked at us like we all just came off the farm. It was a good thing for us because I always used that chip-on-the-shoulder to fire up our players."

The Cyclones were going to need all the inspiration they could get because Lantz, who had provided half of their receiving offense, suffered two broken ribs in the quarterfinal game. He did not practice at all in the week leading up to the semifinal game. His ribs were heavily wrapped, and he was wearing a flak jacket to cushion the blows. Lantz served mainly as a decoy, but Providence Catholic, unaware of his limitations, assigned its top defensive back to cover him and sometimes put two defenders on Lantz.

With Lantz not at full strength, the Cyclones relied more on the run even though Providence Catholic had limited them to just 46 yards rushing the previous year. The Celtics knew that running back Gary Wilson was SHG's top runner. They were caught completely off guard several times when Dondanville faked handoffs to Wilson and took off with the ball himself. The quarterback had run the ball a few times during the season but carried the ball a team-high 15 times on this day. In addition to passing for 146 yards and two touchdowns, Dondanville ran for 133 yards, including a 63-yard romp that set up an 18-yard TD pass to Wilson to go up 7-0.

Gus Bloink added a field goal to increase the SHG lead to 10-0 on the first possession of the second half. At 6-foot-4 and 200 pounds, Bloink didn't resemble your normal kicker. He was an All-

State soccer player who scored 25 goals in 24 games, and he led the SHG soccer team to a second-place finish at state two weeks earlier. He went on to play soccer at Bradley University.

The Celtics responded to tie the game 10-10 with a field goal and an 85-yard touchdown pass. The game remained tied going into the final quarter. That's when Lantz became more than a decoy. He broke free from his defender, slanted to the middle of the field and caught a 25-yard TD pass from Dondanville to put the Cyclones up for good 17-10. They hung on 24-17 to reach the title game for the third time in four years.

Dondanville saluted Lantz for his toughness, noting that many in the SHG camp were unsure if the receiver would even be able to play in the game. "His ribs were dinged up," Dondanville said. "I knew he would get on the field because he's a competitor." Looking back on it, Leonard says, "John looked a little like the Michelin Man with all that protective wrapping. I know he must have been in pain, and we kept asking him if he was okay. John just kept going as best he could. He was one tough dude."

SHG would meet an unbeaten Lemont team in the 6A championship game. The Indians were back in the 6A title game for the second straight year, having finished second in 2007.

The Cyclones had fumbled the ball only once all year, but Dondanville coughed it up on the very first play from scrimmage in the title game, leading to a Lemont field goal. The next time the Cyclones got the ball, Dondanville missed receiver Dominic Walton, who had gotten open deep on the sideline. Leonard dialed up the same pass route on the very next play, and this time Dondanville hit Walton. The receiver caught the ball despite tight coverage, broke a tackle and ran 72 yards to the end zone and a 7-3 lead. "I wasn't going down no matter what," Walton said in the postgame press conference. Walton often burned teams that concentrated too much on stopping Lantz, who turned into a blocking escort on the big play. "Johnny was right in front of me, leading me the whole way."

Lemont answered with a second quarter touchdown but had to settle for only a 9-7 lead when Lantz blocked the extra point kick. The Cyclones immediately responded with a 69-yard TD drive, the big play being a 43-yard pass to Cave, another receiver who made teams pay when they concentrated their coverage on Lantz. Wilson capped that drive with a 10-yard run, and the Cyclones led 13-9 lead when their two-point pass attempt failed. Chris Cox came up with a pass interception on Lemont's next possession, setting Wilson up for another TD run, this one from seven yards out for a 20-9 lead.

Bloink kicked a 30-yard field goal, the only points of the third quarter, and the Cyclones took a 23-9 lead into the final quarter. Lemont went on an 80-yard drive to start the fourth quarter, cutting the lead to 23-15. Though Wilson had two TD runs in the first half, he had been bottled up most of the night by the Lemont defense and had just 20 yards rushing going into the final 12 minutes. In what proved to be a decisive play, Wilson blew through a gaping hole and raced 64 yards to the Lemont 5-yard line. "We just had to be patient and let things come to us," he said later.

Dondanville capitalized on the big run by hitting Lantz on a slant pattern in the end zone, and SHG's lead grew to 30-15 with 6 ½ minutes left. It was a favorite goal-line play for the Cyclones, who perfected it during 7-on-7 summer tournaments. "That was our staple play," Dondanville said afterward in the press conference. "State championship, no matter where, John will get open." The SHG defense got the ball back, and Wilson provided his third TD run, this one a 10-yarder, for the final score of 37-15.

The Cyclones' defense had completed the turnaround Leonard predicted after the stinging loss to Montini in the season opener, which proved to be the only loss. Middle linebacker Blake Pronger had 12 tackles in the title game to lead the SHG defense, as he had done most of the year. Walton had 10 tackles, a quarterback sack and an interception. Cox had five tackles and the big interception that led to a touchdown. In the postgame press conference, he credited the film study and preparation he, his teammates and coaches put in the week leading up to the game. "Their quarterback would kind of look at who he was going to throw to," Cox said. "When I saw who he was looking to, I played the ball." Jake Smith also had an interception to go with five tackles.

The Cyclones' offense put up 37 points despite the injured Lantz catching passes for only 43 yards. Wilson ended up with 122 yards rushing, 102 of them coming in the fourth quarter. Walton had the big 72-yard TD catch and Cave the 43-yard catch that led to a score. Lemont coach Eric Michaelson acknowledged in the postgame press conference that the Cyclones were more than one dimensional. "You stop number 13 (Lantz) and they've still got number 8 (Walton). Number 5 (Wilson) is shifty and does a nice job of seeing an opening," Michaelson said. "The quarterback (Dondanville) is an excellent player. In that kind of offense, the quarterback is asked to make a ton of decisions, and it sure seemed like for the most part he made the right ones."

Dondanville summed up the win by talking about his SHG teammates who never got much ink, guys who protected him such as center Matt Anderson, guards John Root and Jeremy Bertoni, and tackles Aaron Peterman and 6-foot-4, 255-pound Marlandez Harris, who would go on to play for Indiana University. Unsung heroes on defense included linemen Dillon Thomas and Dan Schafer and linebackers Zach Boente and Darryl McMath, the only sophomore starter.

"The thing is, it takes 22 guys," Dondanville told reporters. "The Big Four, whatever people call it, only happens because of the other 18 guys. The offensive line, the defensive line...those players up front won the battle on the line of scrimmage, and that was huge."

Looking back on the Cyclones' third state championship in four years, Leonard points to the team's motto. "Our motto was '*Together as One*,'" he says. "The team really bought into that. It was such an unselfish group, and when John got hurt, others stepped up. The seniors on that team reminded me a lot of the 2006 group. When these guys were sophomores, they had to go against that 2006 group every day in practice. They learned what it took to be champions."

Victorious!

Rocket Ignition

Sean Robinson had every intention of following in his brother's footsteps. Sean hadn't even been born when Joe Robinson was the starting quarterback of the then-Griffin Cyclones in 1986. Joe led them to an 11-1 record, the only loss coming to eventual state runner-up Rock Island Alleman in the Class 4A quarterfinals. But Sean had heard about his brother's football exploits, and he had grown up watching lots of Cyclones games – paying special attention to Eric Peterman, whose run and pass dual-threat game matched his own athletic skill set.

Sean, whose family lived in the Rochester School District, had taken the entrance exam for Sacred Heart-Griffin High School. He had gone so far as to visit the school for a day as a junior high student, shadowing an SHG student to get a feel for the school. In addition to his brother having attended the school, Sean's mother had graduated from Sacred Heart Academy. It just seemed natural that Sean would follow in the family footsteps and go to SHG. All of that changed following a discussion between Sean and Rochester coach Derek Leonard.

Leonard had been following Sean's progress on the Rochester Junior Football League team for a couple of years, and he was aware of the Robinson family's deep connections to SHG and of Sean's tentative plans to play for Derek's father Ken. Derek had been asked to help coach the eighth-grade Rochester track team even though he had no experience as a track coach. No one else had stepped up to coach the team. Not surprisingly, Sean was a track standout in the 100- and 200-meter dashes and the long jump. After one track practice, Derek approached Sean. While Sean's father Dave sat in the school parking lot, Sean and Derek talked for more than an hour. "Coach Leonard came up to me and said, 'Hey, let's chat,'" Sean recalls. "He then laid out the reasons he thought I should stay at Rochester. It was just his tone and who he was as a guy, so genuine. That was the turning point for me."

Sean's father had played baseball, basketball and football at Feitshans High School in Springfield, the forerunner to Southeast High School. For him, the choice for his son Sean was pretty simple: "I told him he could either be a big fish in a small pond or play for a high-profile program like SHG," Dave Robinson says. "At the time Rochester was still just an up-and-coming football program."

Turns out, Sean was one of the players who helped put the fledgling Rochester program on the map in a big way. Sean Robinson's career high school statistics paint a picture of incredible athletic ability and versatility: more than 3,700 yards passing, more than 2,400 yards rushing, and almost 1,000 yards receiving. He ended up being rated the country's 10th-best dual-threat quarterback in the 2010 recruiting class, earning him a football scholarship to Purdue University. Recruited as a quarterback, he ended up playing middle linebacker his final two seasons at Purdue. It's not all that unusual for quarterbacks to be converted to wide receiver or defensive back in college based on size, speed and hand-eye coordination. It's extremely rare for a QB to become a linebacker in college, especially at the Big Ten level where size and toughness are survival requirements.

"I started three games at quarterback my freshman year at Purdue. I kind of just got thrown into a bad situation, and I was terrible. I embarrassed myself," says Sean, who then took a red-shirt year (sitting out a season but retaining that year of college eligibility), using that season to build strength and mature as a player. There had been a change among the assistant coaches, and Purdue had hired a new defensive coordinator. He noticed Robinson, now 6-foot-3 and weighing about 210 pounds, who was working out with some line-backers. "He asked one of the other coaches, 'Hey, who is that kid?' He thought I was a linebacker," Robinson recalls. "The other coach told him I was actually a quarterback, but probably wasn't going to play much. The defensive coordinator said, 'If you don't want him, I'll take him.'"

Purdue head coach Danny Hope delivered the news to Robinson, who still thought of himself as a quarterback. He asked for some time to think it over. He called his brother Joe, his high school coach Derek and his father. "I told him, 'Sean, if you want to play quarterback, I can make some calls to the other schools who had recruited you as a quarterback. I know that quite a few doors would open for you,'" Sean's father says. Sean had received offers from schools such as Northwestern, Nebraska, Iowa and Boston College, among other big-time football schools.

"I told my dad that I had made good friends at Purdue, that I actually loved the coaching staff and that I was going to stay and do whatever it takes to get on the football field," Sean says. He not only got on the field as a middle linebacker his final two seasons at Pur-due, but he ended up making 116 tackles and being named a team captain his senior season.

As of 2022, Robinson was one of only two freshmen ever to start for one of Derek Leonard's Rochester teams. The other was Hank Beatty, who also went on to play football in the Big Ten (University of Illinois). Both were destined to become All-State quar-terbacks for the Rockets, but as underclassmen both were receivers and defensive players, biding their time behind veteran quarterbacks until their junior seasons. Both checked all of the boxes to play quar-terback – passing accuracy, athleticism, arm strength and high foot-ball IQs. Both also were able to handle the heat that comes with playing the most stressful position in Derek's offense. Anyone who has watched many Rochester games has seen the range of emotions and passion with which Derek coaches.

Dave Robinson remembers watching Sean's first game as the starting quarterback at Rochester, more precisely the first time he saw Derek do his Yosemite Sam exploding head impersonation with Sean. "Sean had told me what a gentle, kind, loving Christian man Derek was...and he is," Sean's father says. "But the Rockets had failed to get a first down on a third-down pass, and the coach lit into Sean as he was coming off the field. I stood up and was starting to yell at Derek, but my wife Lori elbowed me and told me to sit down. After the game, Sean told me, 'I had it coming. I didn't make the right decision. Coach has my best interests at heart.' I am so glad everything evolved as it did because, in retrospect, Coach Leonard has had a huge positive impact on Sean as a person."

For his part, Sean thinks of Derek Leonard as a big brother, albeit a demanding one. "I don't think there was one game I quarter-backed at Rochester when he didn't have his hand on my facemask and left some spittle on my face," Sean says with a laugh. "I had a slight case of being a smart ass, and I knew how to trigger him. He was doing it for the right reasons. He knew I could be better, and he expected more out of me. I looked at it as brotherly love...with a little bit of spittle."

His freshman and sophomore years Sean played wide receiver and linebacker because Wil Lunt, who would go on to play for Western Illinois University, was established as the Rockets quarterback. Sean took over his junior year, leading the Rockets to a 7-3 record in 2008. It would mark Derek's first winning season at Rochester after 3-6, 5-5 and 5-5 records in his first three seasons.

Expectations were high heading into the 2009 season, and for good reason. Derek finally had his program, and his offense, established. Sean's senior class and the junior class both were loaded with tough, physical players for the offensive and defensive lines. They also had lots of speed and athleticism at the skill positions. Also, Sean had a full season of experience under his belt as a quarterback. All systems were go!

Rochester opened that season with a 38-22 win over Mahomet-Seymour. The 16-point margin was the closest any team would get to the Rockets as they ripped off eight more wins in a row to win the Corn Belt Conference championship. They then blew past Mascoutah (57-32), Mt. Carmel (42-14) and a previously unbeaten Quincy Notre Dame team (45-26) to reach the Class 4A semifinals. They would travel to meet tradition-rich Metamora, the defending Class 5A state champion. Coach Pat Ryan's Redbirds entered the showdown with a 12-1 record, having compiled a 58-5 record over five seasons.

That pedigree seemed to show itself against the upstart Rockets during the first half. A Rochester team that had never trailed the entire season gave up an early score but bounced back to take the lead on two touchdown runs by Robinson. The Rockets then gave up three straight TDs to go into halftime trailing Metamora 27-13. Some of the damage was self-inflicted, and some was just bad luck, including a phantom Redbirds reception that led to a score.

The questionable catch was a third-down pass that skipped off the grass and into a Metamora receiver's hands. The view from the stands was clear. Review of the game tape afterward confirmed that the ball hit the ground. However, none of the officials saw it bounce. Late in the first half, the Rockets had a fourth-and-4 at midfield. Robinson, who doubled as the punter, was supposed to line up in shotgun formation, run the clock down as far as he could and then drop further back and punt. The ball was snapped early, and a surprised Robinson was tackled for a 9-yard loss at his own 41. Metamora turned that error into a 23-yard TD pass with just two seconds left in the half.

"It was supposed to be a long count, Sean was going to drop back and punt, but there was a miscommunication...you could tell Sean was stunned. It was an accident," Leonard told reporters afterward. A team that had not been challenged all season suddenly trailed by two touchdowns with only 24 minutes left to play. "We were still okay," Derek says. "I told the kids they'd never been put in that situation this year, but that I knew they would fight back. That's exactly what they did."

The second half was a slugfest between two heavyweight football powers. The Rockets finally drew even early in the fourth quarter when Dylan McKinney blocked a Metamora punt, which was scooped up by Chase Tackett and returned 19 yards for a TD. The Rockets went for the two-point conversion, and Robinson ran the ball in to tie the score at 34-34. Robinson had seldom been stopped on a two-point conversion all year.

Metamora methodically drove the ball down the field, eating up yardage and the clock, converting two short fourth-down plays along the way. Facing a third-and-10 from the Rochester 14-yard line, a Metamora pass was knocked down by Rockets defensive back Colt Gass. However, 15 yards away, an official had thrown a flag into the middle of the line, an area where offensive holding usually is called. It was holding. But this time, defensive holding was the call. Instead of facing a fourth-and-10 and likely trying for a field goal, Metamora ended up scoring a touchdown for a 41-34 lead with 2:47 left to play.

It was do-or-die time for Rochester. Robinson calmly led the Rockets on a 15-play, 69-yard drive that included a diving 18-yard reception by Kyle Brozka, an 18-yard run by Colten Glazebrook and a key fourth-and-1 run by Jake Bivens, who hurdled tacklers to get a first down at the 5-yard line. Robinson then found Matt Bane in the corner of the end zone on a third-down pass from the 2-yard line. Bane, who would go on to become a Big Ten champion pole vaulter at the University of Illinois, made a sensational leaping catch with 3.8 seconds left to draw the Rockets within a point at 41-40.

It was decision time for Derek: Kick the extra point and play for overtime, or go for the two-point conversion and win or lose on one play from the 3-yard line. He had roughly 30 seconds to decide...and several factors came into play, including:

➤ The Rockets' kicker, Sean Ryan, a soccer player who turned out to be one of Rochester's best kickers ever, had missed two extra-point kicks that day after having seldom ever missed a kick during the season.

➤ The field conditions were slick in some spots, contributing to at least one of the missed kicks.

➤ The high school rules for overtime called for each team to have four downs from the 10-yard line. Those rules seemed better suited for Metamora's power, run-oriented offense.

Derek's father was on the Rochester sideline that day. Like others rooting for the Rockets, he was frustrated with the officiating crew that flagged the Rockets for six penalties compared to two against Metamora. What further irked Ken was his knowledge that the crew was local and at least one of the members had a close connection to the Metamora coach. The IHSA subsequently made two adjustments to its guidelines. Coaches who were not part of the team's coaching staff no longer would be allowed to be on the sideline. The IHSA also would redouble their efforts to make sure officiating crews had no close connections to either team in a play-off game.

Derek briefly consulted with his father regarding the critical decision. "I told Derek to do what his gut was telling him to do," Ken would say years later. "If it had been me, I would have gone for two points and the win in that spot, but I didn't say that to him then."

After the game, Sean Robinson told reporters that it was the players who decided to go for two points. "He (Coach Derek Leonard) asked what we wanted to do and we said, 'Let's go get it!'" Derek says it is true he asked the players…but that he already had decided to go for two. "I knew what the players would say, I just wanted to hear them say it…to me and to each other," he says. The play he called was one of the team's bread-and-butter plays featuring Robinson, a play that had been successful numerous times during the 2009 season. "It was Sean's team…he deserved to carry the ball on that play."

"The play was for me to fake a handoff to (running back) Colten (Glazebrook), keep the ball and follow the guard and tackle into the end zone," recalled Robinson, the play still vivid in his memory more than a decade later. "When I turned to run into the end zone, all I could see was a wall of Metamora players. They just blitzed everybody and got lucky. It's still a debate between my buddies and me…some of them said there was a hole there, but a wall was all I saw. I knew I wasn't going to make that last yard, and there was no way to jump over so many people, so I just tossed the ball behind me hoping that one of our guys might pick it up and score."

That didn't happen. The two-point try, the Rockets' unbeaten season and their championship dreams fell less than one yard short. As the Metamora crowd erupted, the Rochester players slowly trudged off the field. Robinson headed straight to his head coach. *The State Journal-Register* the next day included a photo of the high school senior hugging and comforting his head coach. Leonard says that is the one loss that haunts him the most. Metamora went on the next week to demolish Geneseo 41-7 for the state championship.

"That team, Sean and the other seniors on that team, it was a better team than some of our championship teams," Derek says. "To this day, I just feel so bad for Sean and that class. In hindsight, that was probably one of the best games I have ever been a part of. Metamora was a great team, and they proved that the next week in the championship game. We were a great team, too. I remember thinking that you just never know if your team will ever be in the position again to win a championship. I had seen Dad's teams come so close for so many years. So many things have to go right. You just never know if you'll have that chance again."

The PlayStation Running Back… and Redemption

One of the poignant photos following Rochester's heartbreaking 41-40 loss to Metamora in the 2009 semifinal game was that of junior linebacker Dan Camp embracing his father. Camp was one of the leaders of a strong junior class that year that included the likes of defensive ends Riley McMinn and Taylor Hill, running back Colten Glazebrook, receiver Blake Gand and receiver/defensive back Michael Gunter. Waiting in the wings for their chance in 2010 were quarterback Wes Lunt and receiver Zach Grant.

The normal routine was for the Rockets to take the month of December off before getting back into the weight room to begin preparations for the next season. Coach Derek Leonard was surprised to find Camp and several other returning players in the weight room after school the Monday after the Saturday loss to Metamora. "That loss left such a bitter taste in their mouths that they could not wait to start getting ready for the (2010) season," Leonard says. "They felt so bad for Sean Robinson and Matt Bane and those other seniors who literally came up just inches short. They vowed not to let that happen again. They were as focused and determined a group as I've ever had."

There were rumors during the summer that Glazebrook was not going to play football his senior year, despite the fact that he had proven himself to be one of the best running backs in the area his sophomore and junior seasons. Truth be told, he preferred video games to football. The irony is that his real-life football moves resembled something right out of a John Madden Football PlayStation game. "Yeah, I heard the rumors, but I never really thought Colten wasn't going to play football his senior year," Derek says. "I don't think the other guys would have let him quit. Colten was a different sort of guy. He didn't much like to practice, and he didn't like getting hit. But man, when the lights were the brightest on game nights, nobody was better than Colten Glazebrook."

There was the time during Glazebrook's freshman year that Leonard asked him to return a kickoff. "He said he'd rather not. I asked him why. He said, 'Coach, I really don't like getting hit,'" Leonard says, chuckling at the memory. "Not wanting to get tackled is probably one of the things that made him such a great running back. He knew when he couldn't gain any more yardage, and he had this knack of relaxing his body and going down kind of softly. But if he saw an opening, he would really turn it on. He had the greatest vision of the field, even going through the line, I've ever seen in my life. With his ability to change direction and accelerate so quickly, he was really hard to tackle. In three years, I think I only saw him get hit hard once."

Glazebrook once described his running style quite simply to a reporter by saying, "I'm kind of scared out there. I don't like getting hit, so whenever I see the opposite (uniform) colors, I just move the other way." During his junior season in 2009, Glazebrook told *State Journal-Register* reporter Dave Kane, "I'm probably kind of weird. I'm not a 'focus' person. I don't care if I do good or not as long as we win and get the game over with. I don't get obsessed with my stats."

Not only did Glazebrook play football his senior year, but he ended up rushing for 1,719 yards, catching passes for 585 yards, scoring 41 touchdowns and breaking the Central State Eight scoring record with 250 points. He was named the 2010 Player of the Year in the CS8 Conference. His career total of 3,430 yards rushing stood as a Rochester record until Jacob DuRocher broke it in 2021. Not bad for a kid who didn't really care about his statistics. Glazebrook signed with St. Ambrose University in Iowa, where he earned playing time in the season opener as a freshman. He was in line to become the starter the next week. However, he ended his college football career after just one game.

With Glazebrook back and the Lunt-Grant duo set to take flight, the Rockets offense was primed for an explosive 2010 season. The defense also was set with returning stars such as McMinn, who would go on to play at the University of Iowa; Camp, who would earn all-conference honors at Quincy University; and Gunter, Gand, and Aaron O'Dell to name a few. The Rockets went through the regular season unbeaten, the only close game being the inaugural Leonard Bowl, in which Rochester hung on by Jon Gilson's fingernails for a 13-10 win.

They began their playoff run by beating Freeburg 49-7 and Effingham 53-2. Their quarterfinal test would be in Quincy against a solid 9-2 Quincy Notre Dame (QND) team. Even though it hadn't rained for three days leading up to the game, when the Rockets stepped onto the field, they found it was a bit of a quagmire. The slower track and windy conditions helped slow the Rochester attack, and the game turned into a nail-biter. QND took a 14-13 lead midway through the third quarter. With the Rockets offense sputtering, it seemed like they might be in for another frustrating premature ending to their season. This time, though, the defense rose to the occasion.

A 28-yard field goal by John Perry put Rochester back on top 16-14, but QND was again on the march late in the third quarter. The Raiders quarterback faded back to pass. Rochester defensive back Gunter couldn't believe his eyes when he saw the ball spiraling right toward him. He cut in front of the receiver, intercepted the ball and raced 42 yards for a touchdown. "I think Riley (McMinn) got a hand on it and swatted it," Gunter told reporters afterward. "I was like, *'Is he seriously going to throw it?'* And he actually did. I was like, *'Here we go!'*"

The nine-point lead did not last long as QND drove 68 yards

for a TD to cut the lead to two points, 23-21. Again, the Rochester defense came through, not once but twice in the game's final few moments. Traves Everly ripped the ball loose from a running back and recovered a fumble to thwart one QND drive with 8:30 left to play. "(The runner) came through the hole, and it was like slow motion," said Everly, who had an interception earlier in the game. "He held the ball out a little bit, I hit it and it popped up right back to me. It was lucky really, that it popped up to me."

QND got the ball right back on an interception two plays later, but up stepped Gunter with his second pick of the game. It would take a third interception by Gunter, the fifth takeaway for the Rockets, to finally seal the win and get back to the semifinals. "It was probably one of the best feelings I've ever had," Gunter said, again acknowledging a teammate's assistance. "Blake (Gand) just tipped it up. He came over to me after the game and said, 'I just don't know how to swat a ball down.' I told him, 'It's all right buddy, I got your back.'"

Leonard had been worried about the matchup with QND, a concern that only deepened when he saw the condition of the field. "I had been telling everybody that we were going to have to win a game like this...almost every championship team has to win one like this somewhere along the line," he says. "They were the most physical team we had played. We're not a good muddy-track team. Between the mud and the wind, we had some things stacked against us. But our defense came through big time."

For nearly a year, the Rockets had been waiting for and hoping for the opportunity to again play Metamora. On the bus ride back to Rochester, one of the coaches heard the news that Metamora had beaten Pontiac 34-7. When the coach shared the score with the players, the cheers and celebration shook the bus. The Metamora-Rochester rematch was set, again with a ticket to the championship game on the line. This time, however, the game would be played at Rocket Booster Stadium in Rochester.

A boisterous crowd estimated at more than 6,000 fans showed

up, most wearing the Rochester colors of orange and blue. The defending state champion Redbirds quieted the crowd when they converted a fourth-and-14 for a 28-yard TD pass to cut the Rochester lead to 13-10 midway through the second quarter. The only noise on the Rochester side at that point was coming from on top of the press box, where some of the Metamora assistants were positioned. One of the assistants taunted Rochester fans with shouts of "How do you like that?"

The Rockets' reply came on the very first play after the kickoff. Lunt faded back and lofted a perfectly thrown 72-yard TD bomb to Everly streaking down the left sideline in front of the Metamora bench. Moments later, Lunt again found Everly, this time for a 68-yard score thanks to a one-handed, fingertip catch by the receiver, and the Rockets led 28-10 at the half. Glazebrook broke loose for a 54-yard TD on Rochester's first possession of the second half and later added a 12-yard TD run. For the game, Glazebrook ran for 206 yards and five TDs. Lunt threw only 20 times but amassed 255 yards and the two long TDs to Everly.

This time, there would be no suspense. The game would be decided by the running-clock mercy rule instead of mere inches as the Rochester lead ballooned to 50-10 early in the fourth quarter. The Metamora assistants had packed up their equipment and vacated their perch atop the press box by the end of the third quarter. Final score: Rochester 50, Metamora 17.

"We bent early on, but we didn't break," Leonard told reporters after the game. "After the middle of the second quarter, we were pretty stinkin' good." Several of the Rochester players noted that the victory over Metamora was as much for Sean Robinson and the other seniors from the 2009 team as it was for themselves. The Rockets were heading to the first-ever state championship game in the school's 15-year football history. The opponent would be unbeaten Rock Island Alleman – that "Green Team" that as a youngster roaming his dad's Griffin sideline Derek never again wanted to face.

Victorious!

A Decade of Dominance Begins

The Class 4A championship game is always the fourth and final game of the first day of the Illinois High School Association football championships the Friday after Thanksgiving. By the time the Rochester and Rock Island Alleman teams took the field for the 7 p.m. kickoff at Memorial Stadium in Champaign on November 26, 2010, light snow had begun to fall and the temperature had dipped into the 30s. The defense would need to stand firm until the Rockets' offense thawed.

Riley McMinn gathered his fellow defensive linemen Taylor Hill, Aaron O'Dell and Ryan Broglin together before the game. All were seniors playing in their final game for Rochester. "Tomorrow is not guaranteed," he said. "What is guaranteed is now, this family and the opportunity we have in front of us.'" McMinn followed his words up with action by sacking the Alleman quarterback on the first series of plays.

That sack and other defensive plays led to the Rockets getting on the scoreboard later in the opening quarter when Colten Glazebrook took in a screen pass from Wes Lunt and weaved his way 23 yards to the end zone. Aided by three penalties that kept its drive alive, Alleman tied the game at 7-7 in the second quarter. Rochester took a 10-7 lead at halftime when John Perry kicked a 25-yard field goal.

Glazebrook accounted for all 90 yards to get the Rockets off to a fast start in the second half. He took the kickoff at his own 10-yard line and returned it 23 yards to the Rochester 33. He then lined up wide left, caught a short pass from Lunt, avoided one tackler and sprinted 52 yards to the Alleman 15-yard line. He covered the final 15 yards by running up the middle for gains of 5 and 9 yards and then ran the ball in from the 1-yard line for a 17-7 lead.

"We made an adjustment at halftime to try and get Colten the ball as often as possible out where he had some space to maneuver," Derek says. "On the pass play, we lined him out to the left as a receiver for the first time all year. We lined up three receivers on the right and sent our running back in motion to the right. That left Colten with one defender, and almost no one could tackle him one-on-one." Glazebrook ran the ball for 208 yards – more yardage rushing by himself than the entire Alleman team accumulated – and caught passes for 89 more yards. He scored all three Rochester touchdowns.

The defense got the ball back again, albeit at Rochester's own 4-yard line. Facing a critical third-and-11, Lunt hit Zach Grant with a 12-yard pass. Then, on third-and-13, Lunt found Traves Everly to keep the drive going. Glazebrook took care of the remaining 74 yards on runs of 63 and 11 yards. The Rockets' lead grew to 24-7.

"Our (offensive) line gave me time, and we made big plays on those third downs," Lunt told reporters later. "We really needed to score and we did." Derek says not enough credit goes to the offensive line when people talk about the Rochester offense. O'Dell, Kyle Kremitzki, David Molohon, Kyle Loprez and Chase Walker all were seniors. They averaged 250 pounds, and all season long they had been opening running lanes for Glazebrook and forming an almost impenetrable pocket for Lunt.

The defense did the rest, harassing the Pioneers quarterback the whole last quarter to secure Rochester's first state championship 24-7. The Rockets defense held Alleman to just 119 yards of offense – only 24 in the second half. Alleman coach Dave DeJaegher summed it up succinctly in the postgame press conference by saying, "As good as they are offensively, I think they were extremely good defensively. We just never did get a push on the line of scrimmage at all, and when we tried to throw, they got a lot of pressure on us."

That pressure included seven quarterback sacks, three by Kremitzki and two by McMinn. "We came out ready to go, and I've got to give it to Kyle Kremitzki and Ryan Broglin. They really stepped up huge," McMinn said during Rochester's press conference. The Pioneers didn't have time to throw the ball, and when they tried to run outside, they were met by Michael Gunter, Everly and Blake Gand. When they tried to run up the middle, there was middle linebacker Dan Camp, who led the team with nine tackles.

"That 2010 team was probably the best defense of any of our teams. Eric (Warren) was really a genius as a defensive coordinator that year. The players on defense kind of took on his personality," Derek says. "Not only were they big, strong and fast, they also were so connected. They cared so much for each other and might have been our closest group of players."

His school's first football championship in hand, Derek Leonard expressed a bittersweet emotion in his postgame press conference. "I'm more sad the season's over than anything," he said. "This is a special group to my heart, and this is for everyone who has played for me. We've worked a lot of years for this."

One of the people who had put in so much blood, sweat and even tears was Sean Robinson, the Rockets' 2009 team leader who came up inches short of reaching the title game on his final high school play. A freshman quarterback at Purdue, Robinson was sitting in a West Lafayette, Indiana, hotel room that Friday night watching his former teammates capture the first football state championship for Rochester. Robinson and his Boilermakers teammates were scheduled to play intrastate archrival Indiana the next afternoon in the annual Old Oaken Bucket series that dates to 1925.

"The Old Oaken Bucket is always the biggest game of the year for Purdue and Indiana, but I was way more interested in watching Rochester play for the state championship," Robinson recalls. For the record, Robinson did not get into the game the next day, and Purdue lost 34-31.

Victorious!

Reloading

One of the challenges to sustaining football success at a public school is the random nature of athletic ability. When a class loaded with great athletes graduates, it's not a given that the next class will have the same type of athletic ability. That's just genetics. Some of those ups and downs can be smoothed out by having a great youth football program, and the high-profile success Rochester has had certainly attracts lots of kids who want to prepare themselves to be a part of Rockets football. However, unlike parochial or private schools, athletic participation in public schools is limited by the geographical boundaries of the school district.

If you want to play for a school like Rochester, you must reside within the school district's boundaries, according to the IHSA by-laws. The only general exception is for neighboring schools that decide to form cooperative teams, in which case the team must count the enrollment from both schools to determine in which of the eight classes the team is placed for football playoff purposes. Because they can enroll student athletes from within a 30-mile radius, parochial and private schools are pushed up in class by a 1.5 enrollment multiplier if their teams have playoff success according to the complex IHSA system.

It is true that schools that develop great programs will attract transfer students, much like realtors will tell you that home buyers tend to migrate toward communities that have strong school districts. Bottom line: Coaches at public schools can field teams only from students who live in that school district.

It's not an apples-to-apples analogy, but the "Blueberry Story" by Jamie Vollmer is a good illustration. Vollmer was president of the Great Midwestern Ice Cream Company in Iowa. Their blueberry ice cream was chosen by People Magazine as the "The Best Ice Cream in America" in 1984. It was served in the Reagan White House after Nancy Reagan sampled a taste. Vollmer also was the founding member of the Iowa Business Roundtable in the late 1980s, and the group focused on improving public schools.

Speaking at a gathering of teachers, Vollmer cited statistics showing how public schools were lagging private schools. Vollmer said, "If I ran my business the way you people operate your schools, I wouldn't be in business very long!" A teacher raised her hand during the Q & A that followed Vollmer's presentation. She congratulated Vollmer on having produced such award-winning ice cream.

"Do you use premium ingredients?" she asked. "Super-premium. Nothing but Triple-A," Vollmer replied proudly.

"So, what do you do when you receive an inferior shipment of blueberries?" the teacher continued. "I send them back," Vollmer said.

"We can never send back our blueberries," the teacher said. "We take them big, small, rich, poor, gifted, exceptional, abused, frightened, confident, homeless, rude, and brilliant. We take them with ADHD, junior rheumatoid arthritis, and English as their second language. We take them all! Every one! And that, Mr. Vollmer, is why it's not a business. It's school!" The exchange so resonated with Vollmer that within a couple of years he had changed from being one of public schools' biggest critics into one of their biggest advocates. He switched careers, founding a company dedicated to helping public schools and writing a widely acclaimed book titled "Schools Cannot Do It Alone."

The Rockets had won their first state football crown in 2010 despite losing Sean Robinson and so many other great players from the 2009 team that came up just inches short. Looking ahead to 2011, the Rockets had many voids to fill because of the graduation of the likes of Riley McMinn, Colten Glazebrook and the rest of that championship class. On the plus side, quarterback Wes Lunt and his favorite target, Zach Grant, were returning for their senior seasons.

"When you lose so many great players from a graduating class, you just never know how the pieces will fit together the next year," Derek Leonard says. "But I knew we had Wes and Zach back, and I also knew that we had some guys people hadn't heard much about because they had been forced to wait for their chances. What we could see that people on the outside couldn't was how the younger players were developing going against those really good older players every day in practice."

Rochester went 7-2 in the regular season, losing only to an SHG team that ended up making the semifinals in the 5A playoffs, and to Chatham Glenwood, whose only two losses were to SHG. The Rockets blasted through the first four rounds of the 4A playoffs, beating Quincy Notre Dame 56-35, Manteno 42-28, Kankakee Bishop McNamara 55-21 and Charleston 42-13. Those wins propelled them into the championship game against a 12-1 Richmond-Burton (R-B) team that was missing its best running back, Jack Dechow, when it lost its season opener 7-0. With the return of Dechow, a tough runner who would go on to earn All-American honors as a wrestler at Old Dominion University in Virginia, R-B won 11 games in a row. The R-B defense had allowed an average of only 11 points per game heading into the title game.

Aside from their excellent records and the fact they both shared the nickname Rockets, the two teams could not have been much more different. R-B relied heavily on the run and set a 4A championship game record that night with 514 yards rushing, led by Dechow's 244 yards and four TDs. R-B did not complete a pass, attempting only three, and one of those was an intentional spiking of the ball to stop the clock late in the game. Rochester had but 48 yards rushing, but Lunt completed 31 of 39 passes for 506 yards and three TDs. Grant caught 13 of those passes for 259 yards and two TDs.

Other statistical oddities occurred in the first half. R-B had the ball for almost 18 minutes compared to six for Rochester, yet Rochester led 21-10 at halftime. Fullback Seth Cronin had given Rochester an early 14-0 lead with two 1-yard TD runs. Those would be the only two times he carried the ball in the game. Cronin was one of those unheralded players who had been biding his time the previous two seasons. But seizing on his expanded playing time in 2011, he was the leading tackler on the Rochester defense. He also played fullback on offense, often being the lead blocker for Garett Dooley, who led the team with more than 1,100 yards rushing and 25 TDs for the season.

"I knew I was going to play defense, but I didn't play offense last year except for two games," Cronin told Ryan Mahan of *The State Journal-Register* a few days before the title game. "This year, coach told me I was going to start on offense, and I thought it was a great opportunity. I either get the ball or I block for someone so they get the ball…There was no jealousy whatsoever. We helped each other, whether (Dooley) was lead-blocking for me or I was lead-blocking for him. It's such a great feeling to have a friend in the backfield with you."

Every time R-B drew close in the second half, Lunt had an answer. R-B's Dechow ran it in from 24 yards out to cut the Rochester lead to 21-16. Just two plays later, Lunt hit Austin Green with a 60-yard TD pass. A successful onside kick by Rochester led to a 4-yard TD run by Dooley that grew the Rochester lead to 35-16. R-B would bounce back when Dechow broke loose for a 68-yard TD run. Lunt's response: a 75-yard TD bomb to Grant.

Instead of folding, R-B scored the next two TDs to close to within 42-39 with a little more than five minutes left to play. An interception in its own end zone of an underthrown pass gave R-B the ball back with 1:17 left on the clock. R-B drove the ball all the way to the Rochester 39-yard line with 34 seconds left, but Matt Swaine and Gabe Ferguson combined to bring the ball carrier down

224

two yards shy of a first down on a fourth-and-8 play. Rochester had secured its second straight state championship.

"This is unbelievable," Grant said in the post-game press conference. "Everyone worked so hard. This whole team is just blessed. I love these guys."

The high-flying combination of Lunt-to-Grant rewrote much of the state's record book in 2011 – despite the fact that Lunt missed the first four games with a foot injury incurred during offseason workouts. Through the 2022 season, Lunt's 3,651 yards passing in 2011 was the 15th best in the state for a single season. Grant's 2,310 yards receiving still stood as the most ever in a season for a high school player in Illinois. Lunt's 31 completions and 506 yards remained 4A championship game records, as did Grant's 13 catches and 259 yards receiving.

"Wes was the best natural thrower I've ever coached," Leonard says. "The ball just came out spinning perfectly. And Zach had the best hands of any of my receivers. The two of them formed the best quarterback-receiver combination I've ever been a part of. Everybody knew what we were going to do that year, and they still couldn't stop Wes from throwing the ball to Zach."

Richmond-Burton coach Pat Elder tipped his cap to Lunt in the post-game press conference when he said, "There's a reason that boy (Lunt) is going to Oklahoma State." Lunt became the first true freshman since 1950 to start an opening game at quarterback for Oklahoma State, and he threw for more than 1,000 yards that season before injuries sidelined him. He transferred to the University of Illinois, where he was the starter in his final three seasons except for missing several weeks of his first year with a broken leg. He was briefly signed to a free-agent contract by the Minnesota Vikings of the NFL.

As great as Wes Lunt was in high school, his older brother Wil still holds some family bragging rights. Wil finished his high school career with the fourth-most passing yardage (8,308) and fifth-most completions (603) in state history from 2005-2007, both still school records at Rochester 15 years later. In terms of most passing yards in a single game, Wes ranks sixth in state annals with 583 versus Springfield High in 2011 – nine more yards than Wil, who ranks seventh with 574 against Bloomington Central Catholic in 2007. One big bragging right for Wes is that he has two championship rings. Wil's three years as a starter were Derek's first three as a head coach, laying the foundation for his program. Those Rockets teams never had better than a 5-5 record, but Wil set a gold standard for quarterback play at Rochester.

Meanwhile, Grant went to National Association of Intercollegiate Athletics (NAIA) powerhouse St. Ambrose University in Iowa, where as a freshman he broke the school records for receptions (91) and touchdowns (16) and was among the top 10 in the nation with 1,190 yards receiving. He was reunited with Lunt at Illinois when he transferred there for his final three seasons and twice earned All-Big Ten Academic team honors. Grant went into coaching after his graduation from the U of I, first as a graduate assistant at Illinois, then as running backs coach at Western Illinois University before becoming the receivers coach at Southern Illinois University in 2023.

Of all his championship teams, the 2011 team is the one that surprised Derek Leonard the most. The 2009 team that fell just short and the 2010 team that won Rochester's first championship were loaded. But those players were gone. "The senior class in the 2011 season had not been all that successful growing up," Leonard says. "As coaches, we were not really thinking realistically about a state championship until later in the season. I give those guys all the credit in the world. They proved even us coaches wrong.

"That wasn't one of our strongest defenses. You don't usually win a championship without being good in most phases of the game. But the one thing we did well – Wes throwing the ball to Zach and the others – we did so well it made up for everything else."

Going for a Three-Peat

As the Rockets prepared for a run at their third straight championship, they would do so without their record-breaking duo of quarterback Wes Lunt and receiver Zach Grant. A host of other standout players also had graduated from the 2011 title team. Other than Garrett Dooley, a running back and big-time linebacker who would go on to play for Wisconsin, the 2012 Rockets didn't feature many well-known players. However, several members of the senior class had participated in 41 games the previous three seasons. They had won 38 of those games.

Derek Leonard was confident in his 2012 team, but he shared a cautionary tale having agonizingly watched some of his dad's best teams fall short in Ken Leonard's first 21 years coaching the Cyclones. "I have lived through it," Derek said. "You don't take this stuff for granted, and it doesn't just happen. You've got to have a lot of breaks go your way. You've got to get lucky, have good (playoff) draws, and you've got to have a great football team."

The 2012 version of the Rockets featured a new quarterback, senior Austin Green, who probably would have started for three years for most teams. He had patiently honed his game as the backup to the record-breaking Wes Lunt, waiting for his turn to run the Rockets offense. "Austin was my first one-year starter at quarterback at Rochester," Leonard says. "He had played linebacker and receiver because we had Wes at quarterback. Austin maximized his God-given ability as much as anybody I've ever had." It was a new challenge for Leonard. His Rockets threw the ball about 60 percent of the time when Wes Lunt was quarterback. They would dial that back to about 40 percent in 2012.

Any concerns about the Rockets offense were dissipated on the first two plays of the season against Mt. Vernon. Dooley took a handoff and ran 50 yards for a touchdown on the first play. The next time Rochester had the ball, Dooley ran 73 yards to the end zone. Green added a 50-yard TD run and threw a 57-yard TD pass to Gabe Ferguson, and the Rockets won 54-22.

Rochester played at SHG in Week Two, the first game at the Cyclones' new state-of-the-art stadium that a few years later would be named "Ken Leonard Field." Green threw for 225 yards, but also was intercepted twice and lost a fumble. The Cyclones' sophomore quarterback Gabe Green (no relation), scrambled out of the pocket for a 36-yard TD run midway through the fourth quarter to give SHG a 29-26 victory. Gabe Green lived in the Rochester school district but had attended Catholic grade schools and chose to continue that educational path and attend SHG. His father, Todd Green, owned several successful car dealerships in Springfield and was a major force in raising the funds to build the school's new stadium.

The Rockets were happy to have their own Green, and Austin rebounded from the loss to SHG to go on one of the hottest streaks in Rochester history. In wins over Springfield High, Lanphier and Chatham Glenwood, he completed 65 of 75 passes for 952 yards. The wins over Springfield and Lanphier were blowouts, but they eked past Chatham 41-35 when Green scored on a 1-yard quarterback sneak with 1:40 to play. The game ended in a rules controversy that wasn't decided until the next day.

Leading by just six points, the Rockets did not want to give the speedy Chatham kick returners a chance to break loose, so instead of kicking the ball deep, they chose to have their kicker just pop the ball up in the air about 15 yards downfield. Drake Berberet caught the ball in the air for Rochester, and the referees awarded the Rockets the ball, allowing them to run out the clock. In the heat of the moment, neither the game officials nor the coaches remembered a new rule that stated the ball had to either hit the ground or be touched by an opposing player before it could be recovered by the kicking team.

Rick Karhliker, the Central State Eight Conference supervisor of officials, confirmed to reporters a couple days later that the call had been incorrect and that Chatham Glenwood should have been awarded the ball. However, once both teams left the field, there was no provision for a do-over. "It is what it is," Karhliker said. For his part, Leonard says, "I wasn't sure about the rule. I asked some people and found out it should have been their ball."

It would be the last time that luck would be needed by the Rockets. They steamrolled through the final three games of the regular season. Green suffered a hamstring injury early in the first-round playoff game against Mahomet-Seymour. Backup quarterback Robbie Kelley replaced him and threw for two touchdowns in what would be a preview of the junior's abilities, and the Rockets won 43-0. Green returned the next week against Charleston, but mainly just handed the ball off as Dooley ran for 141 yards and three TDs and Berberet ran for 99 yards. Blake Pasley opened that game with a 90-yard kick return for a TD, and what was predicted to be a tough test against Charleston turned into a 42-14 blowout. Green remained limited because of his injury, but a 98-yard TD run by Dooley and another kick return of 85 yards by Pasley helped get the Rockets past Peoria Notre Dame 46-21. In the semifinals, Dooley ran for three more TDs and caught a pass for a fourth score as the Rockets defeated Harrisburg 49-22.

Rochester was in the state title game for the third straight year. The Rockets again would face perennial power Rock Island Alleman, the team they beat in 2010 for their first championship. Leonard had kept Green under wraps in the three games following his hamstring injury, but he turned his quarterback loose in the title game. "I really unleashed him," Leonard would tell reporters later. "His hamstring has been bothering him, but I told him today we were going to run him. This shows we're a spread team that is physical and that we can run the football against a great defense."

Green kept the Alleman defense off balance by running for 130 yards, including TD runs of 17 and 22 yards to extend a 14-12 lead to 28-12. After Alleman scored again, Green hit Pasley for a 16-yard TD late in the third quarter, and Dooley sealed the 43-18 win with a 9-yard TD run in the fourth quarter. Dooley had 98 yards rushing and two TDs, while Green threw for 172 yards and two TDs. But it was the quarterback's running – something Alleman's coaching staff had not seen him do during Rochester's playoff run because he was nursing his hamstring injury – that made the most difference in the game.

"It's a dream come true," Green said in the postgame press conference. "I've been waiting for this opportunity my whole life, this moment with my team in front of the whole town here on the biggest stage possible." Green turned his senior-year opportunity into first-team All-State honors and a Division I football scholarship to Eastern Illinois University.

Leonard was left searching for words even though he had plenty of experience talking about championship teams, this being Rochester's third straight title. "What can you say? Words can't describe it," he said afterward. "It's awesome. It's a great feeling. It's great for this program." He would make pretty much the same speech after the Rockets won again in 2013 and 2014 to set a public-school record five straight championships. Then he would prepare his team for a shot at a sixth straight title.

Seeing Double

Derek Leonard got a very pleasant surprise in the summer of 2015 when the Cox twins, Avante' and D'Ante', showed up for football workouts in Rochester. Speedy wide receivers and defensive backs, the brothers had helped the Williamsville Bullets finish second in the 3A playoffs as sophomores in 2014. The Cox family decided to move to Rochester, giving Leonard two more weapons to unleash on opposing defenses.

Derek still recalls the first time he saw Avante' and D'Ante' in person at practice. "My first reaction was 'Wow!' They were so fast and quick. I had heard about them when they were at Williamsville, but when I saw them in person at that practice, my mind started racing." He went home and began working on all the ways he would utilize the Cox twins in the Rockets offense.

Avante' and D'Ante' Cox would leave an indelible mark on Rochester football. Avante' made his presence known in his very first game with six receptions for 157 yards and two touchdowns as the Rockets opened their 2015 season with a 79-48 win over Decatur Eisenhower. D'Ante' did not play in that game but three weeks later caught nine balls for 117 yards and a TD in a 53-14 win over Chatham Glenwood.

The Rockets' record-breaking string of five straight state championships was broken by a 46-42 loss to Belleville Althoff in the quarterfinals. That loss also ended Dan Zeigler's high school career as the latest in a line of prolific Rochester quarterbacks. That baton would be handed to Nic Baker, a junior in 2016. Baker would start the season out in a time share at quarterback with senior Josh Grant, Zach's younger brother. Baker kept progressing and claimed the lion's share of snaps midway through the season.

The 2016 Rockets lost just one regular-season game, 33-28 to archrival and eventual 5A runner-up SHG. In the 4A playoffs, Rochester easily dispatched Bethalto Civic Memorial 52-7, Mt. Zion 63-21, Belleville Althoff in a 48-47 thriller, and Canton 49-21 to return to their normal year-end destination of the state championship game after a one-year absence.

The Rockets and most observers thought the title-game opponent would be Chicago Phillips, the defending state champion and the team Rochester beat in the finals in 2014. However, an unbeaten Johnsburg team surprised Phillips 23-20 in overtime in the semifinals. Johnsburg was led by All-State running back Alex Peete, who had rushed for 2,295 yards and 37 touchdowns, including a couple of 400-yard games rushing. Peete would go on to be a star running back at the University of Wisconsin-Whitewater, a perennial Division III powerhouse.

The 5-foot-8, 205-pound Peete was as good and tough as billed. He carried the ball 35 times for 233 yards and both Johnsburg touchdowns despite the Rockets' focus on stopping him. Those were the only two scores for Johnsburg and not nearly enough to keep up with a Rochester attack that had the Skyhawks seeing double. That's because the twins, Avante' and D'Ante', were uncontainable. They repeatedly used their speed and shiftiness to break free or get behind the Johnsburg defenders. And Baker didn't miss his targets. The quarterback completed 23 of 31 passes for 335 yards and four TDs – two apiece to Avante' and D'Ante', who each caught 10 balls for more than 150 yards. The twins also each caught one of Johnsburg's passes for interceptions.

Avante' caught a 63-yard bomb from Baker on the fifth play of the game and added a 24-yard TD catch a few minutes later in the first quarter. Peete's second TD run tied the game midway through the second period, but it took the Cox brothers only two plays to put the Rockets ahead for good. Avante' returned the kickoff 57 yards, and on the next play D'Ante' got behind the defense for a 40-yard TD strike from Baker. The Rochester defense held, and Alec Ostermeier scored on a 4-yard run to expand the Rochester lead to 28-14 at the half. The Rockets added a 15-yard TD catch by D'Ante' and a 24-yard field goal by Clay Alewelt in the fourth quarter for the final margin of 38-14. A year later, Alewelt would be asked to kick another field goal in the state finals under very different circumstances.

"Once we got up three scores or four scores, we knew Johnsburg wouldn't be able to keep running Peete, that they would have to throw the ball," Derek Leonard told reporters afterward. "Our defensive backs are obviously really good." In addition to the interceptions by Avante' and D'Ante', Skylar Caruso picked off a pair of passes for the Rockets. Caruso credited the interceptions to the constant pressure caused by the Rockets defensive linemen Austin Mathis (a team-high 11 tackles), Sean Brewer (a quarterback sack among his five tackles) and Clay Johnson. Linebacker Mikey McNicholas also had a sack among his seven tackles, and linebacker Sam Baker had six tackles, including two behind the line of scrimmage.

Most everyone connected with Rochester, including Leonard, was delighted with a sixth state championship in seven years. However, the Cox brothers thought the Rockets could have been even more dominating. In the postgame press conference, D'Ante' admitted to not feeling totally confident in the early stages of the game. "We had some ups and downs...but when Avante' scored his first two, I felt like everything started clicking after that." Said Avante': "We could've definitely stopped (Peete) more. He was a great running back, I'll give him that, but we missed assignments and missed tackles. I'm being pretty picky because our goal wasn't just to come to state, but to reach our max potential. We didn't do that, but we were close today."

Despite not quite reaching their goal of perfection, Avante' and D'Ante' put on a championship game performance that won't soon be forgotten by Rochester fans. "They had God-given talent, but they also worked so hard at their craft," Leonard says. "When it came to football intelligence, they were two of the smartest I've ever been around on the football field."

In an interesting interview with Ryan Mahan of *The State Journal-Register* before the semifinal win over Canton, the Cox twins talked about how they each were seeking their own identities. "We play the game together, but that's the only time we're together," D'Ante' said. "I won't say we don't like being around each other, we're just annoyed by being around each other because we've been around each other since we were little. It's always been a competition between us. Everybody sees us as competing against each other and who is better; that's how we've been looked at our whole life."

They both said they would be going their separate ways to play college football, and they did. Avante' originally went to the University of Wyoming for two years before transferring to Southern Illinois University (SIU). D'Ante' went to Division II Missouri Baptist and then to Illinois as a walk-on before joining his brother and Nic Baker at SIU. When the three were finally reunited, they picked right back up as a lethal passing combination, though D'Ante' missed big parts of two seasons due to leg injuries. Avante' became only the 10th consensus All-American in Saluki history. Because he was granted a medical waiver, D'Ante' still had one more year to play and was projected to fill his brother's role as the Salukis' top receiver in 2023.

Like Derek Leonard, Saluki coach Nick Hill realizes what a special combination it was to have Baker and the Cox brothers on the same team. "I think I'll look back and appreciate it more when they're gone," Hill says. "I doubt I'll ever coach a trio like that who played together in high school and won a lot of games, were phenomenal and won state championships. They just have each other's backs, and they are winners. That's the thing that separates them: They don't like to lose, and they're not used to losing because of what Derek Leonard has created at Rochester."

No Way to Measure the 'It' Factor

There has been plenty of discussion about Nic Baker's height. The Rochester football roster listed Baker as 5-foot-8 his junior year and 5-foot-9 his senior year, acknowledging a small growth spurt. Some teammates contend 5-foot-8 might be stretching things a bit. Then there was the little girl who approached Baker after one of Southern Illinois University's football scrimmages. Hall of Fame Saluki broadcaster Mike Reis, who was standing nearby, tells the story: "This girl, who couldn't have been more than 8, looks up admiringly and asks Nic, 'How come you're so tall?' Nic says, 'Thank you!! I don't hear that very often!'"

There is one thing about Nic Baker that no one questions. It is something that simply cannot be measured. It is the "It" factor. Baker has made a believer out of SIU coach Nick Hill, the only Division I coach to offer Baker a football scholarship despite his phenomenal career as a high school quarterback. One example of the "It" gene Baker possesses was in 2021 when Baker led the Salukis on a game-tying drive in the final minute of a game at South Dakota State and then to victory in overtime. Facing a do-or-die fourth-and-6 situation, Baker escaped a heavy pass rush and scrambled just far enough for a first down. Next came a longer fourth-and-11 challenge. Baker sidestepped a couple of would-be tacklers and threw an 18-yard completion.

"Some people have 'it,' and some people don't. Nic Baker's got 'it.' I've been telling people for a long time how much I believe in him," Hill said afterward. "It's fourth-and-6 and you've gotta step up, avoid a blitz, take off and get a first down by one yard. That's not X's and O's. That's resiliency and just having a competitor and a warrior back there at quarterback." Even in talking about the "it," Hill struggles with a definition. "You can measure height, weight and speed. You can scout all the summer camps and combines and watch players run, throw and catch. But you don't play football in shorts and T-shirts. For me, the "it" comes down to a relentless, competitive spirit to win. Nic Baker has that in spades. If he went out to play golf and didn't do well, he'd be mad and go back and work on his golf game."

Baker was back for his senior season at Rochester in 2017, but the Cox twins had graduated. Many observers expected a less explosive passing attack without Avante' and D'Ante' darting around and zooming past defenders. The preseason prognosticators even picked Rochester to finish no better than third in their conference. One of Baker's character traits is unwavering confidence. "I was telling my friends we were gonna be good. Just wait and see!" Baker recalls. "We took it upon ourselves to try and be the best team that's ever come through here. We took it to another level physically, mentally and spiritually."

Baker and the Rockets did take it to dizzying new heights. Baker would put together the most incredible season of any Rochester quarterback and one of the best of any high school quarterback in state history. He would set a school record by throwing for 3,900 yards (7th most in state history) and 54 touchdowns (5th most). The most amazing part is he threw only two interceptions – none during the regular season – in 338 attempts.

Herrin coach Jason Karnes called Baker the best quarterback he had seen in his 12 years of coaching high school football after Baker dismantled the Tigers by completing 24 of 30 passes for 448 yards and five touchdowns in a 56-14 quarterfinal win. "If that kid were 6-4, you're talking about him going to any school he wanted to play for. He's got that special thing that you just can't coach," said

Karnes, who quarterbacked Du Quoin to the 3A state championship in 1992. The Herrin coach didn't just tell reporters his opinion of Baker. He also texted his friend Hill, the SIU coach. Both Karnes and Hill grew up in Du Quoin and both were outstanding quarterbacks for the Indians. "When I was an eighth grader, Jason took me under his wing," Hill says of Karnes, who was 10 years older. "I thought he walked on water."

Hill was one of the people who consoled and shared his faith with the Herrin coach when Karnes' son Chance was killed in an auto accident in 2022. Hill says he had known Chance since the day he was born. Du Quoin High School has retired just four football jersey numbers in the school's history. Jason Karnes and Nick Hill are two of those honorees. Karnes' father Bob coached there from 1968 through 1987 and posted a 136-59 record, good enough for induction into a couple of football coaching Halls of Fame.

Karnes and Derek Leonard double-teamed Hill regarding Baker. Karnes sent the long text message, and Derek sent an email that went to more than 100 college coaches advocating for Baker. One thing Derek said reverberated with Hill. "He said if he had one game to win a state championship, he'd start Nic Baker," Hill says. "That struck me as quite a statement with all the great quarterbacks he's coached. In the end, it came down to me trusting Derek."

One day the next week, Hill and assistant coaches Pat Pour and John Van Dam loaded into Hill's pickup truck and drove to Rochester. It was a cold and windy day in late November, the week leading up to the Rockets' championship game. "It was really crappy weather, but it didn't faze Nic. He threw the ball right through the wind," Hill recalls. "I liked his demeanor and leadership even more." The assistant coaches might not have been completely convinced because of the height issue and the fact the Salukis already had signed a highly touted quarterback in that recruiting class. Pour got so cold he went back to the truck. "I weigh a lot of input," Hill says. "But the good thing about being head coach is I get to make the final decision." Hill called Baker that night and offered him a scholarship.

Hill knows what it takes to be a good quarterback at the college level. His name is all over the records books after being the Saluki quarterback for three seasons from 2005 through 2007. He also played professional football for six years in the Arena League and had brief free-agent stints with the Chicago Bears and Green Bay Packers before beginning his coaching career. He was hired at his alma mater as quarterbacks coach in 2014 and promoted to head coach in 2016.

Taking a chance on Baker despite him not being of optimal height for a college quarterback paid huge dividends for Hill and the Salukis. Heading into the 2023 season, Baker already stood No. 2 at SIU in career passing yardage, touchdown passes and completions. To break all those records at the school that had been playing football since 1913, Baker needed to complete only three passes, average only about 100 yards passing per game and throw 16 TD passes in his final season. He already had broken the school's single-season record with 3,231 yards passing and the single-game record with 460 yards passing in 2021. Those whose records he surpassed at SIU included former NFL star Jim Hart and Hill.

The youngest of three boys in his family, Baker says he had no choice but to learn how to survive playing with bigger kids. "My oldest brother is five years older than me, and my other brother is a year older. I was always playing sports with the older guys, and I would get ticked off because they would just beat me around," Baker recalls. "I had to learn how to be tough and figure out a way to compete because they were bigger and better than me." Some of Baker's toughness comes from his dad Curtis, who served in the Marine Corps. "I was a little bit of a turd head growing up, and Dad would make us do pushups and sit-ups when we got in trouble. He would tell us, 'You are either going to get really smart or really strong!' I never really got it, so I kept doing pushups." He says his mother Nancy instilled compassion in him. If that sounds familiar, the family dynamic Baker describes is pretty much the same as that of his coach Derek Leonard.

Baker played all sports growing up but says he probably was best at baseball. He was the leading hitter his senior season at Rochester, and playing college baseball was Plan B if playing college football did not work out. He says the light went on for him as a quarterback during a 7-on-7 tournament when the Rockets were playing a really good Wheaton Warrenville South team. "I started putting it together in that game, and that's when it kind of clicked for me that I could be pretty good." He says he was nervous when he took the field as the starting quarterback for the first time his junior year at Rochester. The nerves dissipated when he completed his first pass – a short toss to his older brother Sam, who then gained about 15 yards. "When I completed that pass to Sam, I just remember thinking *'It's just football. I've been doing this my whole life.'*"

Baker's self-assessment doesn't mention his ability to throw the ball with pinpoint accuracy to any part of the football field. "I want to be the guy that players rally around, the guy that when something needs to get done, I get it done," he says. "I want to be the guy that never ever blinks, even in the clutch."

Victorious!

Storm Rising in the South

The coaches and players of the Cathedral, Griffin and Sacred Heart-Griffin Cyclones have built a rich football tradition. One part of that tradition is the wearing of gold helmets. The Leonard Bowl showdown with the Cyclones was the game circled in red for Rochester ever since the Rockets joined the Central State Eight Conference in 2010. Another team featuring gold helmets was building a powerhouse 100 miles to the south. Belleville Althoff was attracting players from all over the Metro-East area across the river from St. Louis. For a five-year period from 2013 through 2017, Rochester and Althoff would collide in the playoffs four times with the winner advancing to the 4A championship game each of those years.

The Rockets beat Althoff 50-21 in their initial playoff meeting in 2013 as Rochester was en route to a fourth straight championship. The two teams would not meet in 2014, and the Rockets marched to their fifth straight title. That streak and Rochester's 27-game playoff winning streak came to an end in 2015, when Althoff won a thrilling 46-42 game. The Rockets lost despite quarterback Dan Zeigler throwing for 338 yards and five TDs, three of those scoring passes being caught by Avante' Cox. That game at Belleville hung in the balance until Althoff intercepted a pass in the end zone with five seconds left. Just one play earlier, it appeared a Rochester receiver had caught a game-winning TD pass only to have the ball get dislodged when he landed in the end zone.

The Rockets stewed over that loss for almost a year. Well, 363 days to be precise. Some Rochester players who were returning for the 2016 season had literally been marking the days off the calendar. Until that Althoff game, Rochester football teams had been state champs ever since Nic Baker and classmate Mikey McNicholas had been in fourth grade. "I just thought winning state was how it was supposed to be," Baker says. "I had a lot of friends on that 2015 team and seeing them lose like that made me sad. It made me think about what I needed to do to get ready for the next season." McNicholas was equally determined. "It was really bad. I'm sure you've seen all the pictures of us crying. They weren't tears of joy. On the bus ride home, I was like, 'This isn't happening again,'" he told reporters the week leading up to the rematch.

The 2016 quarterfinal game again would be on Althoff's home field at Lindenwood University in Belleville. The layout of the seating areas there was different. There were about 50 rows of bleachers in one end zone, where many Rochester fans were seated. There were seats only on one side of the field because railroad tracks on the other side did not leave enough room for seating. Althoff chose to be on the side where there were no fans. Most Althoff fans and some Rochester fans were seated behind the Rochester bench. It was a recipe for trouble.

The home team Crusaders led Rochester 47-28 in the third quarter. A comeback seemed improbable for three reasons. The obvious one was the huge deficit. Then there was the matter of having only about 18 minutes left on the clock. Compounding the time issue was that Althoff had a terrific running back in Jason Bester, who would go on to play Division I football at Miami University of Ohio. Bester already had run for five TDs in the game. If the Rockets could not stop Bester, his runs would achieve first downs and drain precious time off the clock. "We had been focusing on stopping Bester the whole game; we just hadn't been able to in the first half," Derek says. "We made a couple of adjustments at halftime, but the biggest thing was the swing in momentum."

The Rockets' late-game surge started when Avante' Cox capped a third-quarter drive by scoring from 1 yard out on an end-around play. His brother D'Ante' made an incredible catch midway through the fourth quarter, leaping as high and extending as far as he could to snare a 27-yard pass from Baker and holding onto the ball when he landed in the end zone. The Rockets still trailed 47-42 with only six minutes left.

But they had gained momentum, and players on the sideline had become animated cheering on their teammates. If the Rockets needed any extra motivation, some of the Althoff fans sitting behind them provided that boost. They were becoming irate at the officials and at the unexpected turn of events. "Those fans were right behind us, and some started cursing at our players," Derek says. "At one point, the police had to break up a fight in the stands. Then I got hit with a hot dog and a bag of Chili Cheetos that someone threw from the stands…I thought about eating them. All those things just made our players more determined."

The Rochester defense stopped the Crusaders to give the Rockets offense one last chance to complete the mission. Baker coolly led his team to a couple first downs. Baker then spotted D'Ante' streaking past Althoff defenders and lofted the ball 45 yards downfield. There was no need for an acrobatic catch this time; the throw was perfect and D'Ante' caught it in stride for a touchdown. Clay Alewelt's extra point kick put an exclamation point on the comeback for a 48-47 win.

"We were really good and they were really good," Derek says. "I don't know if I've ever been at a high school game with more great athletes." McNicholas, who as a sophomore had been part of the Rochester's 2014 state championship team, summed it up by telling reporters, "It was something real special. It was probably better than state."

Victorious!

The Best Rochester Team Ever?

Most coaches will tell you that each of their teams is special in different ways. Most of them will respectfully decline to rank their teams because each team has unique strengths and weaknesses and also because sports evolve in a way that makes it hard to compare teams from different time periods. Sports writers love to make comparisons, though, and *The State Journal-Register* sports editor Jim Ruppert wrote such a column the week leading up to the championship game in November of 2017.

"Comparing Rochester football teams is akin to deciding which of your children you love the best," observed Ruppert, who then listed numerous reasons he thought the 2017 Rockets might be the best Rochester team to that point in time. Facts supported Ruppert's hypothesis. Up to then, only the 2010 team had gone through a season unbeaten. The 2017 Rockets not only were unbeaten on the eve of the championship game, but they had been seriously challenged only once, a 35-28 win over archrival SHG, which would emerge as the 5A state champion. The Rockets also dismissed Belleville Althoff, their biggest playoff obstacle in the south, by a 41-23 score. Their offense had gone the entire regular season without committing a single turnover.

The Rockets' fast-paced, precision offense was built around Nic Baker, who put together a season for the ages. In addition to his other-worldly passing stats that included 54 TD passes, the quarterback ran for 12 more TDs. The Cox twins had graduated, but up stepped receivers Cade Eddington, Riley Lewis, Ben Chapman and Jayden Reed without missing a beat. Reed had not played football his junior year so he could concentrate on his favorite sport of baseball, where he was a college prospect as a sure-handed shortstop. A baseball standout as well, Baker recruited Reed to join him on the football team for their senior year. Just like at shortstop, Reed displayed an uncanny ability to catch any ball he could reach.

Previous Rochester championship teams leaned heavily on featured running backs like Colten Glazebrook in 2010, Garrett Dooley in 2011and 2012, Drake Berberet in 2013, and Evan Sembell, who rushed for a school-record 2,447 yards in 2014. Three Rochester running backs shared the 2017 load, with Nick Capriotti, David Yoggerst and Zach Gleeson combining for more than 1,600 yards and 20 touchdowns.

Of course, none of that could happen without a great offensive line, which included Clay Johnson, Sean Brewer, Clayton Blanshan, Matt Tungett and Hunter Butcher. Highland coach Jim Warneke made note of that after the Rockets dispatched his previously unbeaten team 31-14 in the semifinals. "Everyone looks at the passing yards and the prolific quarterbacks they've had, but what makes the engine run is up front. That makes the passing and everything else open up," Warneke said. "We knew they were a darn good football team on both sides of the ball."

The Rochester defense doesn't get mentioned a lot, mainly because the offense grabs most of the headlines. But the 2017 Rockets defense under defensive coordinator Steve Buecker was solid from start to finish. They gave up an average of only 14 points per game, with SHG scoring the most in a 35-28 Rochester win. Limiting opponents to 14 points is even more impressive because the opponents got the ball back every time the Rockets scored, which was quite often. Also, more than half of the opponents' points came late in blowout games against Rochester's second-team defense. Linebacker Stephan McCree, who moved to Rochester from Chatham before his senior season, led the team with 75 tackles. Junior Riley Lewis was the team's best defensive back. At 5-foot-8, he appeared to be overmatched against Highland's 6-foot-4 All-State receiver Sam LaPorta, who would go on to earn All-American honors as a tight end at the University of Iowa and was the 34th player chosen in the 2023 NFL draft by the Detroit Lions. All Lewis did was intercept two passes intended for LaPorta.

Ruppert included this caveat: "Of course, in order to be in the argument for the best ever, these Rockets have to win the state championship." That looked to be a tall order because the title game opponent was Morris, a perennial 5A football power that had reached the semifinals in that larger class in 2016. Morris had a line that averaged 6-foot-2 and 280 pounds. The Redskins also featured Tyler Spiezio, a 6-foot-5 standout player with great athletic bloodlines in that his father, Scott, and his grandfather, Ed, both had been major league baseball players. Some observers predicted that Morris might be the Rockets' toughest test of any of their championship opponents.

Indeed, the game would be hotly contested literally to the final second. Rochester started fast, marching 67 yards with the opening kickoff. Capriotti broke loose for a 27-yard touchdown run to put the Rockets up 7-0. Morris would answer with a 71-yard TD drive of its own to tie the game 7-7 late in the first quarter.

Baker found Eddington open for a 49-yard TD strike and a 14-7 halftime lead. Eddington would end the night with five catches for 138 yards to account for the majority of Baker's passing yards. Baker hit Reed with a 7-yard TD pass for a 21-7 advantage, but Morris used relentless running back Kameron Dransfeldt (38 carries and 184 yards for the game) and Spiezio to put together 70- and 80-yard scoring drives. Morris tied the game at 21 on a 4-yard TD catch by Spiezio with four minutes to play.

Baker approached his coach on the sideline and said, "Put the ball in my hands and let me run." He knew Leonard only wanted him to run the ball when he had no other choice because the coach didn't want to lose his quarterback to injury. Very few people knew it, but Baker had been playing for over a month with a small hairline fracture of his kneecap.

Derek already had decided to put the ball – and the championship – in the hands of Baker, the player with the "it" factor that is so hard to define. Baker entered the huddle, looked around at his teammates and said, "This is what we have dreamed about. I trust every one of you, and you guys trust me. Let's go do this." Looking back, he says, "Tie game. Fourth quarter. State championship on the line. The ball is in your hands. As a little kid, when I went to sleep, I would dream about things like it's bottom of the ninth, two outs and you are at bat."

Baker steadily led his team down the field as the clock was ticking. On the drive, the quarterback completed three passes for 31 total yards. But on seven of the 10 plays, Baker kept the ball and ran with it, gaining 42 total yards. It was a strategy the Rockets had not employed all season.

The most critical of Baker's runs came on a fourth-and-1 play from Rochester's own 39-yard line with under 2 ½ minutes to play. The Rockets had failed on two fourth-down passes earlier in the game. Leonard never hesitated. "I wasn't going to let anyone talk me out of it," he told reporters afterward. "There are a lot of factors…we were punting into the wind, and I didn't want them to get the ball back. I felt like our defense was tired." He also knew the play he wanted to use. "That's our bread and butter," he says of the play in which Baker faked a handoff to the running back going to the right and then headed left behind his guard and tackle on that side. "I ran it in 2009 with Sean Robinson," Leonard says, referring to the two-point try that ended the Rockets' season inches short of victory in the semifinals that year. "I'd do it again with Sean, and I'd do it again with Nic. It's just how I feel about them."

The fact that Rochester went for it on fourth down did not surprise the Morris coach. "We'd seen them do it on film, so we knew they were going to go for it," Redskins coach Alan Thorson told reporters. "Honestly, I probably would have done the exact same thing with the state title on the line. They made a good play call and had good execution."

Baker says the play did not go exactly as designed, but the quarterback improvised, something Derek gives his players the freedom to do. Baker says the confidence Leonard has in his players allows them to play without fear of failure. "The hole I was headed for kind of got plugged up, so I veered more to the outside, around the left end," Baker says. "There was no way I was not getting a yard for that first down." The play went for seven yards before he was tackled at the Rochester 46-yard line. The clock ticked down toward the two-minute mark.

On the next play, he flipped the ball to Gleeson on a short screen pass, and the running back rumbled 18 yards to the Morris 36-yard line. Baker hit Reed on the sideline for seven more yards, with Reed stepping out of bounds to stop the clock with about a minute left. Baker ran up the middle for 11 yards to the Morris 18 for a first down. Then he ran up the middle for nine more yards to the Morris 9-yard-line. He was stopped for no gain on second down, and the Rockets took a timeout with 20 seconds left. On third-and-1, Baker again ran straight up the middle, gaining six yards to the 3-yard line. The Rockets quickly lined up, snapped the ball and Baker gave it to Capriotti, who immediately went down two yards behind the line of scrimmage so as not to risk contact and so the Rockets could call a timeout before the clock ticked under four seconds.

Leonard sent Alewelt, his field goal kicker, onto the field to try a 24-yard field goal. Extra-point kicks in high school are not a given, much less field goals. Assuming no defender can break through the line to block a kick, three things must happen for a successful field goal. The center must hike the ball seven yards back to the holder, who must catch it and place it properly in position to be kicked. Finally, the kicker must kick the ball high and true through the goalpost uprights. That all takes place in the span of about 1.5 seconds. If there is a breakdown in any of those three actions, the kick fails.

Alewelt had only kicked one other field goal the entire year, mainly because the Rockets usually scored touchdowns and they often eschewed fourth down punts or field goals to instead try for a first down. Morris took a timeout after Rochester's timeout had ended in the hope that making the Rockets' sophomore kicker wait longer before the biggest kick of his life would make Alewelt feel jittery. The TV camera showed Alewelt smiling during the timeout. "I was just trying to keep calm," he said in a post-game TV interview. "If you get nervous, it just makes it worse. When there were about three minutes left, I kind of saw it coming and I mentally prepared for it. When I got out there, it wasn't hard."

When play finally resumed, Zach Lee, a senior role player, snapped the ball to the holder, backup quarterback Clay Bruno. The snap was on target. Bruno caught it cleanly and placed the ball for Alewelt, who kicked the ball squarely between the uprights as time expired. A Morris player was flagged for a roughing-the-kicker penalty for running into Alewelt but didn't faze the kicker; the ball was already airborne. By the time the ball landed, the scoreboard at Huskie Stadium in DeKalb had already changed to Rochester 24, Morris 21. The Rockets had secured their seventh state championship in eight years.

An all-around athlete, Alewelt's role on the Rockets would grow in his final two years as he developed into a good tight end and one of the top tacklers as a defensive end. As a kicker, he would end his career with 279 extra points, which still stood as the state record through the 2022 season. He would make only a handful of field goals in his four years as a kicker at Rochester, where field goal attempts were rare. But the one Clay Alewelt kicked on November 24, 2017, will last forever in Rochester football lore.

Alewelt's reaction when a TV reporter asked how it felt to kick the winning field goal? "Amazing," he said, smiling. "I don't really have the words." Alewelt's father relived the moment in an interview the following fall. "He could barely talk when he was on TV," said Brad Alewelt. "It wasn't like he was overly excited. I know inside he was happy, but he's just a humble kid." A humble kid who would get an opportunity for a third state championship ring before he graduated two years later.

SIU coach Nick Hill, who had offered Baker a scholarship just days before, watched the game on TV. He came away more reassured than ever, even though Baker had what was for him just a pedestrian night throwing the ball (15-for-28 for 223 yards and two TDs). "Seeing how Nic handled that situation and doing what he did when the game was on the line, I loved seeing that," he says. "All you need to know about Nic is this: He has had a couple of outstanding games that we lost here at SIU. He'd rather throw for just 150 yards, no TDs and we win than have great stats and we lose. I was addressing our team after one of those losses when Nic played great. I noticed Nic in the back of the room with tears in his eyes. I told my team, 'That's what a winner looks like.'"

Unbeaten. State champs again. A virtually flawless season. Were the 2017 Rockets the best Rochester team? Probably not, says their coach. He says the 2010 and quite possibly the 2019 Rockets had more overall talent. "The highest compliment I can give that 2017 team is none of my teams ever played better for an entire season," Derek says. "It was the most perfect season I've ever seen any team have in high school, college or the NFL. We did not commit a single turnover in the regular season."

Baker points to an intangible he thinks drove him and his teammates to focus so intently and strive so hard for perfection. All of them knew that their coach was having a tough time dealing with his mother's illness, an aggressive recurrence of cancer that would claim Liz Leonard's life just 37 days after the Rockets' championship victory.

"Derek never brought it up to us, and the players never really spoke about it, but we all were aware of what was going on. You could see it on his face some days," Baker says. "There was nothing any of us could really do to help him except to do our best. None of us wanted to let Coach down. It was just an unspoken understanding."

Victorious!

Derek says he knew what the players were trying to do for him. "It was my toughest year of coaching with what was going on with my mom," he says. "But the way that team played took a lot of the stress out of coaching. Deep down they knew I loved them, and I knew they loved me. I will forever be indebted to them."

Stepping Up in Class

As the 2019 football season kicked off, storm clouds were brewing in Chicago that had nothing to do with football but would have a huge impact on the playoffs. More than 35,000 teachers and support staff had been working without a contract since June, when their previous deal had expired. Issues such as pay, class size, number of support staff, an increase in employee contributions for health care, and the length of the contract made negotiations complicated, difficult and bitter.

The teachers and support staff went on strike October 17 and stayed out until October 31, making it the longest teachers' strike in Chicago in 32 years. Ultimately, the teachers gained a slightly bigger raise than what had been offered as well as promises to reduce class sizes and hire more social workers, librarians and nurses for the nation's third-largest school district. While the strike turned the lives of some 300,000 students and their parents upside down, collateral damage included cancellation of high school football games for the final two weeks of the season. Because of missing games, at least four Chicago high school teams – Back of Yard, Military-Bronzeville, Whitney Young and Vocational – fell short of playoff berths they otherwise would likely have earned.

Those four larger schools not making the playoff field had a cascading effect on the rest of the field, bumping some teams up one class to fill vacancies in the larger classes. When the dust settled, the Rochester Rockets, who had won seven Class 4A state championships in the previous nine years, found themselves in 5A for the first time…by one student. Taylorville ended up being the largest 4A team with a student population of 769. Rochester was the smallest 5A school with 770 students.

It was, for coach Derek Leonard and his team, both a challenge and an opportunity. "In a way, I was excited," Derek says. "I thought we had a group that could handle it, and it would be fun for us to test ourselves against the bigger schools. We had lots of experienced seniors, and we had some size and depth, which are important when you are playing schools that have twice the number of students that you have and don't have to play guys both ways. It really boils down to whether you can hang in there for 48 minutes."

Derek Leonard was well aware that some 4A coaches and fans had been grousing that, voluntarily or involuntarily, the Rockets should be playing up a class given their decade of domination in 4A. He also had heard the whispers that the larger schools would teach the Rockets a lesson about big boy football. That sentiment struck Leonard as kind of odd and uninformed given the fact that the Rockets annually played a Central State Eight (CS8) schedule full of teams with much larger enrollments.

The Rockets had steamrolled through the first eight games of their schedule in 2019, winning those games by an average score of 56-18, including a 56-21 thrashing of archrival SHG in the Leonard Bowl. Then came an eye-opener in the final week of the season when an unbeaten Chatham Glenwood team broke open a close game in the fourth quarter to stun Rochester 56-26.

"That might have been Glenwood's best team since I've been here," Leonard says. "We were down by six points early in the fourth quarter at Chatham, and we dropped a wide-open touchdown pass. You can't miss on those opportunities against a great team. In hindsight, that game might have been a little bit of a good thing for us." Indeed, Chatham Glenwood had crushed CS8 foes by an average score of 51-9 en route to the conference championship. Glenwood then rolled over Danville, Lemont and New Lenox Providence in the 6A playoffs before losing a hard-fought game against perennial power and eventual 6A champion East St. Louis in the semifinals.

A refocused Rochester team made its 5A playoff debut by trouncing LaSalle-Peru 68-26 and then whipped Highland 42-7, setting up a quarterfinal rematch with SHG. This time, SHG gave Rochester all it could handle, tying the game at 35 early in the fourth quarter before sophomore sensation Hank Beatty broke free for an 81-yard TD run. The Rockets then stopped an SHG drive, taking over on downs at their own 15. They used strong runs by Jacob DuRocher to march down the field, eating up yardage and the clock. DuRocher put the Rockets ahead by two TDs when he ran the ball in from 8 yards out with about three minutes to play. On that day, DuRocher carried the ball 27 times for 203 yards and two TDs.

DuRocher would end his career in the COVID spring season of 2021 as Rochester's all-time leading rusher with 3,868 career yards, third most in the history of the CS8. "Jacob was just so good at everything as a running back," Leonard says. "He had great vision running the ball, good size, decent burst and speed. He probably would have gained even more yards, but his sophomore season we also had three good senior running backs. By the end of that year, he was kind of on a level of his own."

The Rockets blasted Mascoutah 56-34 in the semifinals to set up a 5A championship game against Chicago St. Rita from the powerful Chicago Catholic League. St. Rita, normally a 7A team, had dropped to 5A for the 2019 season under the IHSA's complex multiplier rules. The Mustangs featured a standout sophomore running back Kaleb Brown, who would go on to Ohio State as one of the nation's top-ranked recruits. Edgy Tim is the name of a popular high school football blog based in the Chicago area. It is a must-read for coaches and fans who want to be up to speed on Illinois high school football statewide. The fan comment section made for some interesting reading the week leading up to the state finals.

"Has Rochester played anyone with overall speed like Rita?" wondered one poster. "I've only seen a little video of Rochester, but

Rita shouldn't have a problem." "Rochester has not played against a defense as aggressive, fast and powerful as Rita," opined another. "I like Rita in this one, and I really think they'll win by two scores," wrote yet another fan.

Derek Leonard shared some of the "expert" predictions with his players in the week leading up to the game. "I'm not against cheap motivation," he says with a smile. Perhaps the best (as in worst) fan prognostication was this gem: "Rita in 5A after playing a tough CCL schedule is just too much for these teams. The best team Rochester played all year dropped a 50 spot on them and showed how *not* fast the Rockets can be. Taking a look at the MaxPreps roster, I see starting linebacker number 10 clocking in at 5-7 and 170 pounds and number 41 at 5-7 and 150 pounds…yeeeesh!" That one did not age well.

Number 41 was sophomore Johnny Neal, who had seven tackles, a quarterback sack and two tackles for loss. Number 10 was junior Jake Gunter, who had six tackles and two tackles for loss. The Rockets held Brown, St. Rita's uber talented running back, to just 18 yards on 21 carries. The Rockets featured senior quarterback Clay Bruno (3,000 yards and 39 TD passes for the year), who would go on to become the starting quarterback at Western Illinois University, and sophomore Hank Beatty, who would become one of the school's all-time greats and go on to play in the Big Ten at the University of Illinois.

It's understandable why the Rochester defense often goes unnoticed amid all the offensive fireworks Leonard's teams have produced, but the offensive-minded coach has great appreciation for his team's defense. "Our defenses have been extremely undervalued," he says. "You don't win the championships we've won without a good defense. I've had three defensive coordinators since I've been here – Charlie Brown, Eric Warren and Steve Buecker – and they are the absolute best at coming up with a game plan and teaching our players the right reads and techniques."

Derek says he has never forgotten one coaching lesson his father taught him: Let your assistant coaches do their jobs. "You can't do it all or you won't be great at anything…and it will just wear you down. I stick with the offense, and I let them do their thing on defense. Of course, I have the final say, but if they have a good reason for doing something, I stay out of their way. I have never called a blitz on defense. All I said about defense heading into that St. Rita game was that we had to stop Brown."

Neal, the undersized linebacker, epitomized the Rockets' toughness and tenacity in that 5A championship game. For the next two years, Number 41 would be in on more tackles than any Rochester player. "Talk about undervalued. Johnny Neal was as undervalued as anyone I've ever coached," Leonard says. "He may have only been 5-6 or 5-7, but he was one of the smartest and toughest players I've ever coached…and one of the best defensive players we've ever had here."

With the Rockets' defense stymying St. Rita, Leonard's offense did its thing. DuRocher, who earlier in the season had broken Colten Glazebrook's school record for career rushing yards and touchdowns, opened the scoring with a 7-yard TD run midway through the first quarter. The Rockets had planned to run the ball a lot because it was windy and rainy the morning of the game. However, the Bruno-to-Beatty connection worked early so the Rockets kept using it. The two went on an incredible hot streak as St. Rita simply could not stay with Beatty.

Bruno threw for 313 yards and four TDs, while Beatty had 12 catches for 212 yards and three TD receptions. The two traded roles in what proved to be one of the key plays in the game. Leading 7-0 near the end of the first quarter, Bruno handed the ball off to Beatty in what looked to be a running play around right end. However, Beatty stopped and threw a 21-yard TD pass back across the field to a wide-open Bruno. "I was kind of nervous at first. I threw the ball two times this year, but they were both incomplete," Beatty said in the postgame press conference. "Coach trusted me to throw it. I saw that he got wide open, and he made a great catch." For Bruno, it seemed like an eternity for the ball to arrive. "As soon as Hank threw the ball, I looked down for a moment and saw the defensive end is hauling right at me," he said. "I thought my head was going to be taken off. But he threw a good ball."

"We had seen a similar play that had worked against them in our film study of St. Rita," Leonard says. "We noticed that their players would really flow toward the ball carrier, and no one stayed on the back side. Usually when a team plays man-to-man coverage on the receivers, no one picks up the quarterback." The trick play worked to perfection for a 14-0 lead.

The Rockets delivered the knockout punch early in the second quarter. With the ball at the St. Rita 23-yard line, Beatty lined up in the slot to the right side of the field with only one player assigned to defend him. Few high school players could cover the speedy and shifty Beatty one-on-one. It was a mismatch he and Bruno recognized instantly. Bruno used his thumb and forefinger to form the letter J, silently changing to a pass play called "Jenny."

"Coach would name some plays after the quarterback's girlfriend," Beatty says. One of the assistant coaches had seen that Bruno had changed the play call and brought it to Leonard's attention. Leonard, who makes almost every call on offense, did not intervene. "I didn't see the hand signal and wasn't quite sure what they had called. But they seemed confident, so I trusted them." Beatty easily separated from the defender and Bruno hit the receiver with a perfect TD pass.

The Rockets built an insurmountable 42-7 margin before St. Rita scored three times in the final eight minutes to make the final 42-28 score seem closer than it really was. So much for Rochester not being able to hang with the big boys in 5A.

One year earlier, the Rockets' push for another state title ended in the semifinals on a sloppy, muddy field in Kankakee, where Bishop McNamara running back Tyshon King just ran over, around and through the Rockets for 337 yards and four TDs on a whopping 48 carries. The game was tied 35-35 before a couple of untimely turnovers sealed a 52-42 loss to the Irish. Bruno, a junior at the time, threw for 317 yards and three TDs and ran for 92 more yards and a TD – but he also threw an early interception that stopped a deep Rochester drive and had a fumbled snap.

Fast forward a year, and Bruno and his teammates were celebrating the 5A state championship. But the quarterback had not forgotten that loss at Kankakee. "This championship is also for the seniors on last year's team," Bruno said. "I still feel bad for them that we lost that game." Leonard was not surprised at Bruno's response.

"Clay Bruno is just a winner, plain and simple," Derek says. "It was never just about him. He just kept quiet and did his job, never blaming anyone else and always crediting his teammates on the offensive line, his running backs and his receivers. His teammates loved him and would do anything for him."

Victorious!

The Unicorn

Gossip was making the rounds in Rochester back in 2012 about a sixth grader in the Junior Football League (JFL) who was going to be the next great player for the Rockets. Hank Beatty was a boy who excelled at all sports, especially soccer. He didn't even start playing football until he was in sixth grade. His mother, Helen Kwong, was concerned about the possibility of serious injury. The evolution of strength and conditioning training in high school football was producing bigger, stronger and faster players. She understood the simple physics of Force = Mass x Acceleration. Hank's mother and his father, Mark Beatty, were both emergency room doctors and had seen the injuries resulting from that formula in car crashes...and in football collisions.

Rochester assistant coach JC Clark, who was also coaching one of the Rochester JFL teams, talked Beatty's mother into letting Hank play football. "Everybody was annoying my mom about letting me play when I was in sixth grade," Hank says. "But it was Coach Clark who talked her into it." Even with Beatty, his Rochester JFL team didn't dominate as much as one might have expected. "We always lost to Rashad Rochelle's (Springfield team)," Hank says, alluding to the quarterback who would become a rival at Springfield High and who would go on to earn a football scholarship at Rutgers University.

"I had heard what everyone had heard about Hank," Derek Leonard says. "He had played with JC's son in JFL, and I trusted JC when he told me that Hank was going to be a great player, a great quarterback. Hank wanted to play quarterback. But we had a Division I quarterback in Clay Bruno, and I explained to Hank that he could help the team best by being a wide receiver. Hank is a team-first guy. He just nodded his head and went out and became one of the country's top receivers his sophomore year." In fact, Beatty's 1,949 receiving yards as a sophomore ranked sixth in the nation among high school players in 2019 according to the National Federation of State High School Associations record book.

Beatty would become a hybrid threat as both a quarterback and a wide receiver in his final two years at Rochester. He finished his high school career as the all-time leading scorer in the Central State Eight Conference with 440 points despite the COVID-shortened season in 2020. He was a three-time All-State selection and was named the Gatorade Player of the Year in Illinois after his senior season. He is the only player in CS8 history – quite possibly in state history, according to available records – with more than 2,000 career yards passing (2,697), rushing (2,365) and receiving (2,923). No player in league history had previously finished their career with 1,000 yards in all three of those offensive categories.

When Beatty signed his letter of intent to play for the University of Illinois in December of 2021, Leonard compared him to a mythological creature as a football player. "He is that unicorn," Derek remarked at the signing. "He was almost over 2,500 (yards) in every category...I think that's the first time in Illinois history to be so dominant at all three things. There are five-tool baseball players (who excel at hitting for average, hitting for power, speed, throwing-arm strength and fielding)...he's a five-tool football player."

At least one rival coach, Jacksonville's Mark Grounds, agreed. "Hank Beatty is the most versatile athlete I've ever coached against," said Grounds, the president of the Illinois Football Coaches Association at the time. "He could be the best wide receiver in the state, and he's currently one of the best quarterbacks. He's a complete game-changer, no matter where he is."

The most complete player in the first 27 years of Rochester football history, Beatty's only state championship came in 2019, his sophomore year, when the Rockets stepped up a class to 5A and beat Chicago St. Rita 42-28. In that game, Beatty displayed his rare versatility by catching three TD passes and throwing for another TD. During Beatty's freshman season of 2018, the Rockets were eliminated in the semifinals by Kankakee Bishop McNamara. COVID wiped out the playoffs in Beatty's junior season of 2020. His high school career ended in November of 2021 because of sheer exhaustion in the semifinals against Sacred Heart-Griffin.

Beatty had volunteered to play that entire game on defense as well as offense for the first time in his career to try to help slow down the Cyclones' potent passing attack. It worked, at least for most of the game. The Rockets built a 25-7 lead as Beatty ran for 189 yards and two TDs, caught a 34-yard TD pass and covered speedy Cyclones receivers all over the field on defense. The Cyclones battled back and led 42-39 midway through the fourth quarter, but the Rockets had the ball and were moving to retake the lead. However, Beatty remained on the ground on the SHG sideline after a second-down play. He had cramped up so badly that he had to be helped off the field.

"My hamstrings and quad muscles in both legs really cramped up. I couldn't get up. All I could think of was *'Crap!'* I didn't want to let my teammates down," Beatty recalls. "Coach Leonard and I talked in his office about me playing both ways the week leading up to the game. He was worried about how my body would hold up. I told him I would be just fine. I only remember cramping up one other time ever, and that was a 7-on-7 camp one summer in Kentucky when we played seven or eight games in one day."

Trainer Pete Stoll poured pickle juice down Beatty's throat to help relieve the muscle cramps. Beatty was able to return with about three minutes left in the game, albeit with a still noticeable limp. By that time, SHG had built its lead to 10 points and not even Beatty could help the Rockets overcome that deficit. The Cyclones won 49-

42 to advance to the championship game.

Ken Leonard jokes about what he was thinking as he looked down at Beatty getting medical attention on the SHG sideline. "I remember thinking *'You need to stay down, Hank…you have a great career ahead of you and you don't want to risk that!'"* Truth is, there are very few players, friend or foe, the Cyclones coach puts on the same level as Beatty.

"Having him out for several plays certainly helped our chances. We couldn't contain him; not many teams could," Ken says. "Hank Beatty was as good as it gets for a high school football player. I had the utmost respect for him, and so did our players." The coaching staffs normally form a separate post-game handshake line from the players. Ken broke away from the coaches' line that day to track down Beatty and shake his hand.

Beatty says it was during a couple of 7-on-7 summer camps between his freshman and sophomore years that he first realized how well his blend of speed, shiftiness in running pass routes and ability to catch the ball might translate into something special. "We played against a lot of 7A and 8A teams, and we were winning most of those games," he recalls. "The game didn't feel so rushed to me, and I started to be kind of the guy the quarterbacks were looking to throw the ball to. Coach Leonard and I talked toward the end of my sophomore season about what position would give me the best chance to play in college. Given my size (5-foot-11 and 165 pounds at the time), he said being a receiver would be my best shot."

Says Leonard: "It doesn't matter who's guarding him, when the ball is in the air, he has a special gift to get to the ball. Grades-wise, he is smart, he's one of the nicest kids you'll ever be around, a great leader, one of the best football intelligences I've ever been around, and one of the best receivers I've ever been around." The Rochester list of great receivers includes the likes of Zach Grant, whose 2,310 yards receiving in 2011 still ranked as the most ever in a season in Illinois high school history as of 2023, and Cade Eddington, whose 1,594 yards in 2017 ranked No. 9. Beatty's 1,949 yards and 25 TDs in 2019 rank No. 4 and No. 5, respectively, on the state's all-time single-season list.

Leonard's advice proved prescient. Beatty received numerous Division I scholarship offers, including ones from the Air Force Academy and Iowa State. He chose Illinois, his parents' and his grandmother's alma mater. He says he may follow in his parents' career footsteps and study pre-med. He was one of new Illini coach Bret Bielema's first in-state recruits after the former Wisconsin and Arkansas coach was hired at Illinois in December of 2020.

Beatty describes his bond with Derek Leonard similarly to many of the Rochester players interviewed. "We are close," Beatty says. "It was almost like a father-son relationship; he was almost more of a life coach than just a football coach."

Victorious!

The Lost Season

The first cases of the 2019 Novel Coronavirus Disease, known as COVID-19, occurred in China's Hubei Province in the city of Wuhan around December 12, 2019. A cluster of patients began to experience symptoms of an atypical pneumonia-like illness that did not respond well to treatments. By January 19, 2020, 282 laboratory-confirmed cases were reported with 278 in China, two in Thailand, and one each in Japan and the Republic of Korea. The first confirmed case in the United States was reported in the state of Washington a day later, on January 20.

Little did anyone know at that time the havoc that COVID-19 would wreak in this country and throughout the world. According to the Centers for Disease Control (CDC), as of May 2023, more than 1.1 million in the U.S., or one out every 300 Americans, had died from the disease. Impacts from other things such as remote schooling, isolation, business shutdowns and deepening divisions within the United States won't fully be known for years to come. It pales by comparison to families losing loved ones to COVID, but the disease also robbed a lot of high school athletes in Illinois of competing for championships.

The Illinois High School Association (IHSA), taking its lead from public health officials, postponed the 2020 fall football season until the spring of 2021, when it allowed teams to play six-game schedules. But there would be no statewide football playoffs for the first time since their inception in 1974. Every football team in the state was affected. It was especially frustrating for the seniors on those teams because it would have been their last chance to compete in the playoffs after rigorously preparing for those moments for four years of high school.

Rochester was coming off a state championship in 2019, the Rockets' eighth championship in 10 years, and had another contending team featuring junior superstar Hank Beatty. A few miles away in Springfield, the senior class at SHG was considered by most observers to be one of the most talented classes of football players ever to play for the Cyclones.

"We had everything a high school football team would want. We had speed, size, strength...and we had a special bond," says Reese Edwards, an All-State linebacker who would go on to play for Illinois State University. "I have no doubt we would have won the state championship. Our senior class was a special group; we loved and played for each other." As it ended up, the Cyclones would win all six games in the shortened spring season of 2021 and would be ranked No. 1 in Class 5A. Rochester would go 5-1, the Rockets' only loss coming against SHG, and would end up being ranked No. 1 in Class 4A.

Both Ken and Derek Leonard helped organize football coaches from around the state to push state officials and the IHSA to reconsider the postponement of the fall football season. They held a rally at the state capitol in Springfield. Ken also made remarks on a Springfield radio station that ended up being controversial.

Noting that his father, John Leonard, had fought in Europe during World War II, Ken said, "He told me ... and he told all my brothers and sisters ... don't ever let them take your guns, and do not let them get you like sheep where they just tell you what to do, because that's what the Germans and the Jewish people did at that time. And that's kind of what's happening a little bit. I mean, our governor right now is telling our parents that he knows how to parent their kids better than they do, and he's going to keep them healthy. Well, you know what? That's a parent's job."

The response on both sides was what you might expect given the polarization that had taken hold in the country. Many cheered Leonard's remarks and agreed the players in Illinois should be allowed to compete as players in surrounding states were able to do. Many others, including officials at SHG, were quick to condemn the analogy to Nazi Germany. Subtract the voices of people who staked out positions based solely on politics, and most reasonable people probably can understand why public health officials erred on the side of caution, given that no one really knew where COVID was headed in the fall of 2020. Reasonable people might also extend that grace to Leonard for standing up for his players.

Leonard says he never meant to compare Governor J.B. Pritzker, who happens to be Jewish, to Adolf Hitler. He says he was just trying to represent his players and voice his opinion that the decision whether to play should be left to parents. The fact that his players could not play while teams in Missouri, Iowa, Michigan, Indiana and Kentucky, all of the states that border Illinois, were allowed to play rankled him then…and still did three years later.

As of May 2023, only a relatively small number (1,060) of children ages 5-18 had died of COVID. That's no consolation for those families hit by the unthinkable tragedy of losing a child. Looking back three years later, it appears that teenagers probably could have played football in the fall of 2020, with concussions and other sports-related injuries being more of a risk to them than COVID. But that's with hindsight.

Edwards, the All-State linebacker, says despite what people on the outside thought of Leonard's comments, it was never about the coach wanting to add more victories or another championship to his coaching resume. "In all of my years playing for Coach Leonard, he never made it about him," Edwards says. "He was one of the leading voices in the state trying to make it possible for us to play. He put his neck way out there for us. He got a lot of blowback and there were a lot of nasty comments made about him. I respect the hell out of him for speaking up for us."

Upon reflection, Edwards says he can understand both sides of the issue. He even sees a silver lining. "Look, I'm still bummed that we didn't get the chance to play for a state championship. I think about it a lot, my teammates and I still talk about it. But, in a weird way, I wouldn't change anything. I am grateful that we got to play six games in the spring. I'm thankful that we got to play football pretty much all year, because we practiced all fall and then got to play in the spring. The seniors on that team had a special connection, and the COVID experience made that bond even stronger."

One of Edwards' classmates on that team was Devin Hale, an All-State offensive lineman who ended up playing at the University of Illinois. "That team was very special and loaded with talent. It was hard to accept that we were the number-one ranked team in the state but never got to play for a championship," says Hale, who is majoring in pre-medicine at the U of I. "Looking back, I could see where the public health people were coming from, where everyone was coming from. It was an extreme time."

One enduring memory for both Hale and Edwards was participating in mandatory Zoom strength and conditioning workouts each day during the time that schools were shut down. Those sessions were led by strength and conditioning coach Doug Ludolf and assistant coach Dan Schafer. Leonard would monitor the workouts, requiring the players to keep their computer cameras activated. "Sometimes one of the guys might angle the camera toward the ceiling or turn it off," Edwards says. "Coach Leonard would call that player out by name and say, 'Hey, we need to see you!' He held everyone accountable just like he always did. We continued to train as a team each day as though we were going to be able to play the next week."

One of Leonard's attributes, according to former players, is that he never quit caring for them even after their playing days at SHG were finished. Leonard's efforts on behalf of players were not just limited to his own team. Illinois State Police Master Sergeant Tony Webster said Leonard made unsolicited calls to college football coaches and helped Webster's son, Peyton, a defensive back at rival Springfield High, get a football scholarship to the Missouri University of Science and Technology. Rival coaches related similar stories.

Hale had been selected to play in the Shriner's All-Star football game in June of 2021. He also had qualified for the state track and field finals in the shot put and discus. Both events were scheduled for the same weekend. The state track meet would be held Friday and Saturday in Charleston, and the all-star football game on Sunday in Bloomington. Leonard was coaching Hale's all-star football team the week leading up to the state track meet. "After football practice, Coach Leonard would put me in his pickup truck and drive me across town to another school in Bloomington so I could get ready for the state meet. He would retrieve the shots and discs and just kept on encouraging me. He was always very caring of me," Hale says. "And I will never forget that faith always came first with him. When I first came to SHG, I didn't have that faith background. Through his FCA (Fellowship of Christian Athletes) group at school, and in other ways, he poured his faith into us."

Edwards and Hale were among the 15 or so members of that COVID senior class of SHG football players on hand at Memorial Stadium on the campus of the University of Illinois when Leonard coached his final game in November of 2022. In the postgame press conference following the Cyclones' state championship victory, Leonard and some of the players said they were dedicating the championship to that team that never got the chance to play for a title.

"Some of those guys were starters on that 2020 team as sophomores, and others played on the scout team against us in practice my senior year," Hale says. "I was so happy for them to win that championship, and the fact that they remembered us in that way made my heart feel full."

Edwards had attended one of the Cyclones' regular-season games during a week when Illinois State was not scheduled to play.

He talked with some of the players after the game had ended. "I was saying my good-byes to some of the guys, and a couple of them said, 'We're going to win this (championship) for you guys that never got the chance to win yours.' Then, I heard some of their comments about us after they won the championship game. They did not have to do that. It was their moment. It was so humble and selfless for them to remember us at that moment. That's the culture that Coach Leonard created in the SHG football program,"

The Last Dance

Ken Leonard broke out in a sweat during Mass on Friday morning. It had nothing to do with the message at Mass or the upcoming second-round playoff game the next day at Waterloo. Chills and a fever followed, and by early Saturday morning he phoned assistant coach John Allison to let him know that he was going to have to assume the role of interim head coach. It would be only the second time in his 43-year coaching career that Ken would miss a game. The other time was for his father's funeral, the season opener in 2007. The Cyclones lost that game.

By the time kickoff rolled around on Saturday, Leonard felt well enough to listen to the radio broadcast and watch a livestream of the game on his computer. The video stream lagged a few seconds behind the radio call, meaning he would hear the outcome of a play before he could see it unfold. Not ideal for his visual coaching mind. Also troubling was a flashback to Chenoa and the time he was an interim coach because the head coach had been suspended for one game. It would turn out to be the only loss for that 1979 Chenoa team until the state championship game.

Leonard had complete faith in Allison. He had turned the offensive play-calling over to the assistant coach years earlier and had recommended Allison be named his successor before the 2022 season began. Still, it was kind of unsettling to not be on the sideline for what could be the final game of his storied career. He also knew something not even Allison knew until after the game, that a favorite uncle of Allison's had died that morning in Arizona. Allison's mother waited until after the game to tell him about the death of her brother because she did not want him to be distracted.

Allison's background is not typical for a football coach. He was a 1998 graduate of Lincoln High School, better known in the Illinois high school sports world for its basketball teams. During Allison's three seasons starting on the offensive line for Lincoln, the Railers football team won only two of 27 games. He went on to be an undersized offensive lineman at Illinois College, where quarterback Derek Leonard was his teammate. Allison earned an undergraduate degree in biology and pre-med from Illinois College and a master's degree in physics and education from Southern Illinois University-Edwardsville. It was a path his high school counselors helped guide him toward given his excellent grades.

His detour from the medical profession into coaching began innocently enough when he found a part-time job as a freshman coach at Edwardsville High School near the campus of SIU-E while he was working on his master's degree. He became hooked on coaching. He really enjoyed mentoring and teaching kids and found it rewarding in ways over and above the paycheck, which was considerably smaller than those found in the medical profession.

Doug Martin, one of the Cyclones assistant coaches who had been a teammate of Allison's at Illinois College, left SHG during the semester break in December of 2003 to take a job in Texas. The timing of Martin's move in the middle of the school year resulted in a small pool of candidates available to fill the opening immediately, and Martin called Allison about the job. Allison was hired at Sacred Heart-Griffin in January of 2004 to fill an entry-level position on Ken's football staff. Allison would rise through the ranks until he was promoted to offensive coordinator, a position he held for all six of the Cyclones' state championships. In addition to his football duties, which ultimately would include filling the shoes of a coaching legend, Allison taught honors physics at SHG.

Those who know Allison well describe him as unflappable. His reaction to that 7 a.m. phone call from Ken was in keeping with that character trait. "I just said, 'I hope you feel better Coach. Don't worry, we got this.' Our game plan had been finalized earlier in the week. As a coach, the games are the easy part…other than the heart-break you feel for your players if you lose. Of course, the magnitude of it being Coach Leonard's final season wasn't lost on me."

Allison had a premonition during the pregame warmups that the Cyclones might be in for a tough battle despite being heavily favored. "You could just feel it in the air. I told the players that this (Waterloo) community has never experienced this kind of football excitement. Their team felt like they had already been written off by a lot of people, that they had nothing to lose. I told our guys, 'You can't let them get any momentum, or we will be in for a dogfight.'"

SHG's first drive saw a touchdown nullified by a penalty. A catch in the end zone was ruled to be just out of bounds, wiping out another TD. There were overthrows and dropped passes. Mean-while, Waterloo was executing its game plan to keep the ball away from the Cyclones' offense by running the ball and grinding out first downs, eating up yardage and minutes off the game clock. The Bull-dogs kicked a pair of field goals and took a 6-0 lead at halftime.

Already feeling guilty for missing the game, Leonard's sense of unease grew as the Cyclones continued to struggle. He placed a phone call to Allison during the halftime break and a couple more calls to assistants on the sideline during the second half. "I just wanted to encourage John. He was very calm; that's just who John is. But I knew it had to be tearing him up inside. I have been in that situation," Leonard says. "I shared with him some things I noticed. Several times Waterloo moved their inside linebacker out on the edge to try and slow down our passing game. I suggested we run the ball if the linebacker kept moving outside. But John was already planning to make that adjustment."

Allison said he and the team felt confident, trailing by only six points at the half. The biggest offensive change was to have quar-terback Ty Lott run the ball more in the second half. "We were not having our usual success throwing the ball against their defensive alignment, so how do you get an advantage if they are committing so many people to try and stop our receivers? The way you do that is run your quarterback. Going into the game, it was not our plan to run Ty that much, but it ended up being what we needed to do."

The last thing Allison told the team before they went out for the second half was that they were going to be fine...as long as they didn't turn the ball over anymore. Waterloo promptly intercepted a pass and returned it to the SHG 10-yard line. The home crowd was in a frenzy. "Of course, the one thing I said we couldn't let happen happened," he said afterward. "Now you start wondering how the players are going to respond." The fact that more than 20 of the team's key players were battle-tested seniors gave Allison hope. SHG's defense stiffened to keep Waterloo out of the end zone after the interception, and the Bulldogs had to settle for another field goal and a 9-0 lead.

Watching the ensuing Waterloo kickoff sail deep toward Colin Johannes, SHG assistant coach Chris Flaggs thought to himself, *"Waterloo just messed up..."* Timed in under 4.3 seconds in the 40-yard dash, Johannes was the fastest player on a team filled with blazing speedsters. Johannes fulfilled Flaggs' prophecy. Taking the kickoff at the 10-yard line, he saw a lane open up, broke a couple of tackles and outran everyone 90 yards to cut the deficit to 9-7. The Cyclones finally had momentum, but momentum in sports can be fickle.

Waterloo running back Bryce Reese broke free for a 69-yard TD with just seconds left in the third quarter. The Cyclones had never trailed in a game all year; their closest call to that point had been a 35-point win over Rochester in the season opener. They entered the final quarter behind 16-7. As news of the stunning score spread across the state via social media, the livestream was joined by a surge of new viewers.

Looking back weeks later, several SHG players said that not having Leonard on the sideline gave the game a strange sort of vibe, but Lott says that it was no excuse for the flat performance. "Coach Leonard built us as a team to where even if he's not there, we and the other coaches had been prepared to stand on our own," the quarterback says. "Even in his last season, Coach Leonard never made it all about him. He always put himself last. Coach Allison was there, and all our position coaches were there. We knew what we were supposed to do."

When he notched his 400th win in October of 2021, Leonard had hinted at retirement, saying, "I don't know exactly how long I've got, but I can see the end from here." He had seriously considered retiring a few years earlier, but when his wife Liz was diagnosed with cancer, she urged him to keep coaching. "Even through the toughest part of her battles, Liz just wanted to make sure everyone else was taken care of," Ken says. "She knew that we were not going to be able to do some of the things we had planned to do when I retired, and she knew that coaching would help me get through what we were facing."

After Liz's death at the end of 2017 and his later marriage to Angie, Ken began to recalibrate when and how he would step away from the game. A big family consideration was that one of his grandsons, Bradley's son John Patrick (JP), soon would be entering high school, presumably at SHG if Ken was still coaching. Soon after that, Derek's oldest son, Blake, would be going to Rochester High. Coaching against his son had taken enough of an emotional toll on him, and Ken vowed he would never coach one grandson against another grandson. He submitted his retirement letter to school officials in February of 2022 and recommended that Allison be named the coach-in-waiting. The fact that his final senior class was loaded with elite athletes was certainly part of his calculation, but he also wanted a smooth transition for the players, Allison and the school. Now, tracking the Waterloo game at home, he had a nagging concern that his announcement might have placed too much pressure on his players.

"When the game moved into the fourth quarter, I began to think about how I was going to handle it if it was my last game," Ken says. "I have always told my teams after a tough loss that if this is the worst thing that ever happens to you, you will have had a wonderful life. I would just have felt bad for the kids, especially the seniors, and for putting John in that situation."

A core group of senior players – Lott, defensive back J'Veon Bardwell, running back Richard Jackson, and wide receivers Jake Hamilton and KeShon Singleton – had been part of SHG's first-ever state champion basketball team in March of 2022. Along that March Madness trail under coach Tim Allen, their character as competitors had been tested repeatedly. They:

- ➤ Trailed archrival Lanphier by 11 points in the fourth quarter of the regional title game before storming back to prevail 63-57 in double overtime. ("Watching that game, I thought there was no way we could come back, but they did," Leonard says.)
- ➤ Nipped Decatur MacArthur 55-53 in overtime in the sectional, and
- ➤ Pulled away from East St. Louis late for a 60-50 win and a trip to state after the Flyers had pulled within two points in the fourth quarter.

"There were some points where it got a little nerve-wracking, but we stayed composed," Jake Hamilton said after the super-sectional win over East St. Louis. "You saw it in the Lanphier and MacArthur games, too, so I think one of our strong suits is being able to stay composed when it gets like that."

The Class 3A state basketball championship game against Metamora was the ultimate baptism by fire. The Cyclones rallied from six points down at the end of the fourth quarter to send the game to overtime. They sent the game to double overtime on a layup by Zack Hawkinson with 2.5 seconds left. The championship finally was decided at the end of the second overtime when Singleton accidentally dribbled the ball off a Metamora defender's foot, recovered the ball beyond the three-point line at the top of the key, spun around and tossed up a prayer that hit the front of the rim...then the backboard…bounced twice more on the rim…and fell through the basket with 1.4 seconds left on the clock for a 53-50 state title victory.

It was about perseverance for Singleton. "It comes down to pure will," he says. "We were in a lot of tight situations in basketball. Both (basketball and football) programs preach at us, asking us how badly we want to succeed, and what we are willing to do to keep going, to keep pushing when things get tough. Those are sports lessons, but they are life lessons, too."

Prior to the start of the 2022 season, Leonard predicted that the reservoir of experience gained by surviving those tense situations in basketball would help his football team if it ever found itself in a really tough spot. As the game entered the final 12 minutes, the Cyclones were facing their Waterloo moment, to borrow a bad Napoleon pun. They had to dig deep or their state football title dreams – and Ken Leonard's incredible career – would come to a shocking end.

Senior running back Richard Jackson scored on a 1-yard TD plunge to cut the margin to 16-14 with 11 minutes to play. Waterloo again moved the ball near midfield and needed only about a yard on fourth down to keep the drive going. Rather than trying to pin SHG deep in its own end of the field with a punt, the Bulldogs decided to go for the knockout punch. They had succeeded running the ball most of the day. A first down would have drained precious minutes off the clock, and if Waterloo scored again, one of the biggest upsets in Illinois football playoff history would be achieved. When the ball was snapped, 6-foot-4, 400-pound nose tackle PJ Smysor and the other Cyclones defensive linemen won their individual battles along the line of scrimmage. With Waterloo's blockers occupied, two-time all-state linebacker Cory West shot through the line to tackle the Waterloo ball carrier in the backfield for a 3-yard loss.

"The game was on the line right then, and I knew they were going to try running up the middle. It's what they had been doing the whole game," West says. "The coaches scooted me and Hud (Mc-Mann) up closer to the line. When the ball was snapped, PJ (Smysor) just went low and stuck his nose in there and sealed the middle, and that allowed me to run right through a gap into the backfield. That's how our defense works. Our defensive linemen keep blockers off us linebackers, and that's how Hud and I get so many tackles. They don't get a lot of credit publicly, but I'm thankful for those linemen."

The Cyclones offense also was thankful. The fourth-down tackle gave the Cyclones the ball near midfield with a chance to take the lead for the first time. SHG senior running back Bill Sanders capped a 50-yard drive with a 1-yard TD, followed by a two-point conversion. The Cyclones finally overtook Waterloo for a 22-16 lead with just over five minutes left.

The defense got another stop. Just when Leonard and Cyclones fans were about to exhale, disaster almost struck. The Waterloo punt sailed over the punt returner's head. Rather than let the ball bounce deeper into SHG territory, the returner tried to make a difficult over-the-shoulder catch. The ball caromed off his hands and bounced around precariously inside the SHG 20-yard-line with a couple of dark-clad Bulldogs in hot pursuit. Seemingly from out of nowhere, Johannes flew in to fall on the ball. Johannes had been blocking a Waterloo player but turned in time to see the ball glance off his teammate's hands. "All I could think of in that moment was *'We can't go out like this!'"* he recalls. He sprinted after the ball, sliding the last couple of yards to secure the football.

A few plays later, Lott, who had suffered through his most uneven passing game of the season, broke loose for a 67-yard TD run and a 28-16 lead with just over three minutes to play. Cyclone Nation could finally exhale. The Cyclones outscored Waterloo 21-0 in the fourth quarter. Coming into the game, the SHG offense had averaged more than 56 points per game and had never been held below 49 points. When a team scores points at that pace, the defense can tend to go unnoticed. But on this day, the defense, featuring key tackles and sacks by the likes of West, Smysor, McMann, Reggie Thomas and Jake Kepler, simply refused to buckle. Limiting Waterloo to field goals the first three times the Bulldogs had driven deep into SHG territory kept the game within reach and bought time for the offense to finally get going.

Survive and advance. That's really all that matters in the play-offs.

Outwardly at least, Allison appeared to keep his cool though it all. "I'm pretty sure he (Ken Leonard) was more nervous than I was," Allison told reporters afterward. "The first half we could not have been a whole lot worse. We just kept shooting ourselves in the foot with stupid mistakes. I wasn't too worried at halftime because I could see the look in the eyes of our seniors. They were not going to let this be Coach Leonard's last game when he's not even here. I just told that core group of seniors, 'We're gonna put this on you.' I knew they would come through."

Immediately after the game, Leonard sent a message to the entire team and coaching staff telling them how proud he was of them for their perseverance. Later that evening, he sent a private text message to Allison. In part, it read, "John, I am sorry you had to go through everything you had to go through today. And this weekend and the loss of your uncle. You are a great father, husband, coach and Christian man. Everything will be fine. Turn it over to the Lord."

Victorious!

A Wake-Up Call...Literally

The quarterfinal opponent would be Murphysboro, which had come from a 16-point halftime deficit to eliminate previously unbeaten Macomb. Any hope Murphysboro might have had to catch the Cyclones napping pretty much vanished with the punch in the mouth Waterloo delivered. The odds of SHG coming out flat for a second straight week were slim to begin with, but Leonard was taking no chances. He called for an all-coaches staff meeting at 7 a.m. the next morning before church. He then called a seniors-only meeting with his players before school started on Monday morning.

He apologized to the coaching staff for missing the game, and he congratulated them on the win. He then pivoted to observe that the Cyclones had looked "a little lax," adding, "We all need to look in the mirror and ask ourselves what we need to do better...and that starts with me."

Lott and Singleton both approached the Monday morning meeting of senior players with Leonard with a bit of trepidation. "We thought maybe he was gonna be yelling and stuff," Lott says. "But when we got there, he was all cool. He apologized for not being there, and he congratulated us on keeping our calm and getting the win to move forward. He said he wasn't mad at us, but he was mad about the performance. There is a difference."

Leonard turned his attention to a litany of little things that needed corrected, including items as seemingly innocuous as players making sure their knee pads were properly in place and that their

T-shirts weren't hanging out. The main point wasn't lost on Singleton. "He was just telling us that the little things always matter," Singleton says. "Things like having your knee pads and mouthpieces in, all the way to all 11 players knowing their assignment and doing their job on every play. He said to put the Waterloo game behind us and that this was going to be one of our toughest weeks of practice."

The Waterloo game was not only the first time the Cyclones had truly been tested all year, but also literally the first time the starters had to play a full 48 minutes. In every other game, the Cyclones had earned a running-clock or mercy rule designation because they were more than 40 points ahead. Reserves and underclassmen played most of the second halves in those games while the game clock ran uninterrupted by incomplete passes or plays that went out of bounds.

"When you win games like we did all season, it's easy to get a little lazy," Leonard says. "You're not trying to drop a ball or commit a penalty, but your focus might not be completely there. That's just human nature. The Waterloo game was a wake-up call for all of us."

Leonard closed that meeting with the seniors by saying, "You're special to me because for the first time in my career, we're all in the same boat. When it's over, we're all done, you and me. But this is not about me. I have had my seasons. This is your senior year, your team. Somebody may beat us, but we can't allow beating ourselves. Waterloo did a great job, but what almost beat us was us." No one said anything. He could tell by the look in their eyes that the message had hit home.

True to his word, practice that week was perhaps the most rugged since the twice-a-day workouts in the summer. Normally, underclassmen serve as the "scout" team, running the upcoming opponent's offense and defense against the starters. Now, Leonard ended up pitting seniors against seniors in practice for the first time all season. "We even had some of our seniors yelling at the scout team guys because they weren't giving us good enough looks at what

Murphysboro might try to do," he says. "So, some of the time we ended up having our number one offense going against our number one defense."

Leonard lost his temper that week in a way that he seldom had since his younger days as a coach. The center, junior Burke Wilkin, also happens to be coach Allison's nephew. The center is a critical component of a team's offense. He must make sure the blocking assignments match the defensive alignment, snap the ball on the right count and then block. Every play starts with the center's snap of the ball, and accuracy is especially important when the quarterback is lined up a few yards behind the center in the spread offense SHG uses. If the snap is off target, the timing of the play can get disrupted. Wilkin's snaps had been precise all season, but on this day at practice, he had uncharacteristically snapped a few balls too low to the quarterback. Leonard finally sent him to the sideline to practice snapping the ball. He overheard Wilkin ask one of the assistant coaches if his snaps had really been that bad. The assistant's reply was "well, maybe not that bad..."

"I just snapped. My temper got the best of me," Leonard says. "There was a hush over the whole field. I immediately apologized. I said, 'Guys, I screwed up and I'm sorry.' One of the players spoke up and said, 'Don't worry about it, Coach. It just shows you're human.'" Coach McMann, the defensive coordinator, had a unique perspective, having played for Leonard at SHG almost 40 years earlier. "You're lucky he's 69," McMann told the team. "I had him when he was 29."

"I love Burke Wilkin and he knows I love him. I've often joked with him that if he moved his feet as quickly as he does his mouth, he'd be an All-American. He's been a big part of our success on offense," Leonard says. "You know, when one of the players tried to let me off the hook by saying it showed I was human, I said, 'No, it's not okay. That's not what I am supposed to do as a Christian.' I tell my coaches and my players that when you screw up, don't make excuses. Accept your mistakes and get better. I had to own this because if you're telling them not to do something and then they see you doing it…you have to be real with them."

Ken Leonard unabashedly professes his faith, but he has never proclaimed himself to be a saint. He fully understands that others are carefully watching for any chinks in his Christian armor. There have been times, such as losing his temper, when he has fallen short of his own expectations. "The motto for our football team here at Sacred Heart-Griffin is *'Our goal is to be champions. Our purpose is to be Christ-like,'*" Leonard says. "Guess what, we're all human and we all sin and fall short of the glory of God. And that certainly includes me. In that moment on the practice field, God humbled me."

The SHG team that took the field against Murphysboro was laser focused. The Red Devils just happened to be the unlucky recipient of the Cyclones' pent-up frustration. Singleton returned the opening kickoff 75 yards for a touchdown, and the Cyclones built a 38-0 halftime lead en route to a 51-13 win. Three hours to the south, Rochester rolled over previously unbeaten and top-seeded Carterville 41-28 to set up a Leonard Bowl encore in the semifinals.

The Encore

One reason many thought the season opener between Rochester and SHG would be the final Leonard Bowl was that 2022 looked to be a down year for the Rockets. All-time great Hank Beatty had graduated and was playing for the University of Illinois. Several other key players also graduated, leaving many voids to fill. Derek Leonard was not playing it coy before the season when he said he could envision his team possibly going 6-3 considering the number of good players teams like SHG, Chatham Glenwood and Jacksonville had returning.

A 6-3 record would represent the ceiling for most teams, but it would not be up to Rochester standards. After getting rolled 62-27 by SHG in the opener, 6-3 might have looked realistic, maybe even optimistic, to some Rockets fans. In some ways, the score of that season-opening loss was a bit misleading. At the end of the first half and the start of the second half, the Rockets had controlled the ball for almost 12 straight minutes, scoring at the end of the half and again to start the third quarter to narrow the gap to 27-21. A 91-yard kick return by Johannes, a fumbled kick return by Rochester and a long fourth-down pass completion by Lott blew the game open. The Rockets improved week by week as the new starters, including a strong junior class, gained experience and grew into their roles. They would carry an 11-game winning streak into the rematch with SHG.

"That was a long time ago," Ken Leonard said on the eve of the rematch, referring to the earlier blowout win. "I know Rochester has gotten so much better, and so have we. I think we both showed what this conference and what these two programs mean to high school football in Illinois."

Indeed, Rochester had improved. But no one expected to look up at the scoreboard at the end of the first quarter and see Rochester 21, SHG 0. The Cyclones had run only six plays and had zero yards of offense. The deficit grew to 28-0 when Rochester quarterback Keeton Reiss scored on a 3-yard run to start the second quarter. At 5-foot-11 and weighing 255 pounds, Reiss didn't look like your typical quarterback. But he had a strong, accurate arm, surprisingly quick feet and once he had a full head of steam, he was a nightmare to tackle.

Derek Leonard speaks of Reiss with admiration. "Keeton was just a team-first player. His ideal spot, and what he probably wanted to do, was to play fullback and linebacker. But, man, whatever I asked him to do to help the team, he did it. His might be one of the most impressive years of any quarterback we've had based on expectations. The transformation from his sophomore year to his senior year is as remarkable as any quarterback I've had. I would say Keeton and Dan Zeigler (quarterback on the 2014 state championship team) would be in that conversation." For the year, Reiss completed 70 percent of his passes for 2,923 yards and 29 TDs. He also ran for 689 yards and 20 rushing TDs. Those numbers compare favorably to anyone in the star-studded lineage of Rockets quarterbacks.

A squib kick recovered by Rochester helped the Rockets build that 28-0 lead before the Cyclones finally scored. The ensuing onside kick recovered by SHG in the second quarter was key to the Cyclones getting back into the game. The onside kick was unusual in that the kick was dribbled straight ahead and was recovered by the kicker, Mason Grove. Most onside kicks are aimed at one side or the other of the field and are seldom recovered by the kicker.

"I was supposed to try and softly kick the ball straight ahead and then follow the ball. I had never executed it well in practice, but when Coach Leonard called for the onside kick, he came up to me on the sideline and told me to relax," Grove says. "Jake (Kepler), who was lined up next to me, knocked the nearest Rochester player away from the ball so I could recover it." The Cyclones capitalized when Bill Sanders scored on a 4-yard run to make the score 28-14.

Derek reached into his rather large bag of schematic tricks to keep the Cyclones at bay. He had added a new formation to the Rochester passing game a couple of years earlier, lining a receiver up some 15 yards behind the line of scrimmage, well behind the quarterback. The formation looked strange, and it was just one more thing opposing teams had to spend time preparing for in practice. The quarterback could hit the receiver in full stride before a defensive back could close the gap, or fake that pass and throw it deep if the defenders overreacted. In this case, unveiling a brand-new wrinkle, Reiss threw the ball behind him to receiver Parker Gillespie, who stopped…and lofted the ball to a wide-open Jack Swaney for an 81-yard TD. The Rockets led 35-14.

The Cyclones added a touchdown with just 20 seconds left in the first half when Lott found Singleton in the end zone on a fourth-and-7 play to close the gap to a more manageable 35-21. At halftime, the SHG character development coach Charlie Brown, who had played for Ken Leonard, told the team that their comeback would be "legendary."

Cory West describes it as an inner battle when the Cyclones found themselves so far behind in the semifinal. "I had two mindsets," he says. "On one side it was like, *'Man, are we just going to give up?'* That was the devil talking, as Coach Leonard says. Then I've got the other voice saying, *'Hey, the game's not over yet. It's your senior year. Do it for the other guys. Do it for Coach Leonard. It's his last ride.'*"

Jake Hamilton, the senior wide receiver/free safety, admits he also had his doubts at times during the semifinal. Hamilton had been through the basketball wars back in March alongside his twin brother Will, who didn't play football but was a starter and key cog on the state basketball championship team. "Sure, there were times in that Rochester game where I thought this might be it," Jake Hamilton says. "But Will and I and the others faced a lot of adversity on the basketball court. Coach Leonard and his family had been through so much adversity, and he would talk to us a lot about how out of adversity can come greatness. I wasn't about to give up and neither were the other guys."

During the post-season banquet, Jake Hamilton was described by one of the assistant coaches as perhaps the smartest free safety he had ever coached. That high football IQ may have helped save the SHG season. Rochester still led 42-28 as the game moved into the fourth quarter and the Rockets had the ball. The Cyclones simply could not give up another score.

Earlier in the game, Rochester had run a "bubble" pass, so named because the formation kind of looked like a bubble with two receivers on the line of scrimmage and a third receiver lined up a couple of yards behind them. The ball would be thrown quickly to the third receiver, with the two in front serving as blockers. Hamilton almost had gotten there in time to intercept the ball, but the play had gone for a decent Rochester gain. When he saw the Rockets line up in the same "bubble" formation, he quickly diagnosed what might happen.

"It looked like the bubble pass again, but I know what an intelligent coach Derek Leonard is, so I thought it might be a fake bubble," Hamilton says. "I told Madixx (Morris, the other safety) that I was going to move up in case it was that bubble pass, so he really needed to get over to my side of the field because they might fake the short pass and try to throw it over me."

Derek at first said he had just made a bad play call. It happens. But, after viewing the game film, he said it was more a great defensive call by the Cyclones because of how well they disguised the coverage. "I can't fault Keeton for making that throw because the way they lined up, it looked like the deep pass would be open. I would have made the same throw," Derek says. Reiss' performance that night included 190 yards passing and four rushing TDs. He had thrown only four interceptions all season.

Part of the reason Reiss thought for sure the pass would be open was a slight hesitation by Morris, who had only started playing the safety position a few weeks earlier because J'veon Bardwell had been slowed by a minor knee injury suffered late in the Waterloo game. Morris had to process not only what Hamilton had told him but also the fact that his coaches had warned him to be ready to respond if Reiss ran the ball. "My responsibility was to cover the middle of the field, but their receivers were so far out toward the sideline that I was going to really have to work hard to get over there," Morris says. "I trusted what Jake told me. When I saw Keeton pull his arm back to throw the ball, I just took off as fast as I could. I don't think he ever saw me until it was too late."

Morris cut in front of the intended receiver, intercepted the ball and returned it about 15 yards to the Rochester 37-yard line. Morris had been battling calf cramps in the second half of the Rochester game and tried to take himself out of the game after the interception return. But the play clock was running down, and the coaches were waving to him to stay on the field, so he stayed in the game as a receiver. He caught a 37-yard TD pass from Lott on the very next play. "I was kind of blessed because I ended up wide open and didn't have to break any tackles or anything," Morris says. "I'm not sure I could have gotten by anybody because of my calves being so tight, but I was just all alone in the end zone." On back-to-back plays, Morris intercepted a pass and then caught a TD pass to cut the Rochester lead to 42-35.

On Rochester's very next play from scrimmage, the Cyclones produced another turnover when DeAndre Stewart stripped the ball from a Rockets receiver who looked like he might run for a big gain. Bardwell fell on the loose ball near the sideline. Lott then found Hamilton open in the end zone for a 27-yard TD pass. In a span of four plays that took less than a minute on the game clock, the Cyclones had wiped out a 14-point deficit to tie the game at 42 with 10:33 left to play. Rochester would not recover.

The Rockets had come into the game minus senior Grant Wisecup, who was injured in the quarterfinal win against Carterville. He was in concussion protocol and not cleared to play. Derek called Wisecup "the heart and soul" of the Rockets. Because he started on both the offensive and defensive lines, Wisecup's absence created two vacancies. Another key two-way player, senior fullback and linebacker Ian Lichtenberger, had to be helped off the field against Carterville a couple of times after getting banged up. Similarly, he had to be helped off the field a couple more times against SHG.

"In the end, we just wore out," Derek Leonard says. "Man, this team really came on and gave it everything they had. I'm as proud of this team as any team I've coached given where they came from to where they ended up."

The final Leonard Bowl was the epitome of a no-win situation for Derek. His first responsibility, of course, was to his players, staff, school and community. Each of the previous 15 father-son games had been emotionally draining, especially the two playoff meetings that the two teams had split because a loss in the playoffs meant the end of someone's season. This time, it wasn't just a season that would end. Beating SHG this time would end his father's career.

"Either way, I was going to feel terrible," says Derek, who did not speak with his father the week leading up to the game. "If we lost, I would feel so bad for my players, especially those seniors. And if we won, I would have felt so happy for my players but so sad for my dad's career to end that way. I told my staff and my players not to worry about me, that I was going to give it my all to win this game. I know Dad understood that I was going to do everything I could to win the game for my players…and we did. We just wore out at the end."

For his part, Ken Leonard's final game on the field that bears his name goes down as one of the wildest and most memorable of the 499 games he had coached to that point. "For a while, it was like

'Whoa, we're not going to make it!'" he told reporters afterward. "But these kids were just not going to quit. We've had some comebacks here at SHG but never to come from so far back to win a game that meant so much."

What it meant was that Ken Leonard's career was going to end with perfect symmetry. The championship game the following week would be the 500th game of his coaching career. The opponent, New Lenox Providence Catholic, was the same school he faced in his first title game appearance back in 1995. The Cyclones led late in the game by 10 points only to see their first-ever state championship slip from their grasp when Providence Catholic scored two touchdowns in the final three minutes. In a series of gut-wrenching playoff disappointments up to that point in his career, that one stung the most.

"I was just devastated," he says, recalling those final minutes at Hancock Stadium on the campus of Illinois State University. "You never know if you ever will get back there again. The way things had gone for us, I was starting to think we might never get a championship. But then I probably hadn't walked 20 yards before I had this feeling of calm come over me. It was the peace of Jesus Christ. I wanted that championship for our kids and for our school…and I wanted it as a coach. But I knew in that moment that God had a bigger plan for my life, and that plan might not include a football state championship. I was okay."

Victorious!

Leaving a Legacy

Ken Leonard wasn't always okay not having a state championship. Even though he ended up with six of them, the first one proved to be so elusive that it haunted him at times. Of course, he savors those victories as he looks back on what he describes as a "blessed" career. But those championships did not end up being what gave him peace.

"For people on the outside looking in, they probably think the Leonard family must be the happiest people on earth...and it has been an unbelievable career and life," Ken says. "But when you get down to the core of it, we all are human and our family has suffered through some of those heartbreaking times everybody has to go through in life." The loss of Liz Leonard to cancer and the death of adopted son Philip Pearson in an auto accident represent a toll of tragedy that would test anyone's faith.

"The only way you can get through those horrific times is not by football wins. Wins, status, money – and we never made much money, by the way – they are not bad things. But none of those will get you through life," Ken says. "If those things are your ultimate goals, you will never be happy. You know, when we finally won that first state championship, it wasn't long before I started thinking about next year's challenge. I was always searching for the next championship. There's nothing wrong with that, but it won't get you eternal happiness. I think that is what led me to Rick's barber shop that day. It's also why I shared my faith with my family. I know without any doubt that I will see my family members who have gone on before me in heaven one day because they accepted Jesus as their Savior."

For Ken Leonard, there would be no more worrying about the coaching challenges next year would bring. Win or lose, his 500th game would be his final one as a coach. The final Leonard Bowl behind them, Ken and Derek reopened their normal daily lines of communication and shared their thoughts about how to attack Providence Catholic. The Celtics' 9-4 record entering the 4A championship game was kind of deceiving. Their losses had been to:

➢ Loyola Academy, which went on to win the 8A championship;
➢ Chicago St. Rita, which reached the 7A semifinals;
➢ Wheaton North, which reached the second round of the 7A playoffs; and
➢ Joliet Catholic, the defending 4A champion, having beaten SHG in the 2021 title game. Providence Catholic avenged its regular-season loss by beating Joliet Catholic in the playoffs. Along the playoff trail, the Celtics also had knocked off unbeaten and third-ranked Wheaton St. Francis as well as unbeaten and top-ranked Richmond Burton.

"I can usually tell from talking to my dad how he feels about a game," Derek said a few days before the championship game. "Talking to Dad and looking at film, Providence Catholic plays mostly a man-to-man defense. That's what they do, and they do it well. They're not going to change what they do. I'm just not sure they've seen the type of speed SHG has all over the field. If it was me, I would try to get Ty (Lott) going early."

Ken and offensive coordinator John Allison came to the same conclusion. From the outset, it was clear that the Cyclones were going to spread the field and take several shots downfield. "We knew it wasn't going to look pretty at times because those long passes are lower percentage throws," Ken said afterward. "But when you hit one, it really pays off."

Lott, who had completed more than 70 percent of his passes

during his career at SHG, missed on four of his first five throws. Those first few incompletions were a combination of a couple of balls slightly overthrown and Providence Catholic defenders physically impeding receivers to slow them down and throw off the timing of passes. It was a sound strategy designed to neutralize the speed of the Cyclones receivers, especially when it became apparent that the officials were going to allow the physical style of pass coverage. There were no pass interference calls on either team the entire game.

The first explosive play came on first down at SHG's own 12-yard line, a byproduct of being able to stretch the Celtics defense horizontally by spreading the Cyclones receivers sideline to sideline. The Cyclones emptied the backfield, sending running back Richard Jackson out to the right with the receivers, leaving only the quarterback Lott in the backfield. The running play they called gave Lott two options. If the defensive end on the left stayed outside, Lott would keep the ball and run inside. When the end chose instead to take an inside route toward the quarterback, Lott handed the ball off to Jackson, who was coming from right to left. Jackson got a couple of blocks as he ran around the left end, and he then used his speed to outrun everyone down the sideline. He ran out of gas 84 yards later at the 4-yard line. It didn't matter because he took a handoff on the next play and followed a block by center Burke Wilkin to run into the end zone.

Providence Catholic answered with an 11-play, 80-yard drive, scoring on a 4-yard TD pass on the first play of the second quarter to tie the game 7-7. It was at this point that SHG's wide-open approach began to pay dividends. Jack Western made an acrobatic over-the-shoulder catch for a 36-yard completion and, on the next play, Jake Hamilton shed a clutching defender for a 28-yard TD catch. On the very next series, Lott looked to his right to move the defense that direction, pivoted back to his left and flipped a short screen pass to the running back Bill Sanders, who had slipped out of the backfield. Sanders sprinted 54 yards untouched to the end zone. The first half ended with the Cyclones ahead 21-14.

Victorious!

SHG extended the lead to 28-14 halfway through the third quarter when Lott faked a short throw and then lobbed an 18-yard TD throw to a wide-open Morris, who simply ran by the Providence Catholic defenders who had hesitated when Lott faked the short pass. The Celtics attempted to catch SHG napping with a fake punt on a fourth-and-9 from their own 21-yard line. The pass fell incomplete thanks to a heady play by SHG's Andrew McDowell, who stayed with the intended receiver. Three plays later, Sanders ran the ball in from 1-yard out for a 35-14 advantage.

When the next SHG drive stalled at the 30-yard line, Cyclones coaches debated whether to try and pin Providence Catholic deep in its own territory with a punt or try a 47-yard field goal, which would be the longest of Mason Grove's career. As the coaches conferred, Grove approached and said, "Don't worry. I've got this." True to his word, he drilled the ball between the uprights for an insurmountable 38-14 lead.

Sanders added a 15-yard touchdown run, his third TD of the game, early in the fourth quarter for a 44-14 lead. The Celtics added a late consolation score halfway through the final quarter to make the final 44-20, but the game was never in doubt in the final quarter. It was simply a countdown to Ken Leonard's final victory, and a sixth state championship.

Ken declined to rank his 2022 champions above his previous five title teams, or even above other great Cyclone teams that fell short of a state championship. He said the 2020 team that was denied a chance to play for a championship because of COVID might have been the most complete team he had ever coached. Several players from that team were in attendance to watch the 2022 championship game, as well as players from other Cyclones teams. Leonard did allow that his final team was "a special group of players… and probably the most athletic team I've ever coached." One of the most telling postgame comments came from a Providence Catholic player who, when asked what made the biggest difference in the game, shrugged and said, "They were really fast."

Some of the SHG players had noticed a Twitter post from one of the Providence Catholic accounts. The Tweet said the Celtics would be reprising their 1995 championship win over the Cyclones. Of course, none of the 2022 Celtics or Cyclones had even been born in 1995. And it wasn't as if the Cyclones needed any additional motivation. Losing the title game to Joliet Catholic the year before had left a bitter taste in their mouths. That feeling drove them through winter weightlifting, grueling summer workouts, an undefeated regular season and along the treacherous playoff trail. Of course, sending Coach Leonard out on a winning note was also on everyone's mind.

KeShon Singleton had gone from player to player during the pregame warmups on championship night. His message was simple: "We've got 48 minutes left. Let's leave it all out there on the field and have no regrets. Do it for the teammate standing next to you, do it for Coach Leonard." As the clock ticked down the final few minutes, with the game in hand, Singleton said he felt tremendous relief. "Everything that we had worked for, bled for and cried for…those games when we were down late and came back to win. We always believed, and now it was coming true."

When the final horn sounded, the teams lined up to shake hands. The Cyclones then gathered in the center of the field and knelt together. "Get ready to order those (championship) rings baby!" Leonard said to loud cheers. "Hey, we're gonna be taking some of you to the press conference. Remember, Jesus! Jesus!" Removing his hat, he then turned to Singleton and asked him to lead the team in its final prayer.

"Dear Lord, thank you for this day and thank you for the opportunities you gave us. We thank you for letting us put our bodies on the line to get this win," Singleton prayed. "Lord, we ask that you bless Coach Leonard for all that he has done for this program… We just thank you for all that you have done and for letting us get this victory and do it all in the name of Jesus." The whole team then joined in the Lord's Prayer.

Singleton would continue his football career as a full scholarship player at the Air Force Academy. Leonard compared Singleton's physical attributes as a receiver to Malik Turner, a 2014 SHG graduate who went on to play for University of Illinois and then in the NFL. With all of his great sports memories at SHG, including state championships in basketball and football, Singleton says the most important things he will carry with him are the life lessons from Leonard.

"Coach Leonard is just a Godly man. It's what he consistently preached in practice and at team meetings. That's just who he is," Singleton says. "He never speaks highly about himself. He constantly put into our brains to stay grounded and humble, and that God is always there for us. Coach Leonard has been through a lot in his life. We know as we become adults, we are sometimes going to have struggles in our lives. He taught us to rely on Jesus when we have those tough times."

Ken has five siblings, his sister Sheila Easley at three years younger being the closest in age. She is not surprised that faith eventually came first in Ken's life.

"Mom and Dad raised all six of us kids as Catholics," Sheila says. "Ken was always the most religious one in the family, even as a kid. When he does something, he goes all in. When he had his born-again conversion, I thought at first that maybe he had gone a bit overboard. But his faith is real...and he has shared it with all of us over the years. If you asked me in the 1970s if Ken would end up being a preacher, I probably would have said no. But I always figured there would be some kind of way he would follow God. I just didn't know his pulpit would end up being a football field."

One of the biggest honors in Ken Leonard's career came in July of 2023 when USA Today named him the 2022 National High School Coach of the Year for all sports, citing his extraordinary career culminating in another state championship in his final game as a coach. In addition to talking about his victories, the show's hosts talked about the hundreds of young men's lives he touched during his coaching career.

Ken paused when asked how he would like to be remembered. Finally, he said, "I hope my family will remember me as a good husband, a good father and a good grandfather. Of course, I hope my coaches and players will remember me as a good coach and a good person. But the ultimate thing for me is that I am a follower of Jesus Christ. He is the most important thing in my life. I view myself as a vessel to carry that message to my family and to others in my life. It probably took me longer than it should have to become that vessel. As I have tried to say after almost every game since I became a Christian, I give all glory and praise to Jesus Christ."

When the Kansas City Chiefs defeated the Philadelphia Eagles 38-35 in the 2023 Super Bowl, former Cyclones player Brendan Daly collected his fifth Super Bowl ring as an assistant coach for the Chiefs and the New England Patriots. Daly says Leonard's legacy is about the young men he has mentored. "The impact Coach Leonard has had cannot be measured by wins and losses. He has helped literally thousands of people to go on to be successful professionally, personally and civically. His stamp on the Springfield community is as powerful as anyone I can remember."

Marty Lomelino was a sophomore on that first team Leonard coached at Gridley. He sums up Leonard's legacy this way: "He is by far the best high school football coach in Illinois history. He has, what, 400-something wins? But he has helped some 4,000 boys become better men. I am one of those. I know Coach Leonard would say he is prouder of how those kids turned out, the lives they have had, than any win on the football field."

Lomelino went on to coach football, as have many of Ken Leonard's former players. In fact, of the more than 100 coaches on his staff at SHG through almost four decades, about half played for Leonard. His son Derek went on to become one of the most successful football coaches in state history at Rochester, a career that was still going strong when his dad retired. Regardless of what career path they chose, most every former player contacted talked more about what they learned from Ken Leonard about faith and family than they did about football.

One of those players on whom Ken had a profound impact was Eric Peterman, one of the best players ever at SHG. A dual-threat quarterback whose running and passing from 2001-2004 made him the all-time leader in total offense for the Cyclones, Peterman went on to have a great career as a wide receiver at Northwestern. In 2008, he received a national award given to the Division I player who best exemplifies sportsmanship on and off the field. He was signed to a free-agent contract by the Chicago Bears, but injuries ended his football career. It wasn't the football heroics that meant the most to Peterman when he reflected on his time at SHG.

"My parents were divorced, and my father really wasn't a part of my life. So, Coach stepped forward and helped play that role," Peterman said in a 2022 interview with Scott Reeder of *Illinois Times* magazine. "I had the unfortunate experience of losing my son as well. When I was going through that a couple years ago, Coach Leonard was there for me. My son was 4 years old. He had muscular dystrophy, and that ended up taking his life. He was my first child. I was really looking forward to seeing him play football. Just going through that experience was pretty difficult. But seeing how Ken lived his life and got through (losing a son) gave me inspiration and helped. I talked things through with him. He was there for me.

"Football isn't forever, but life is," Peterman said. "He wants us to be good husbands and fathers and be successful in our careers. And he wants us to know Jesus."

Ken often refers to Bryan McKenzie as one of the Godliest men he has ever known. He asked McKenzie to officiate at Philip's and Liz's funerals and at Ken's marriage to Angie. When asked about Ken's legacy, McKenzie's words reflected what Jesus said were his two greatest commandments: "Ken Leonard is a man who passionately and persistently sought to grow in loving God with all his heart, soul and mind – and to love his neighbor as himself. The overflow of his love spilled over into his family, his athletes and his fellow coaches. Everyone who was in his sphere of influence was blessed so that they would be a blessing."

So, the impact of Ken Leonard's career could not fully be measured when the University of Illinois Memorial Stadium scoreboard clock hit 00:00 on November 25, 2022. The contemporary Christian song titled "The Blessing" by Kari Jobe, Cody Carnes and Elevation Worship contains lyrics that speak to the greatest legacy of all:

> *"May His favor be upon you*
> *For a thousand generations*
> *And your family and your children*
> *And their children, and their children."*

Victorious!